MANAGERIAL ECONOMICS

MANAGERIAL ECONOMICS

PETER J. CURWEN

Macmillan

First published 1974 by
THE MACMILLAN PRESS LTD
London and Basingstoke
Associated companies in New York Dublin
Melbourne Johannesburg and Madras

SBN 333 15727 3 (hard cover)
333 15888 1 (paper cover)

Printed in Great Britain by
THE ANCHOR PRESS LTD
Tiptree, Essex

To my parents

Contents

Introduction

The teaching of economics has traditionally been regarded as falling within the province of the university sector of higher education. For this reason the great bulk of all material published in this field has been, and is being, written by university staff at a level suitable for undergraduates and postgraduates pursuing single-discipline courses in economics. Over the past few years however there has been a rapid proliferation of courses in the non-university sector which incorporate economics as a compulsory subject. The majority of these courses are in the fields of Business Studies and Management Studies and involve many thousand students. Despite this fact virtually nothing has been published in the field of economics of direct relevance to these courses. The reason for the paucity of material beyond the introductory level is not hard to discern. Staff in the non-university sector are so overburdened with long teaching hours, administration, and course development, that writing is an unwarranted intrusion upon their free time – unwarranted because it would appear that promotion prospects are poorly correlated with academic endeavour.

This book is an attempt to fill some of the most noticeable gaps in the available literature. It is intended for use by students on Higher Diploma courses in Business Studies, Higher Certificate courses in Business Studies, and Diploma courses in Management Studies. It should also provide useful material for Degree students in these two areas. The level is broadly intermediate, i.e. second year undergraduate level, but care has been taken to make the book acceptable to students with no prior formal training in economics, for example students on the Diploma course in Management Studies. This requirement has meant that some topics traditionally discussed in introductory texts reappear in this book. Nevertheless where this occurs, for example in the chapter on the traditional Theory of the Firm, the analysis has been extended well beyond the usual bounds of introductory texts. Besides which the author feels, as a result of personal experience, that it is unwise to progress to more advanced concepts purely on the supposition that students have both fully understood, and can still remember, topics discussed in a previous course.

Obviously, in a book of this nature, the author has had to exercise his personal judgement concerning the topics to include, and also concerning the content of individual chapters. Almost all of the material in this book has been used for teaching purposes on the courses mentioned above, and has been well received. The principle with respect to the selection of material has been to exclude anything more likely to put the student off continuing further than to motivate him to continue. In order to cater for students who wish to refer to the original publications upon which the book is based, full reference is made to all source material by way of footnotes. Where relevant a full bibliography is attached at the end of each chapter, and the author hopes that this will save both teachers and students considerable effort in tracing relevant material where they seek a fuller knowledge of specific areas of the text.

The book is in no way intended to be comprehensive. The decision was taken to concentrate on those aspects of microeconomics which are loosely referred to under the general heading of 'Managerial Economics', a term which has come to encompass a multitude of topics and approaches. Essentially the book is about decision making within a modern firm, and two broad approaches are contained in different sections of the book. Firstly reference is made to a body of generalisations applicable to the operations of a firm (for example in the chapter on modern theories of the firm), and secondly there is a discussion of decision rules which are of practical use in decision making (e.g. in the chapter on Investment Appraisal). The author believes that the two approaches are compatible, and also regards it as important that a would-be manager can handle concepts as well as apply pre-ordained criteria to problems.

The author has found it convenient to divide the book into individual sections which can largely be read as independent units, but the main intention is that the book should be seen as a cohesive whole. For the most part conceptual matters are dealt with in the earlier chapters, and decision rules are dealt with in the latter part of the book. The book culminates in a chapter on Monopoly Policy which pulls together many of the threads in earlier sections, since obviously a firm can only be judged as acting in, or against, the public interest, in the light of its objectives, cost conditions, pricing policies and so forth.

In summary therefore this book aims to provide students with a relatively non-technical introduction to an important area of economics which has steadily become clouded in obscurity. The author wishes to thank the (for the most part anonymous) referees who have commented on earlier drafts of the book, but wishes to retain full responsibility for all that is contained therein.

I

Basic Concepts in Decision Making

It almost goes without saying that the purpose of any management education must be to help managers reach the best possible decisions subject to the many constraints upon their actions. Such constraints encompass typically the time period within which the decision must be made, the nature of the available information, which is unlikely to be exactly what is needed, and the resources available for use, whether in the form of human or physical capital. In other words every decision has its own unique environment, and it is only through an accurate and thorough understanding of that environment that a manager can make the best possible choice from amongst those which are available. The environment of most decisions frequently lies within the bounds of the firm's own activities, e.g. the capacity of existing machinery is a purely internal constraint affecting a decision, but decisions which affect the objectives of the firm as a whole can only take place within a much wider environment such as the U.K. economy, or even the world economy. Thus a decision concerning the construction of a new factory requires an analysis of demand conditions in whatever parts of the world happen to constitute the firm's markets and also an analysis of factors likely to affect sources of supply of raw materials.

Yet whatever the scope of the environment of a decision, the approach required to establish the optimum course of action remains essentially the same. It is unrealistic to take account of every possible constraint which might feasibly affect the outcome of a decision. Some constraints are manifestly more important than others, and the manager must therefore focus his

attention upon those factors which will above all others determine the success or otherwise of his actions. To do this he
traditionally constructs a model which contains all of the important data necessary to reach a decision. The fact that the
model neglects less important aspects of the environment of
the decision is unimportant of itself. If the really crucial elements of a decision have been carefully identified, and if they
have been correctly juxtaposed, then the model presents a true
reflection of the real world. This being so it is possible to substitute any number of possible values for its components into
the model in order to try and predict how changing the values
of the components will affect the outcome of the decision.

The use of models is commonplace in industry, since the
term applies to any situation where the businessman expresses
the relationship between variables in some sort of mathematical
terms. Often the form of the relationship is geometrical, where
variables are plotted on graphs. Sometimes the relationship
appears in the form of a set of equations. When for example a
manager talks about the total cost of production he is in fact
referring to the relationship between the number of units which
he is selling and the average cost per unit produced. Similarly
terms such as total revenue and total profit can be reduced to
their component parts. It is therefore logical to go about an
analysis of decision making by first identifying the variables
which are an integral feature of most models used by managers,
and subsequently combining these variables in ways which provide managers with an insight into the workings of their firms.

COST CONCEPTS

It is useful to start this section by running through the general
cost concepts employed by all firms.

The *Total costs* of any given output are simply the aggregation of all costs incurred which can be reasonably attributed
to the output in question.[1] If we then divide total costs by the

---

[1] Where a firm produces its products independently one from
the other, total costs are relatively easy to assess. But where any
elements of costs are common to the production of several products
it can be extremely difficult to attribute a fair proportion of
common costs to each individual product.

quantity of output to which the costs refer we derive the *average cost* per unit of output. Total cost and average cost can thus be used interchangeably, since if we know the value of either one together with the appropriate level of output we can derive the value of the other by a simple calculation.

Marginal cost refers to the addition to total costs which results from increasing output by one unit. We can thus derive the schedule of marginal cost by calculating the change in the total cost schedule as we increase output. This does not however add any information which is not already supplied by the total cost schedule. Furthermore a knowledge of the marginal cost schedule is not sufficient for us to be able to draw up a total cost schedule, due to the fact that marginal cost includes no fixed costs as defined below.

A fixed cost is one which is in general unaffected by variations in output. The term 'fixed' can however be interpreted as fixed in total amount or as fixed in relation to output changes. In the latter case fixed costs can change, but only for reasons not associated with output changes.

Sizer[1] accordingly breaks fixed costs down into three categories.

(1) Costs which are not susceptible to any substantial change within the short period, usually a year: for example certain types of depreciation and other such costs.

(2) Costs which are fixed for short periods in terms of providing the necessary facilities to produce, but which are liable to change if volume changes appear likely to continue in the future: for example supervision salaries, which although they may be fixed in relation to volume, may be affected by changes in wage rates.

(3) Costs which are fixed by the management and bear no functional relationship to the current volume of output: for example pure research and design engineering costs.

Variable costs are costs which in general are directly affected by output changes. Thus, unlike fixed costs which are usually taken to be wholly incurred before any production is forthcoming, variable costs are incurred only while output is being

[1] J. Sizer, *An Insight into Management Accounting* (Penguin Books, 1969) pp. 312–13.

produced. Now we have already defined marginal cost as being
the addition to cost when output is increased by one unit.
Hence marginal cost is a purely variable element of costs and
cannot by definition contain any element of fixed cost. Consequently if we know the schedule of marginal cost we can use
it to derive the schedule of *total variable cost*, but not that of total
cost itself because the latter schedule contains elements of
fixed costs.

Given that total cost can be split down into its fixed and
variable components, we can also derive a schedule of *average
fixed cost* from the schedule of total fixed cost, and a schedule of
average variable cost from the schedule of total variable cost.

In illustrating the above concepts graphically a number of
points need to be borne in mind. Firstly we note that average
and marginal cost refer to individual units of output, whereas
total cost refers to all units produced. These concepts cannot
therefore all be plotted on the same graph, and the vertical
axes for graphs of average cost and total cost will not be labelled
identically, as is shown below.

Total fixed costs must be drawn as a horizontal straight line
because fixed costs do not alter as output alters. Total variable
costs however will increase as output increases, and the level of

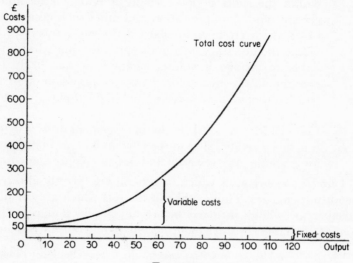

Fig. 1.1

variable costs will therefore dictate the shape of the total cost curve as shown in Fig. 1.1.

The average fixed cost curve must continually decline as output increases because we are dividing a constant total fixed cost by an increasing quantity of output. Average cost however depends upon the shape of the total cost curve as shown in Fig. 1.1. The schedule of costs per unit might appear as in Table 1.1.

TABLE 1.1

Output	Total fixed cost	Total variable cost	Total cost	Average fixed cost	Average variable cost	Average cost	Marginal cost
10	50	10	60	5·00	1·00	6·00	
							1·50
20	50	25	75	2·50	1·25	3·75	
							2·50
30	50	50	100	1·67	1·67	3·33	
							4·00
40	50	90	140	1·25	2·25	3·50	
							5·00
50	50	140	190	1·00	2·80	3·80	
							7·00
60	50	210	260	0·83	3·50	4·33	
							9·00
70	50	300	350	0·71	4·29	5·00	
							10·00
80	50	400	450	0·62	5·00	5·62	
							12·00
90	50	520	570	0·56	5·77	6·33	
							15·00
100	50	670	720	0·50	6·70	7·20	
							18·00
110	50	850	900	0·45	7·75	8·20	

Marginal cost, by definition, refers to the change in cost as output changes from one level to another level. Hence it appears in Table 1.1 *between* the row values for output. Average cost on the other hand appears alongside output values because it refers to the average value *at* that output. Marginal cost is in practice a schedule which rises in steps, although it is usually represented by a curve for simplicity. Average cost is the aggregated value of average variable cost and average fixed cost. It is important to remember that the slope of each curve in no way depends upon the slope of any other curves in the diagram (Fig. 1.2). It is commonly presumed that marginal cost and average cost are causally interdependent, with the slope of one curve determining the slope of the other curve, whereas in practice both curves are simultaneously derived from the same total cost curve, as is apparent from Table 1.1.

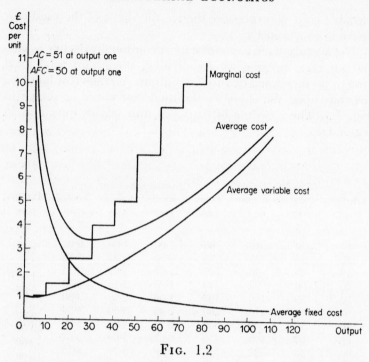

Fig. 1.2

It can be proved by simple geometry[1] that the marginal cost curve must bisect the average cost curve at its lowest point. The relationship of other points on the two curves one to the other can be summarised as follows:

(*a*) Where marginal cost exceeds average cost, average cost is rising.

(*b*) Where marginal cost is less than average cost, average cost is falling.

Note that this implies that both curves can be falling or rising together, or alternatively one can be falling while the other is simultaneously rising (as illustrated in Fig. 1.2).

Not all costs fit into the fixed–variable breakdown as defined above. An additional supervisor may for example only be taken on when the workforce increases by a given percentage. His wage is therefore neither a part of fixed cost (because he

[1] See K. Lancaster, *Introduction to Modern Micro-Economics* (Rand McNally, 1969) pp. 120–5.

is not taken on before production begins) nor a variable cost (because his wage remains constant over a wide range of output). Such costs are known as *semi-variable* costs. The effect of semi-variable costs upon the average cost curve is to make it rise in steps, with sudden increases in average cost occurring at specific output levels. In many texts the terms *prime costs* and *overheads* are treated as synonymous with the terms 'variable' and 'fixed' costs respectively. Prime costs are costs directly attributable to a specific unit of output, and for accounting purposes are split into direct material, direct labour, and direct expenses categories. It is however possible to use the terms prime costs and variable costs interchangeably only where for example direct labour costs are treated as purely variable. The validity of the splitting up of costs into fixed and variable elements is however often in question. Overhead costs include indirect materials, indirect labour and indirect expenses categories, and are costs which cannot be directly attributed to a specific unit of output. In practice many firms will lump together a number of semi-variable costs into the overheads classification, thus producing a different definition of fixed costs and overheads. The economist however finds it simplest to use the two expressions interchangeably.

A Question of Scale

We shall have much to say in later chapters about the relationship between the scale on which a firm operates and the level of its costs. It will therefore be useful at this point to clarify the concept of scale as it affects a manufacturing concern.

For every firm there is a relationship between the rate at which raw material inputs are fed into the productive process, and the rate at which the finished product appears at the end of the production line. This relationship between quantities of input and quantities of output is technological in nature, and will vary according to the scale at which the production process operates. At the simplest possible level a firm may be able to produce twice as much output by feeding in twice as many inputs, or three times as much output by utilising three times as many inputs. If the input–output relationship is fixed in this manner we have what is known as *constant returns to scale.* We can generalise this relationship by stating that constant returns to scale describes any process where, as a result of multiplying the basic input unit by a factor x (where x is used to represent any finite number), the output level will as a consequence increase by a multiple x.

It is quite possible however for the input–output relationship to vary as the scale of operation itself varies. Thus for example a doubling of all inputs may result in a less than doubled output or alternatively in a more than doubled output. In the former case we have what is known as *decreasing returns to scale,* and in the latter case we have *increasing returns to scale.* The numerical examples shown in Table 1.2 will help to clarify the distinction between these terms.

TABLE 1.2

Constant returns to scale					
Inputs	10	20	30	40	50
Output	10	20	30	40	50
Output ÷					
Inputs	1	1	1	1	1
Decreasing returns to scale					
Inputs	10	20	30	40	50
Output	10	19	27	34	40
Output ÷					
Inputs	1	0·95	0·90	0·85	0·80
Increasing returns to scale					
Inputs	10	20	30	40	50
Output	10	22	36	52	70
Output ÷					
Inputs	1	1·1	1·2	1·3	1·4

We can interpret these figures in another way by stating that if we wish to double output we need twice as many inputs under constant returns to scale; more than twice as many inputs under decreasing returns to scale; and fewer than twice as many inputs under increasing returns to scale.

Returns to scale are affected by changes in any of the inputs which go to make up the production process. Thus for example, where a firm wishes to double its throughput of a particular product, it may possibly be able to do this by purchasing a machine less than twice the size of the machine handling the original level of output. Alternatively an increase in scale may enable a firm to redeploy its labour and machine inputs in such a way as to increase efficiency and thus obtain increasing returns to scale.

The principle of Common Multiples is often relevant here. Many products require to be processed through several machines before they are in a saleable condition. The capacity of different machines may however create bottlenecks in the smooth flow of the production line. Let us suppose that the raw materials initially pass through a machine which produces 5 units of semi-finished product per hour, which must then pass through a machine which can handle 7 such units per hour. This latter machine is clearly not being fully utilised. If the firm buys a second machine of the former type, the second-stage machine will be unable to handle the new total output of 10 units of semi-finished goods. If however the firm were to purchase 7 machines of the former type and 5 machines of the latter type, the total output of 35 units of semi-finished goods per hour (the common multiple of the capacity of the two types of machine) would keep all the available machinery fully employed simultaneously.

The technical relationship between inputs and output can be converted into an output–cost relationship by making appropriate assumptions concerning input prices. Let us begin by assuming that no matter how many units of an input are purchased, price per unit of that input remains unchanged.

This now enables us to draw up a table as follows, where we assume that one unit of inputs is sufficient to produce one unit of output at a cost of £1.

Inputs	Total costs	Output	Cost per unit
2	£2	2	£1
2	£2	1·5	£1·33
2	£2	4	£0·50

If price per unit of input remains constant, doubling all inputs must exactly double costs, as illustrated. If output then also doubles, cost per unit (average cost) clearly remains constant. Thus we see that constant average cost is associated with constant returns to scale as previously defined. But where doubling all inputs produces less than twice as much output, average cost is seen to be rising. Hence rising average cost is associated with decreasing returns to scale. Finally, where doubling all inputs produces more than twice as much output, average cost is seen to be falling. Hence falling average cost is associated with increasing returns to scale.

Now we have already drawn an average cost curve, above, which fell for small output levels and rose for high output levels. On the other hand it was flat only along a very short portion of its length. This implies that the way in which cost curves are traditionally drawn allows principally for the possibility of either increasing or decreasing returns, but rarely for constant returns to scale. In practice this is a somewhat doubtful representation of a firm's average cost curve, and we should therefore briefly consider wider aspects of scale effects in industry.

Returns to Scale and Economies of Scale

A distinction which is often made is that between returns to scale and economies of scale. The term economies of scale is used to refer to any circumstances which permit a firm to produce large quantities of output at a lower unit cost than small quantities of output. In other words it describes the relationship between output and costs. The term returns to scale is, as we have seen, purely a technological relationship between inputs and corresponding output. If we then make certain assumptions about how input prices vary in response to quantities bought we can convert the technological relationship into a cost relationship. It is therefore valid to argue that returns to scale are a very important source of scale economies. On the other hand they are by no means the only source of scale economies.[1]

[1] See for example C. F. Pratten, *Economies of Scale in Manufacturing Industries,* Dept of Applied Economics. Occasional Paper No. 28 (Cambridge University Press, 1971). C. F. Pratten and R. M. Dean,

Traditionally scale economies are subdivided into four categories as follows:[1]

(a) Internal Scale Economies. These arise purely as a consequence of cost-savings obtained within the firm itself as it expands. Specialisation is particularly important here, and the advent of production-line methods, as typically used for example in car manufacture, have been a major source of internal economies in the past. The ability to use all machines continually at full capacity will also be a source of internal savings.

(b) External Scale Economies. These arise when the price of inputs to the firm is reduced for any reason, thus enabling the firm to produce more cheaply for reasons external to the firm's own operations. Typically these will occur where a firm's supplier is subject to internal scale economies and passes on the benefits in lower selling prices.

(c) Internal Scale Diseconomies. These arise where a firm becomes progressively more inefficient as it expands. The quality of supervision or management may deteriorate, or the workers may feel alienated in what used to be a small family concern but which grows to become a large impersonal corporation.

(d) External Scale Diseconomies. These arise where for example input prices go up for any reason (such as a supplier subject to internal scale diseconomies) when the firm purchases additional factors of production.

Now in practice the shape of a firm's cost curves will depend upon all those circumstances which produce either economies or diseconomies of scale, and not simply upon technological factors. It is therefore necessary in practice to drop the assumption of constant input prices which we used for illustrative

---

The Economies of Large Scale Production in British Industry, Dept of Applied Economies. Occasional Paper No. 3 (Cambridge University Press, 1965). B. Lloyd, 'Economies of Scale', *Moorgate and Wall St Review* (Autumn 1972) pp. 22–48.

[1] A full breakdown based on a new framework of categories is to be found in A. Silberston, 'Economies of Scale in Theory and Practice', *Economic Journal* (Special issue, March 1972) pp. 369–90.

purposes above. On the one hand a firm may well be able to lower the price per unit of an input by bulk purchasing, which is generally associated with an increase in scale. On the other hand it will get progressively more difficult for a firm to obtain suitable skilled labour as it expands the scale of its activities, so that costs per unit of labour inputs will tend to rise once the firm finds it necessary to attract suitable workers by offering better wage rates. Some costs rise and some costs fall simultaneously, but overall there will generally be a clear-cut movement in average cost as output is expanded. Empirical studies of the way in which the average cost curves of different firms vary as a result of scale effects will be discussed in detail in the final chapter of the book where we are concerned more with policy than with concepts.

Relevant Cost Concepts

So far we have been at pains to build up a catalogue of different cost concepts. But in practice different types of problems require radically different interpretations of which costs need to be taken into account before a decision is taken. This is the 'relevant cost' problem, which has several facets. We may note to begin with that if we buy a good and use it immediately, its cost is what we pay for it. But suppose a firm buys raw materials, puts them into storage, and withdraws them from stock a year later, during which time the present-day cost of the raw materials has steadily risen.

Is the firm to regard the cost of those raw materials at the time at which they are actually used up as being the original purchase cost (known as historic cost), or as being the cost of replacing the raw materials at present-day prices? There are many different rules which can be applied in such circumstances. The economist however will in general be more interested in replacement costs than in historic costs, because past experience has only limited applicability to present or future operations. We might ask further whether, if a machine has been fully depreciated, the cost of using it for further production is zero? The answer here is that the firm is still involved in a choice situation. Either it can sell the machine in the present, or use it for further production and sell it at the end of the year. But if, as is to be assumed, the machine's resale value will have fallen during that year, the cost of using the machine must be equal to the difference between the selling price today and the selling price at year-end.

The above example conjures up the notion of *opportunity cost* which we will meet again in the following chapter. This concept is based upon the principle that all decisions involve choices among available alternatives. If, as is customary, it has limited available resources, the firm cannot purchase everything it wants. Therefore, if it decides to buy one thing it cannot by implication buy something else. Alternatively, if it decides to use its available machines or men to produce one product, those resources are no longer available for the production of other products. It is therefore possible for the firm to assess what it has lost as a result of taking one decision rather than another. The value of lost opportunities is known as the 'opportunity cost', where the opportunity cost will in general be the value of resources, which have been put to their most profitable use, in their next most profitable use. The opportunity cost is therefore *the value of the best opportunity foregone through using scarce resources in one way rather than another*. The opportunity cost is also known as an *implicit* cost of a given action, meaning that it involves no actual monetary transaction. If for example a farmer uses his land for growing wheat, the implicit cost of the land is what it would have been worth if planted with a different crop. Since the alternative crop has not actually been planted no financial transaction is involved. Nevertheless the farmer has supposedly assessed the implicit cost of planting wheat rather than a different crop, since he is presumed to be seeking to maximise his income.

The opportunity cost concept is therefore a useful guide for a person wishing to determine how best to commit his available resources. Reconsidering the question of inventory valuation in this context the problem now requires an estimation of the value of raw materials in stock if they are not to be used for the job under consideration. In this event the cost of using the materials then becomes either their value if sold less selling costs, or the expense that would be avoided if the material were used on some other job. Whichever of these two amounts is the greater may be taken as the cost of using the material.

Other problems may often be related to the time period involved because, for example, many costs are in practice semi-variable (i.e. fixed in the short term but variable in the long term, however defined). The weekly wages of employees are normally treated as variable costs, but this may not be acceptable in all circumstances. Suppose for example that a firm holds on to its skilled workers even though the firm is working well below full capacity, because the firm anticipates difficulties in rehiring suitable workers should trade improve in the future. These workers are then being paid for a full working week irrespective of whether or not they are gainfully employed. Suppose further that a new client appears who wants to buy the type of product made by the firm, but who is not prepared to pay the firm's current prices for that product. Instead he makes an offer which works out at just below the average variable costs of production, which are defined as usual to include all the money which the firm is paying out in the form of weekly wages. Should the firm then accept the offer? Now according to traditional thought on the matter a firm cannot afford to operate at all unless it is covering all of its variable costs in the short run, although it can afford to delay the recovery of fixed costs so long as they are recouped by the time the original capital equipment needs to be replaced. It is argued that if a firm is unable to pay for its raw materials and labour inputs on a weekly basis the supply of all factor inputs will come to a halt. This logically is a very acceptable argument. But notice that, in the example under consideration, *the firm is already paying its full wage bill.*

Therefore, if the firm takes on the order and is able, as a result, to gainfully employ its workers rather than let them sit idly by, it will incur no *additional* wage costs as a result of the extra production. In other words wages are not a variable cost in this particular example. Hence the firm will be able to cover all of its true variable costs by accepting the order, and will probably also be earning enough to contribute to the recovery of fixed costs. The offer is therefore acceptable, although the firm will presumably wish to keep such cut-price agreements as secret as possible.

In the above example we can regard the workers' wages as *sunk* costs. This means that the money to pay for the workers' time has already been laid out by the firm, and is therefore no longer relevant when considering additions to output which do not necessitate any change in available resources. Costs which can be defined as sunk costs will differ for every decision which the firm makes. Obviously wages will not constitute sunk costs if the firm has to employ additional workers in order to meet the extra order. The additional wages will in this case constitute avoidable costs, that is costs which can be avoided by taking no action. Where a machine is lying idle, its costs of obsolescence (the capital loss which is incurred irrespective of whether or not a machine is utilised, because the machine is becoming progressively more and more out of date) are a sunk cost which results from the original decision to buy the machine. Costs of depreciation through use (the capital loss resulting from wear and tear over time while a machine is in actual usage) however are avoidable costs at all times and are as such relevant to a decision as to whether or not to produce a good. The question of the distinction between sunk costs and avoidable costs is thus clearly an empirical matter. Whenever a decision is to be made the firm must assess the incremental costs incurred by that decision. Since the only relevant costs are incremental in nature we often refer here to *marginal costing*.

It is evident that marginal cost will apply only to changes in variable costs. But if a decision is likely to have long-term implications or to result in significant short-term changes in the level of production, marginal cost will include costs generally regarded as elements of fixed costs by cost accountants. A sharp increase in the level of production may for example result in the need for additional supervisory staff. A supervisor's pay is a fixed cost in the sense that it will remain unaffected by changes in the quantity of output, and it will have to be provided even if no output at all is forthcoming. But the pay of an additional supervisor, the employment of whom specifically results from a decision to satisfy one particular order, must be treated as a relevant cost of that order.

It is also worth noting that marginal costing simplifies analysis where a choice has to be made between competing projects in order to determine which is the more profitable, after allowance is made for differences in the incremental output likely to be forthcoming from each project. To the extent that both projects require the same factory space, the same number of supervisory staff and so forth, these costs can be excluded from the marginal cost calculations. The firm will only be interested in those avoidable costs which are different for the two projects.

It will be useful at this point to summarise the above discussion. We have seen that the traditional splitting up of costs into fixed and variable categories is not a useful criterion for decision making, since many costs do not fall easily into one category rather than the other, especially over extended time periods. The economist is interested in discovering which costs can be avoided if a decision is not taken. This is another way of saying that he is interested in discovering the incremental cost which would arise purely as a consequence of making a specific decision. Once however the decision to produce has been made, the firm is interested in determining the value of the resources required by that decision in their next most profitable usage (their opportunity cost). Combining these two concepts we can state that firstly, if the firm has spare resources of any kind no sacrifice is involved in using these resources for a job which was not previously on offer, and secondly, if the firm has alternate uses for its available resources, then the cost of assigning resources to a specific job is equal to the greatest sum they would earn in their best alternative usages.

DEMAND CONCEPTS

So far we have been concerned with the nature of costs, which are the major determinants of any decision affecting the supply side of a firm's operations. The firm can incorporate its knowledge of its costs into a schedule of supply, or supply curve, which indicates the quantities of a good which the firm would be willing to supply at various prices. A supply curve is essentially hypothetical in nature, since in practice a specific quantity must be supplied at a specific price, and this is represented by only one point on the supply curve. The actual price–output combination can however only be determined by considering both demand and supply conditions simultaneously, so that we must now turn to consider some concepts related to demand.

The demand curve facing a firm represents the quantities of the product which customers would be willing to purchase at various prices. Once again it is hypothetical in nature since in practice a definite amount will be bought at a specific price. Customer demand is made up of a wide variety of constituents, of which the most important is probably the income levels of would-be purchasers. Traditionally however we concentrate upon the price charged for the good in order to bring into equivalence the supply and demand curves for that good, which then illustrate the relationship between price and quantity for sale, and between price and quantity demanded respectively. It is customary to assume that where price is increased suppliers will want to increase the quantity supplied, whereas purchasers will want to buy fewer units of any good. This results in demand and supply curves such as appear in Fig. 1.3.

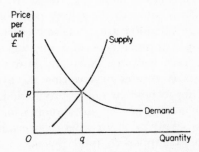

Quantity Oq is purchased at a price of £Op per unit.

FIG. 1.3

Knowledge of demand conditions is essential if a firm wishes to estimate how much revenue it can obtain from selling its products. Its total revenue can be found by multiplying the total quantity sold by the average price per unit of the good. This calculation is very simple where the entire output is sold at a constant price, although in practice many firms indulge in price discrimination, whereby different prices are charged to different groups of buyers for the same product. It must however be true at all times that total revenue is equal to the quantity sold multiplied by its selling price. Thus we have

$TR = p \times q$. Given a figure for total revenue, we can determine the average amount of revenue earned by each unit of output by dividing total revenue by the number of units bought. Thus average revenue is equal to $TR \div q$. But we have already noted that TR is equal to $p \times q$, so that average revenue is equal to $p \times q \div q$ which is the same thing as average selling price. Hence $AR \equiv p$.

Now when we consider that a demand curve constitutes a whole host of possible price–output combinations, it becomes clear that each point on the curve also represents a combination of a level of output with its associated average revenue. This being so the firm's demand curve is necessarily also its average revenue curve, since each point on the curve tells us both how much is being demanded and also the average revenue associated with each unit demanded.

Marginal revenue is equal to the increase in total revenue which occurs as a result of increasing output by one additional unit. It is therefore equal to the selling price of the marginal unit sold. Where all units are being sold at the same price marginal revenue will remain constant, and will also necessarily be equal to average revenue. Normally however a firm can only expect to expand sales by lowering the average price at which it is willing to offer its entire production, and this will cause total revenue to alter by an amount which is no longer equal to the new selling price. In order to ascertain more clearly what exactly does happen to total revenue when there is a change in quantity sold we need to consider the concept of *elasticity*, and this is discussed below.

ELASTICITY

What elasticity seeks to do is to relate two variables to one another in such a way as to enable the firm to determine how *sensitive* one variable is to changes in the other variable (e.g. how sensitive demand is to changes in the price of a good). Once we have determined the sensitivity of a relationship between variables it can be used for predictive purposes. Thus we can use the measured sensitivity of demand to price changes to enable us to predict whether or not total revenue (price × quantity sold) will rise or fall for any given change in price.

This can most easily be done if we know the values of price and quantity exactly, measured in appropriate units, since we can then multiply price and quantity sold both before and after a price change and compare the results. But in general we wish to make predictions which will hold good for a *range* of values of the variables – not merely because this saves us working out large quantities of computations, but also because predictions are at best imprecise. Thus we will always be interested in a range of possible results, because we rarely know exactly the effects upon certain variables of changes in other variables.

Technically elasticity can be defined as

$$\frac{\text{the proportionate change in a variable } x}{\text{the proportionate change in a variable } y}$$

This formula can be broken down as

$$\frac{\text{change in value of } x \div \text{original value of } x}{\text{change in value of } y \div \text{original value of } y}$$

Normally we use the symbol Δ to mean 'change in', which enables us to express the above formula much more concisely as

$$\frac{\Delta x / x}{\Delta y / y}$$

The letters x and y are simply symbols which are given their meaning only in the context of a specific elasticity formula. Most commonly y is used to represent price and x to represent quantity sold, in which event the elasticity of demand or supply, otherwise known as *price elasticity*, is represented by the formula

$$\text{Price elasticity } (E) = \frac{\text{proportionate change in quantity sold}}{\text{proportionate change in price}}$$

The value of E is to be found at all times through the substitution of values for price and quantity into the above formula. Such values must clearly be empirically determined. Nevertheless these are a number of general statements which can be made without recourse to specific problem data.

Let us first consider Fig. 1.4(*a*) from which we can see that

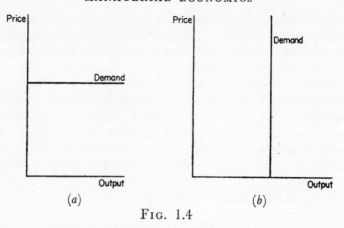

FIG. 1.4

demand expands infinitely without any change in price. In other words, at the ruling price, any quantity of output can be sold. Quantity demanded cannot be said to be measurably responsive to price changes because price in this case does not change. In terms of our formula above this means that the proportionate change in price is equal to 0. But any finite number divided by 0 yields a quotient of infinity. Hence the value of the proportionate change in quantity sold is of no importance because E will always be equal to infinity. The curve is thus said to be *infinitely elastic*.

In Fig. 1.4(*b*) we can see that no matter how big the change in price, quantity demanded remains the same. This means that the proportionate change in quantity is equal to 0. But if $\Delta q/q = 0$ the proportionate change in price is of no importance because E must always equal 0. Notice that the elasticity value must in the above two cases be invariable irrespective of which part of the curves is under study, because only one of the two variables is able to alter in value. This allows us to draw the general conclusion that any horizontal function whether it measures demand or supply, has an elasticity value of ∞ along its entire length. Likewise a vertical function has an elasticity value of 0 along its entire length.

These curves are however not all that useful for practical purposes. A firm is unlikely to find itself able to sell as much as it likes at a constant price, nor is it likely to be unable to affect purchasing behaviour by increasing or decreasing its prices. Most firms find themselves faced by a schedule of demand which falls to the right, signifying that more goods can be sold at low prices than at high prices. A typical demand schedule will be curvilinear, but for analytical purposes it is easier to work with linear functions (see Fig. 1.5).

Every point on the demand curve represents a different

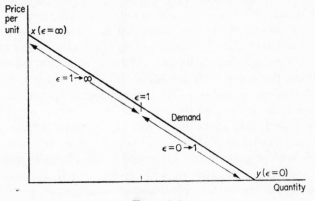

FIG. 1.5

price–output combination. Any change in price must have associated with it a change in output of opposite sign and vice versa. The problem of determining the elasticity value of the curve is therefore of a different order to that in the examples above, where either price or quantity, but not both, was subject to change. It can, however, be demonstrated mathematically that any curve which cuts both the horizontal and vertical axes will have the following properties: (*a*) at the point at which it meets the vertical axis it will have an elasticity value of ∞, (*b*) at the point at which it meets the horizontal axis it will have an elasticity value of 0; (*c*) at its mid-point it will have an elasticity value of 1. Taking these three properties together it becomes clear that (*a*) that part of the demand curve above its mid-point has elasticity values ranging between 1 and ∞, and can therefore be described as *elastic*; and (*b*) that part of the demand curve below its mid-point has elasticity values ranging between 0 and 1 and can therefore be described as *inelastic*

It is very important to remember that the *whole* of the above demand curve cannot be described as elastic or inelastic. It is commonly thought that, if a horizontal demand curve is infinitely elastic, a demand curve which slopes very gently (i.e. is almost flat) must be very elastic along its entire length. Likewise that a demand curve which is almost vertical must be very inelastic at all points. Horizontal and vertical demand curves are, however, exceptions rather than the norm. Any demand curve which cuts both price and quantity axes *has every elasticity value between 0 and ∞,* and elasticity is *different at every point* along the curve. Nor is it permissible, when comparing points on two demand curves having different elasticity values, to designate the point with the higher elasticity value as elastic and the other as inelastic. Rather the former point must be described as *relatively elastic* and the latter point as *relatively inelastic,* and this description will apply even where both points are elastic or both inelastic as defined above.

Now we are particularly interested in the elasticity value of a demand curve because of what it has to tell us about the effects upon the firm's revenues of changes in price and

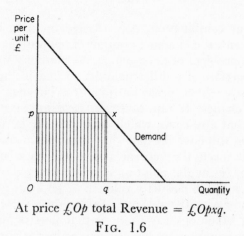

At price £*Op* total Revenue = £*Opxq*.

FIG. 1.6

quantity sold. Revenue is equal to price multiplied by quantity (bought and sold). Hence total revenue is represented by the area lying *under* a demand curve as illustrated in Fig. 1.6.

When price is altered there will be a corresponding change in quantity sold, but of opposite sign. Thus we normally expect total revenue to alter in conjunction with price changes.

As a result of a price rise from £0a to £0b per unit, the firm has increased its revenues for the output 0d, originally selling at £0a but now selling at £0b, by £abyz (Fig. 1.7).

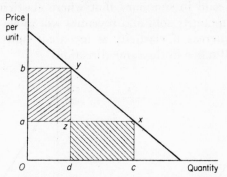

At price £0a original revenue = £0axc.
At price £0b new revenue = £0byd.

FIG. 1.7

On the other hand purchases have fallen by cd, resulting in a loss of revenue, at original prices, of £cdzx.

By comparing the revenue gained with the revenue lost we can discover whether or not the firm has made a *net* gain of revenue as a result of its price alteration. (This cannot however have any implications for *profits* until we take into account changes in costs per unit sold which result from the altered volume of sales.)

But we know that wherever the elasticity value of the demand curve is greater than 1 the proportionate change in quantity sold is greater than the proportionate change in price. Hence if price has risen, and quantity has fallen, revenues will as a result have fallen, because the positive price effect, which increases revenue per unit sold, is outweighed by the negative quantity effect. Conversely of course, if price has fallen, quantity will rise and so will revenues.

Where the curve elasticity value is less than unity the proportionate change in quantity sold is less than the proportionate change in price. Hence if price has risen revenues will also have risen, because the positive price effect outweighs the negative quantity effect. Similarly if price has fallen revenues will have fallen. In other words the results are the exact opposite of those which we derived where elasticity is greater than unity (Fig. 1.8).

It can be said in summary that where elasticity is greater than unity, quantity sold and revenues will move in the same direction, whereas if elasticity is less than unity, price and revenues will move in the same direction.

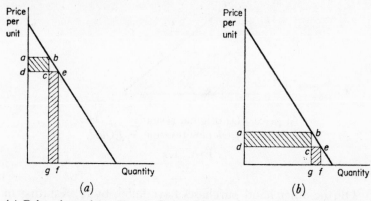

(*a*) Price rises where $E > 1$. Gain of revenue $= abcd$. Loss of revenue $= cefg$. Net revenue *falls*. (*b*) Price *rises* where $E < 1$. Gain of revenue $= abcd$. Loss of revenue $= cefg$. Net revenue *rises*.

FIG. 1.8

It is therefore apparent from the above analysis that when a firm is considering the effects of price or output changes, it can determine the direction of change in net revenues provided it knows the approximate section of its demand curve over which it is operating. A firm will not be able to draw a representation of its demand curve without a significant margin of error, as will be explained in the later section on forecasting. Nevertheless it can reach useful conclusions about the effects upon revenues and profits of changes in sales policy through the application of the above concept. Basic concepts can be applied by a firm at a relatively simple level in order to produce rules for decision making. We will therefore conclude this section by looking at one such decision rule.

BREAK-EVEN ANALYSIS

Break-even analysis, or profit contribution analysis as it is sometimes called, is a way of illustrating the relationship between costs, revenues and profit. The usual method of constructing what is known as a break-even chart is to plot graphically the firm's fixed and variable costs in order to derive a total cost curve, upon which is superimposed the firm's total revenue curve. The vertical distance between the total cost and total revenue curves is then a measure of profit or loss.

In Fig. 1.9 there are two break-even points. The second is

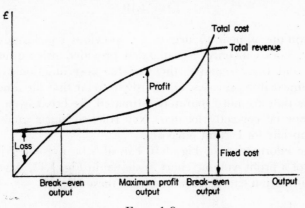

FIG. 1.9

clearly preferable to the first since all production between the two points can be sold at a profit. The most profitable output can be determined by measuring the distance between the revenue and cost functions and choosing the output corresponding to the greatest distance so measured. The object of the chart is basically to determine the relative profitability of different output levels, but, as we shall see, it can be adapted for other purposes.

Now, in practice, break-even charts are customarily drawn with linear relationships, as shown in Fig. 1.10, principally because it greatly simplifies the analysis. The implication of drawing a linear total revenue curve is that price per unit sold must remain constant. The linear total cost curve implies that variable costs per unit sold must also remain constant. These

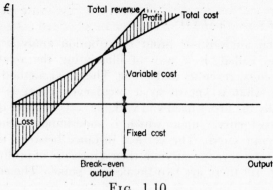

FIG. 1.10

assumptions appear to negate our previous conclusions that firstly, sales can only be expanded provided price gradually falls, and that secondly, the variable cost function will be curvilinear in most cases. Obviously in so far that the functions in question are not accurately estimated the break-even point will not be correctly located. Nevertheless linear analysis is appropriate for certain purposes.

The information in Fig. 1.10 can also be presented in the form of a profit–volume chart as shown in Fig. 1.11. A variety of information can be obtained from these charts.

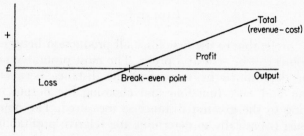

FIG. 1.11

The Break-Even Volume

This is calculated by substitution into the formula below

Break-even volume =

Total fixed cost ÷ $\dfrac{\text{Total revenue } less \text{ variable cost}}{\text{Units of output}}$

The lower part of the formula indicates how much each unit of output can contribute to the covering of fixed costs (i.e. the surplus which each unit earns over and above that needed to cover variable costs). Hence, by dividing the unit contribution into the total of fixed costs we obtain an estimate of how many units need to be produced in order to fully cover fixed outlays.

The Profit–Volume Ratio

This tells us by how much profits can be expected to increase for any given change in output, all other things remaining constant. It is thus a measure of the slope of the profit line in the profit–volume chart (Fig. 1. 11), but it is more commonly calculated by using the formula

$$\frac{\text{Sales } less \text{ Variable costs}}{\text{Costs}}$$

The Safety Margin

Where a firm produces beyond that output which will enable the firm to cover all its costs (the break-even output) the firm is said to enjoy a safety margin. This is calculated using the formula below, and will, as is also true for the profit–volume ratio above, yield a result in the form of a percentage.

$$\text{Safety margin} = \frac{\text{Actual sales } less \text{ sales at break-even point}}{\text{Actual sales}}$$

The major drawback to the use of measures associated with break-even charts is that cost, revenue and profit variables are assumed to vary only in relation to the volume of output produced. Thus it is considered acceptable by many accountants that projected cost and revenue functions in future periods be based upon unadjusted historical data. It is unlikely however that other factors affecting the cost and revenue functions will be so obligingly static in nature. There are likely to be changes over time both in the technology employed, leading perhaps to changes in the types of machines used or to changes in the labour–capital ratio, and in the organisation of the

productive process. Furthermore prices may well vary, especially on an annual basis, and costs are at the very least subject
to the vagaries of inflation and industrial action.

BIBLIOGRAPHY

D. HAGUE, *Managerial Economics* (Longman, 1969).

J. HARVEY, *Modern Economics* (Macmillan, 1969).

K. LANCASTER, *Introduction to Modern Micro-economics* (Rand McNally, 1969).

R. LIPSEY, *An Introduction to Positive Economics*, 3rd edn (Weidenfeld & Nicolson, 1971).

F. LIVESEY, *Economics* (Polytech Publishers, 1972).

B. LLOYD, 'Economies of Scale', *Moorgate and Wall St Review* (Autumn 1972).

C. SAVAGE and J. SMALL, *Introduction to Managerial Economics* (Hutchinson, 1970).

J. SIZER, *An Insight into Management Accounting* (Penguin Books, 1969).

2

Introduction to the Theory
of the Firm

In the course of this chapter we are going to discuss three theories of competitive behaviour, namely perfect competition, monopoly, and oligopoly. Many readers will already be familiar with the first two of these theories, but it is our intention to set out the models in such a way as to facilitate the discussion of alternative approaches to the theory of the firm and of monopoly policy which appears in subsequent chapters, thus permitting the student to refer back to points originally made in this chapter.

PERFECT COMPETITION

In order to construct a theoretical model of how firms behave under circumstances of perfect competition, we need to make the following set of assumptions.

(a) The typical unit of production is a small firm both owned and managed by an entrepreneur, and no one firm supplies more than a very small share of total market demand.

(b) The products of all firms supplying the market are regarded by customers as identical in all respects.

(c) An individual firm is able to alter its rate of production and sales without this having any effect upon the price of the product which it sells. The firm is a passive price-taker.

(d) The *industry* displays freedom of entry and exit in the sense that there are no impediments upon the ability either of new firms to enter the industry or of existing firms to leave the industry.

(e)   The sole objective of the firm is to maximise profits.

(f)   In order to attain its profit maximising output the firm equates its marginal cost with its marginal revenue.

Although the above may appear to be a somewhat lengthy set of preconditions for the existence of perfect competition, it does in fact neglect many of the assumptions found in more traditional texts. It is further to be noted that we are going to assume that all firms are using the same technology, so that they are all operating over the same average cost curve. This is purely a simplifying assumption and leads on from the presumption that all firms within the industry have full knowledge of all relevant market information. The discussion as to whether or not firms in a competitive industry can be expected to be inventive or innovative has been put back to the later chapter on Monopoly Policy. Now the assumption that the firm is a price-taker implies that alterations in its output have no effect upon price. But if price does not vary irrespective of quantity sold this produces an infinitely elastic (horizontal) demand curve, and we have already determined in the previous chapter that firstly, the demand curve and average revenue curve are synonymous, and that secondly, in the exceptional case where average revenue is a constant, marginal revenue is also constant and equal to it. This you will remember is because marginal revenue is equal to the price of the additional good sold, which in perfect competition must remain constant at the level set for all previous units sold.

We can now turn to consider the equilibrium position of the firm in the short run under conditions of perfect competition. According to assumption (e) above, the firm's sole objective is to maximise profit. For the purpose of analysing competitive behaviour we need however to clarify the meaning of the term profit by splitting it up into (a) normal profit and (b) abnormal profit. Normal profit is in reality a part of *costs* so far as the firm is concerned; that is to say it is not a surplus payment to factors but a payment necessarily provided to prevent any factor from choosing to be employed elsewhere. We have come across this concept before in the guise of an 'opportunity cost'. To illustrate this concept in the present context we note that, if a person runs his own firm and works full time at his business, he should count the value of his own labour as a cost of production, because, in effect, it is as much a labour cost as the wages paid to his employees. The value which he places upon his labour should be the maximum wage which he could potentially earn while working for someone else, such that if he finds that he cannot earn as much working for himself as he can earn by working for someone else, he should logically cease to be self-employed. Likewise, where a person sinks his capital into his own firm, he should count as a cost

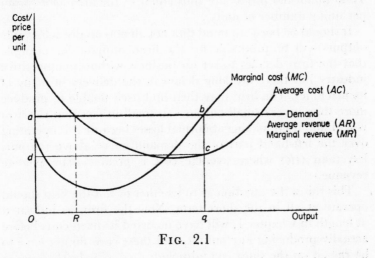

FIG. 2.1

the maximum return that his capital can earn if invested elsewhere.

Abnormal profit accordingly represents any payments accruing to a person or to his assets over and above payments incorporated in the notion of normal profit.

With the aid of Fig. 2.1 we can illustrate the short-run equilibrium of the firm in perfect competition. We have superimposed upon the revenue curves as previously defined a set of average and marginal cost curves in the relationship postulated in Chapter 1 (MC cutting AC at its lowest point).

Now so long as marginal revenue is greater than marginal cost (that is to say above it in the diagram), an increase of output by one further unit must increase abnormal profits (given that normal profit has been incorporated into the cost curves). Thus if profits are to be maximised more output must be produced if $MR > MC$. Likewise, if marginal cost is greater than marginal revenue, an increase in the level of output by one further unit must cause losses. Hence where $MC > MR$ output must be curtailed. Thus we can conclude that profits will be maximised at output Oq where marginal cost and marginal revenue are equal.

At output Oq abnormal profit per unit will be equal to average revenue less average cost, equal to bq less cq or bc per unit. Total abnormal profits are thus equal to the area $abcd$ (profit per unit × number of units).

It should be borne in mind that not all potentially achievable outputs will be profitable for the firm. Suppose for example that the firm decides to set up business within a competitive industry but there are long delays in the delivery of many of its machines. The firm may then find itself unable to produce more than a very small output – so small in fact that the firm would find itself making abnormal losses because it is operating over the left-hand part of the demand curve above (outputs less than OR) where average cost is greater than average revenue.

This raises the question as to whether or not the firm should operate at all in the short term. Now the firm, as indicated at length in Chapter 1, will have incurred its fixed costs before actually producing any output, and these costs do not have to be repaid on the short run, although they will clearly have to be repaid eventually if the firm wishes to replace its fixed capital. On the other hand a firm must pay for its variable inputs as and when they are employed, because failure to do so will result in a shutting off of sources of supply of these inputs, especially of labour inputs which generally only work in return for a weekly wage. Thus variable costs do need to be covered at all times, which suggests that a firm must either earn sufficient revenue in the short term so as to cover variable costs or cease production altogether. Provided variable costs are being covered however, the firm should continue to expand production as much as is possible until it is producing that output at which marginal cost and marginal revenue are equated.

It is also possible for the firm to be making abnormal losses in the short run (i.e. less than normal profits), as indicated in Fig. 2.2. The firm produces output OQ where $MC = MR$. However, it will as a result be making on average a loss of ab per unit sold. Should average revenue remain below average cost for some time the firm would want to withdraw its resources from this industry. In the long run all costs need to be recovered. As firms withdraw so the total supply of the product sold by all

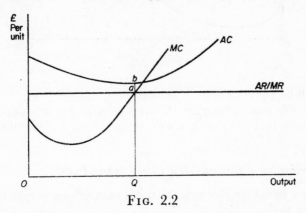

FIG. 2.2

the firms in that industry will diminish, which will cause the price to rise, assuming demand for that product is unchanged. The price will continue to rise as the number of firms diminishes until it is sufficiently high to provide the surviving firms with normal profits.

Furthermore, where any firms in the industry are earning abnormal profits there will be an incentive for resources to shift into that industry either in the form of new firms entering the industry for the first time, or in the form of an expansion of output by already existing firms.

In either event the total supply of the product by all firms combined will rise, and price will fall as a consequence of this, until all firms within the industry are earning only normal profits. There will then be no further incentive for additional increases in output.

Thus, provided there is freedom of entry into and exit from this industry, each firm will in the long run earn only normal profits (Fig. 2.3). Each firm produces where $MC = MR$ in order to maximise profits, but at the same time AC and

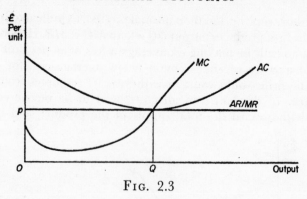

Fig. 2.3

AR will be equal because only normal profits are being earned. Notice also that for output *Oq* average costs are at a *minimum*, indicating that the firm is operating as *efficiently* as possible.

The Derivation of the Individual Firm's Supply Curve

We must next consider how the profit maximising output varies as price varies.

We wish to derive a supply curve which tells us the quantity which the firm wishes to supply at every price (Fig. 2.4). For prices below Op_1 the firm will supply zero units because it is not covering its variable costs. For prices in excess of *AVC* the firm will try to maximise profits by equating marginal

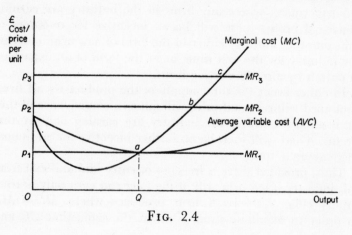

Fig. 2.4

revenue, which is here equal to price, and marginal cost, thus producing a continuous sequence of equilibrium points along the curve *abc*. From this it follows that the supply curve of a competitive firm is that part of its marginal cost curve above its average variable cost curve.

Turning finally to the competitive *industry* there are two comments which need to be made. Firstly we note that the industry supply curve will be equal to the horizontal summation of the marginal cost curves of all the individual firms within the industry (i.e. we add together the total quantity sold by all firms at each price). Secondly the industry demand curve will not be horizontal but will fall to the right in the usual way. This results from the fact that although any individual firm has no effect upon price as it alters its output, when the total output of the industry increases more than marginally it will be possible to sell the extra output level only if the price per unit is correspondingly lowered.

MONOPOLY

According to traditional theory a monopolist is taken to be the sole supplier of a particular good. It is, however, in practice more realistic to define a monopoly as a firm which controls an industry in the sense that, even when other firms do exist within the industry, their operations have negligible effects upon the monopolist's objectives and their attainment.

Now control over its markets enables a monopoly to operate rather differently from a competitive firm. The absence of important competitors will enable the monopoly to set its price without fear of being undersold, and hence we would expect the monopoly to vary its selling price until it is maximising its profits. Each price will have associated with it a certain level of sales depending upon the shape of the demand curve for the monopolist's product, and this curve will fall to the right in the usual way because the curve represents demand for the whole of the output of the industry.

It is perhaps worth noting in passing that the monopolist is often thought to be able to *control* the level of demand for his product, largely through the medium of advertising, whereas it would not pay a firm in a perfectly competitive industry to advertise since it can already sell as much as it wishes at the going market price.

It is clear, therefore, that price will be variable rather than constant, and that any attempt by the monopolist to expand his sales level will cause the price to fall because of the nature of the demand curve. Obviously different price–output combinations will yield different revenues to the monopolist, but only one combination will yield maximum profits depending upon the shape of the cost curves. Thus the monopolist will adjust price and output until he is maximising profits.

Notice that we have so far made no mention of the monopolist's supply curve. This is because such a curve does not in fact exist in a monopoly situation. Remember that a supply curve is merely a representation of what a producer would *like to sell* at different price levels. In practice he will in fact supply a definite amount. A monopolist, given the shape of the demand curve for his product, will always choose a specific price–output combination, and this will represent a point on the demand curve. Hence in monopoly we have *point supply*.

Let us now turn to consider the shape of the monopolist's revenue and cost curves. The average revenue curve will, as always, be identical with the demand curve. Assuming that whatever output is sold is all sold at the same price, price and average revenue will be synonymous, and hence every point along the demand curve will represent the average revenue at which different levels of output can be sold. It can readily be proven that the marginal revenue curve corresponding to any linear average revenue curve which falls to the right will cut the horizontal axis midway to the point at which the average revenue curve cuts that axis. This implies that MR will always be smaller in value than AR, whereas the two were of course equal in value in perfect competition. The essential point to remember here is that if the monopolist lowers his price in order to expand output, he will be losing some revenue on all the units which he could have sold at the original price level but which he is now selling at the lower price level, as well as gaining some revenue as a result of selling more output. The marginal revenue, or *net* increase in total revenue, will therefore be less than the price which is being charged on each unit. The extent to which average and marginal revenue will diverge depends upon the elasticity of the demand curve at the price level in question, as we saw in our discussion in the previous chapter. It is of course quite possible for marginal revenue to be negative in value even where price is positive.

So far as the cost curves are concerned, if we assume them for the moment to be U-shaped as before then it is almost certain that the monopolist's cost curves will initially fall more sharply than would have been true for each of a large number of small firms supplying in total the same output. This largely reflects the much greater capitalisation (fixed costs) which we would expect to find in a firm which intends to supply the whole of, rather than only a small part of, the market. In other words we would expect the monopolist to have access to economies of scale not available to a small competitive firm, and hence for the cost curves to differ in shape. We thus derive Fig. 2.5.

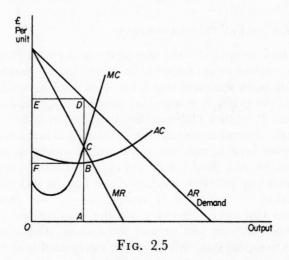

FIG. 2.5

Note that this is both the *short*-run and the *long*-run equilibrium model for the monopolist. We assume that it is not possible for other firms to freely enter the industry in question because the monopolist erects barriers against entry. Hence there is no reason to suppose that there will be any change in the monopolist's circumstances over an extended period of time.

The monopolist is assumed to be a profit maximiser, and

hence, as was also true for firms in a perfectly competitive
industry, he will equate marginal revenue with marginal cost
in order to determine his profit maximising output (OA). In
order however to discover the selling price we must extend the
vertical up from point A through the intersection of MC and
MR (C) until it reaches the average revenue curve, yielding
an average price of OE for each unit sold. The average cost
per unit sold is however only AB, so that the monopolist will
be making abnormal profits (as previously defined) of DB per
unit sold, or a grand total of $BDEF$ for all units. Since there is
no freedom for competitors to enter the industry, there will
be no forces acting upon the monopolist to reduce the level of
these profits in the long run.

Two further issues arise from the monopoly analysis as laid
out in Fig. 2.5.

The Marginal Cost Pricing Controversy

If we turn to compare the monopoly model with that of the
firm in perfect competition in the long run, we find that for
the monopolist marginal cost is less than price in equilibrium,
whereas the perfectly competitive firm has marginal cost *equal*
to price. It is thus claimed that in the monopoly situation
productive resources are not being allocated to best advantage.
The point here is that the value which society attaches to
consumption of a good is reflected in the price that people are
willing to pay for that good. But the cost to society of the
production of that good is represented by the producer's
marginal cost curve (ignoring for the moment the possible
divergence between private and social costs). Hence, if price
exceeds marginal cost, this should be interpreted to mean that
society's satisfaction will be increased if that marginal unit of
the good is produced, since the value which society attaches
to that good exceeds the cost attached to the good. Hence
where the monopolist curtails production before MC and price
are equal, he is preventing society from obtaining a potential
increase in welfare. In perfect competition on the other hand
price and MC are equal in equilibrium, implying that society's
satisfaction is being maximised, while at the same time all
firms are covering their total costs (including normal profit)

since AC and AR are also equal in equilibrium. This conclusion has led critics of monopoly to suggest that monopolists should be either requested or compelled to produce up to the point where MC and price are equal – known as the Marginal Cost Pricing principle.

From the point of view of its practical implications this principle has a great deal more validity for the public sector (nationalised industries) than for the private sector. It is most unlikely that marginal cost pricing would ever catch on in the private sector, not merely because attempts to calculate marginal costs are often subject to considerable error in practice, but also because either

(i) the monopolist would be producing beyond his most profitable output (though still making some profit) and hence would have to be closely supervised in his operations, or

(ii) in some cases, notably those in which the monopolist is operating under conditions of falling average costs, a subsidy would be required to keep the monopolist in business, since at the point where MC and price are equal, average revenue is less than average cost, as illustrated in Fig. 2.6.

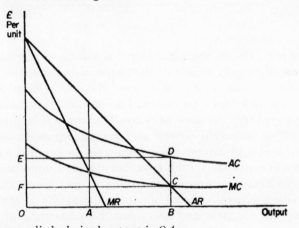

The monopolist's desired output is OA.

The marginal cost pricing output is OB.

Loss per unit for output $OB = \pounds CD$, yielding a total loss of $\pounds CDEF$.

FIG. 2.6

Price Discrimination

Price discrimination occurs when a producer sells a particular commodity to different buyers at varying prices despite the fact that each unit of the commodity is produced at constant cost.

It occurs because different buyers may be willing to pay different amounts for the same commodity, and it may prove profitable for the seller to take advantage of this fact (Fig. 2.7).

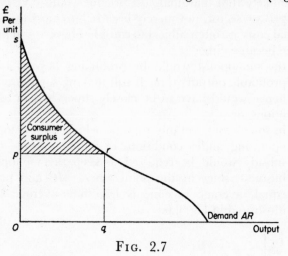

FIG. 2.7

At a price Op the marginal buyer is willing to purchase the qth unit of output. However the shape of the demand curve indicates that there are customers who are willing to pay more than Op for their purchases. Thus in effect the monopolist, were he to charge the same price to all buyers, will be foregoing the revenue indicated by the area *prs*, known as the *consumer surplus,* which he would have been able to acquire were he in a position to charge each customer the maximum price per unit which that customer was willing to pay. Successful discrimination generally rests both upon the ability of the seller to select his clientele and also upon the prevention of resale from the customer who buys cheaply to the customer who pays a high price. It is of course extremely difficult to resell services anyway, so discrimination is much easier to practise in the services as against the goods sector. Also it is easier to discriminate if markets are physically separated (e.g. home and foreign markets).

In such circumstances the monopolist will be discriminating only among a few, large, markets. It is also possible however for the monopolist to discriminate on an individual basis, e.g. a lawyer can charge different amounts to different customers in return for representing them in court, since the service rendered is specific to the individual and cannot hence be resold. An interesting example of a different sort is where a firm sells part of its production to a manufacturer for incorporation in his output, and part direct to consumers at much higher prices (e.g. car parts).

The positive benefits to the monopolist are as follows:

(1) For any given output level, any form of discrimination will enable the monopolist to acquire for himself part of the consumer surplus which would be denied him were he to sell his entire output at the same price.

(2) The monopolist who charges a single price produces less than the perfectly competitive industry, as we have seen, because he is aware that any attempt to expand output beyond the point at which $MC = MR$ will diminish his profits, the expansion in output being inevitably accompanied by a fall in average and marginal revenues. Discrimination will result in a much slower fall in these variables,[1] and hence make it profitable to expand output, since MC and MR will then cross at a higher level of production.

In the diagrammatic representation shown in Fig. 2.8, we will consider a monopolist operating in two markets, both of which are characterised by falling demand curves. It is however a very simple matter to interchange one of these diagrams with one representing a perfectly competitive market, or indeed to add as many extra markets to the model that we so wish, since the economic principles involved will in all cases remain unchanged.

We have drawn in Fig. 2.8 initially two sets of average and marginal revenue curves, appropriate to markets I and II respectively. The MR_T curve in the third diagram is the hori-

---

[1] Because the slope of the revenue curves becomes flattened.

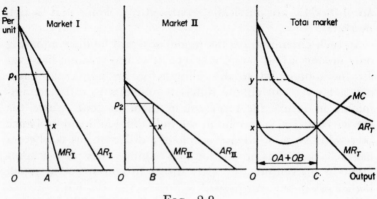

FIG. 2.8

zontal aggregation of MR_I and MR_{II} and its kinked shape reflects the fact that no sales take place in market II yielding a marginal revenue in excess of Oy. In this diagram we have also drawn the monopolist's marginal cost curve. Note that there will only be one MC curve since costs of production are assumed to be invariable irrespective of where the goods are sold. In order to determine his profit maximising output the monopolist will equate MC and MR_T, which produces an optimum output of OC. The monopolist's next task is to decide where to sell this output, or, in other words, how to allocate it to best advantage over the two markets served. What he will in fact do is to allocate the output so as to *keep marginal revenue equal* in both markets at a value of Ox. Thus we find from the diagrams that he will sell a quantity OA in market I and a quantity of OB in market II, where $OA + OB$ are equal to total sales of OC.

Let us try to explain what the firm has been doing in economic terms since this should help to clarify why the monopolist has acted in the manner shown.

The firm has two markets to serve. Each time that it is considering the addition of one more unit to its output, it must consider in which market to sell it. Since it will cost the same to produce irrespective of where it is sold, the incremental unit of output will logically be sold in whichever market offers the higher addition to revenue, i.e. the greater MR. Thus if MR is greater in one market than in the other the firm will expand sales in that market. But if *MR* in that market eventually falls to the point at which it is less than the *MR* available in the other market (*MR* must decline as output expands because of the shape of the *MR* schedule), then the firm will wish to sell further units of output in the other market. Hence, where the firm has a limited output to sell (limited to a total of *OC* above), it will theoretically switch from one market to another depending upon where the *MR* is the greater, and in so doing it will end up supplying *OA* to one market and *OB* to the other. This implies that at the margin the firm would derive as much extra revenue from selling the final (*C*th) unit in market I as it would from selling it in market II. Obviously, if this was not true, and *MR* was greater in one market than in the other for the final unit produced, the firm would find it profitable to transfer output from the market where *MR* was relatively low to the market where *MR* was relatively high, and would continue to do so until this disparity disappeared, at which point no further transfers of output would be profitable because *MR* would be the same in both markets.

However, selling price will *not* be the same in both markets. This results from the fact that the elasticity of demand for the product is different in the two markets, being rather higher in market II at any given price. It is thus a precondition for profitable discrimination that the elasticity of demand should not be the same in all markets.

The rationale for discriminatory behaviour is thus that the monopolist obtains in the two markets sales to those people in each market willing to pay the highest prices for his goods. Were he to sell in only one market, he would be obliged to also sell to people who do not value his goods very highly, and as price would have to be the same for all customers, it would have to be set at a low level.

OLIGOPOLY

Neither perfect competition nor monopoly is commonly to be found in the real world. Most industries are characterised by competitive behaviour which reflects elements of both models, and it would be extremely useful if we could formulate a general theory of how firms behave in practice. Unfortunately, as we shall discover, it has not been possible to do this in a satisfactory manner. The reason for this is rather complex, but it is perhaps worth pointing out that an oligopolist operates within a much more uncertain environment than does a monopolist or a perfectly competitive firm. A monopolist controls the industry, and therefore is able to predict in advance the expected effects of a change in policy, for instance a cut in price, with a great degree of certainty. The perfectly competitive firm is largely passive in its operations, accepting the going price, but it is also able to predict its future operations very accurately since it knows exactly how other firms will behave (perfect knowledge of all market variables is assumed in this model). Only the oligopolist is to a greater or lesser degree unsure of what will happen in the future (to a greater degree where there is no inter-firm collusion, to a lesser degree where such collusion exists) since he must allow for competitive reactions to any policy change which he sets in motion, and these are often unpredictable.[1]

The fewer the number of firms within the industry, the more likely it is that any given policy change by one of them will induce a competitive reaction. This becomes clear if we consider a two-firm industry where there is no collusion. Where one firm lowers the price of its product below that of its competitor, the competitor's sales are likely to suffer more heavily than will be true of other firm's sales where the effects of one firm's price cut are diffused over say the sales of a dozen other firms. Nevertheless we ideally want to develop a theory which is general to the oligopoly situation; and it is to the attempts to do this that we must now turn our attentions.

There are three basic ways in which economists have attempted to construct a general theory of oligopoly.

(1) They have adopted the traditional approach to all competitive situations, which is to construct a theoretical model based upon a given set of assumptions, to then hypothesise about a firm's behaviour given these

[1] For this reason it has been held that to understand oligopoly one needs to understand the rules of war: see for example K. W. Rothschild, 'Price Theory and Oligopoly', *Economic Journal* (Sep 1947).

assumptions, and finally to use empirical data to check whether or not firms do behave as predicted in the real world. The major drawback to this method is that it is likely to be rather a hit and miss affair.

(2) They have formulated a series of hypotheses based upon existing empirical data, relating to fairly narrowly defined situations in which a firm might find itself. Each time that one of these hypotheses is proven acceptable, it is added to those previously accepted, such that at some time in the future it is hoped that it will be possible to predict how a firm will react in every conceivable situation. The major drawback to this method is that it is likely to take much too long to collect the hypotheses together for such an approach to be worthwhile.

(3) They have developed what is known as the Theory of Games, which is an attempt to apply mathematical analysis to the oligopoly situation in order to develop a set of precepts concerning rational behaviour, which, if followed by all firms within the industry, will greatly reduce uncertainty with respect to their future operations.

A Theoretical Model of Oligopolistic Behaviour

Traditional Oligopoly Theory began with the limiting case in which there are only two competitors, known as Duopoly. The best-known duopoly model was constructed by Cournot[1] who suggested that each firm would set its own output in the belief that the other firm's output would remain unchanged. All duopoly models however suffer from an inherent lack of realism, and we shall therefore concentrate upon more modern developments in oligopoly theory. These can perhaps best be illustrated by concentrating upon a specific model, of which a number exist. The 'Kinked Demand Curve'[2] model set out in Fig. 2.9

[1] A. Cournot, *Researches into the Mathematical Principles of the Theory of Wealth* (The Macmillan Co., 1897). See also K. Lancaster, *Introduction to Modern Micro-Economics* (Rand McNally, 1969) pp. 168–72.

[2] See for example R. L. Hall and C. J. Hitch, 'Price Theory and Business Behaviour', *Oxford Economic Papers* (May 1939). Also P. M. Sweezy, 'Demand Under Conditions of Oligopoly', *Journal of Political Economy* (Aug 1939).

is an attempt to provide a theoretical justification for the alleged stickiness of prices in an oligopoly situation. In the diagram we have drawn two demand/average revenue curves crossing at point *a*, and we are seeking to analyse why we might expect the price to be sticky at a level of *Op* for every firm, where *Op* is the prevailing price for all firms within an industry at a particular point in time.

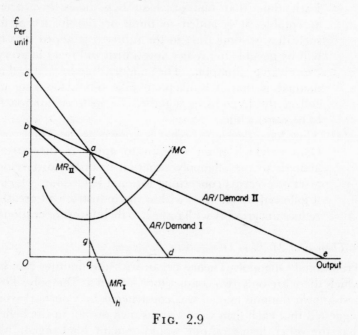

FIG. 2.9

Let us begin by considering what will happen if one particular firm decides to raise its selling price above *Op*. Such a move will make the firm the only high-priced firm within the industry. Hence we would expect price-conscious customers to quickly transfer their custom to other, relatively cheaper, firms with the net result that the price raiser will suffer a significant cut in sales. This is reflected by a movement along the line *ab*, where demand curve II is highly elastic. As a result this strategy will not be considered beneficial by any firm. But suppose that the firm decides to lower its price. It will then be the only cheap firm in the industry and, were its competitors to ignore its behaviour, the net result would be that a large number of its competitor's customers would begin to purchase the products of the cheapest firm. But it is most unlikely that the firm's competitors will turn a blind eye to this strategy, as they did when the firm raised its price. Therefore we must logically expect price-cutting to be competitive, with probably all firms eventually lowering prices to the same extent. If however all firms simultaneously cut their prices there is unlikely to be a major expansion of total sales of the product, unless it is, for example, something particularly desirable which had previously been too highly priced to sell extensively in the mass production market. Thus each firm would suffer a loss of revenue through a downwards movement along the section ad of demand curve I above. In other words demand is now relatively inelastic, so that the marginally greater level of sales multiplied by the significantly fallen price must cause revenue losses to all firms, including the original price cutter. Thus once again this has not proved a profitable strategy for the individual firm to pursue.

Now, in the course of the above analysis, we have discussed movements along a kinked demand curve b, a, d – hence the name of this theory. The precise implications in terms of revenue gains or losses associated with each strategy clearly depends upon the shape of the respective demand curves, and also upon the shape of the firm's cost curves, since falls in output will normally be accompanied by falls in costs, and increases in output by higher costs. It is particularly important to note that the firm's marginal revenue curve, corresponding to the average revenue curve b, a, d, is discontinuous, with section bf corresponding to section ba on demand curve II, and section gh corresponding to section ad on demand curve I. Now if the firm's marginal cost curve passes through the discontinuous section of the curve the profit maximising firm clearly has no incentive to alter its price of Op since even if the firm's costs rise by a reasonable amount the profit maximising output, defined by equating MC with MR, stays the same.

It is apparent however that the above analysis is most readily applicable to the depression phase of the trade cycle, since it is at such a time that any attempt to raise prices will instigate an immediate change of supplier by economising customers. Furthermore, in a depression, a general price cut may do little to stimulate demand overall.

The model is less satisfactory under boom conditions. When people have money to spare, and are competing for available supplies of goods, a price rise by one firm may provide an open invitation for other firms to follow suit, secure in the knowledge that a general price rise will not prove other than a marginal deterrent to customers. In other words demand is relatively less elastic than under depressed conditions, and the firm may find itself operating along *ac* above. In prosperous times prices tend to rise regularly, generally accompanied by an excuse, truthful or otherwise, that costs have risen. Furthermore, price cuts are unlikely in such conditions, firstly because profits can clearly be increased by raising rather than by cutting prices, and secondly because price cuts are unlikely to stimulate sufficient extra sales (which will anyway be accompanied by higher costs) where customers are not price-conscious.

As with any theory it is necessary to compare the prediction of sticky prices against the available evidence, such as it is. We find that between 1926 and 1938 prices remained virtually unchanged in the sulphur industry in the U.S.A., an unusually long period of price stability. Also in 1934 in the U.S. potash industry, one major firm raised its price without its competitors following suit, and the firm's sales fell drastically. As a result it later cut its prices below the level existing in other firms, and all of its competitors followed suit. But in 1947 when G. Stigler[1] investigated seven major U.S. oligopolies, he found that in no case did the above theory accurately portray the way in which these oligopolies were found to operate.

Thus the theory does not, as was hoped, have any general validity[2] although it may reflect reality[3] where inter-firm knowledge is poor, e.g. in a new industry, or where new firms enter an established industry, since they will under those

[1] G. J. Stigler, 'The Kinky Oligopoly Demand Curve and Rigid Prices', *Journal of Political Economy* (Oct 1947).

[2] See for example W. Hamburger, 'Conscious Parallelism and the Kinked Oligopoly Demand Curve', *American Economic Review* (1967) pp. 266–8 and comment pp. 269–72.

[3] See K. G. Cohen and R. M. Cyert, *Theory of the Firm* (New Jersey: Prentice-Hall, 1965).

circumstances have no knowledge of likely competitive reactions to price variations. But even in these cases the firms may quickly learn that they are better off with collusion.

Generalising from Hypotheses about Observed Behaviour

A readily available exposition of how to build up a theory using a collection of hypotheses based upon empirical data appears in Lipsey.[1] He selects as his general hypothesis that of *qualified joint profit maximisation*.[2] He defines this as follows:[3]

> Firms that recognise that they are in rivalry with one another will be motivated by two opposing forces; one moves them towards policies that maximise the combined profits of the existing group of sellers, the other moves them away from the joint profit-maximising position. Both forces are associated with observable characteristics of firms, markets and products, and thus we can make predictions about market behaviour on the basis of these characteristics.

The hypothesis explicitly allows for the fact that the actions of the rivals affect the size of the pie as well as its division among them. This is, of course, not surprising since the group must face a downward sloping demand curve, and unless the elasticity of the market curve just happens to be unity total revenue earned by the group will vary as their collective pricing policies vary. If the firms behave as a single firm they can act just as would a monopolist and adopt that policy which will maximise their joint profits. If all firms depart from monopoly behaviour they will reduce their joint profits. But it may pay *one* firm to depart from the joint profit maximising position if, by so doing, it can increase its share of the profits. If a firm adopts such a strategy in order to raise its share of the profits it must balance what it expects to gain by securing a larger share against what it expects to lose because there will be smaller total to go around among all firms.

Consider the following example:

[1] R. G. Lipsey, *An Introduction to Positive Economics*, 3rd edn (Weidenfeld & Nicolson, 1971).

[2] The notion of joint profits is an integral part of W. Fellner, *Competition among the Few* (New York: Knopf, 1949).

[3] R. G. Lipsey, *An Introduction to Positive Economics*, p. 272.

Let total profits = £100. Assuming there are ten firms in the industry, let profit per firm = £10.

By altering its price one firm may manage initially to increase its profits to £12, or 12 per cent of total profits, as against its original 10 per cent share. The other firms then respond by lowering their prices to the same extent as the original price cutter, but in so doing they will as a group no longer be operating at the most profitable price–output combination. Available profits hence fall, to, say, £92.

The original price cutter now earns 12 per cent of £92, or £11 approximately. Thus it has increased its profits through its original action. All other firms however have taken a cut in profits to just under 10 per cent ($\frac{1}{9} \times 88$ per cent) of £92, which equals £9 approximately.

Lipsey then goes on to enumerate eight hypotheses about behaviour in oligopolistic markets.[1] The most interesting of these has to do with the question of barriers to entry[2] which have been noted in practice to be greater:[3]

(a) the greater the economies of scale;

(b) the greater the degree of existing product differentiation;

(c) the greater the brand-name advertising.

Firstly we note that to produce cheaply may require a large output which normally takes time to achieve, given that existing firms within the industry will already be operating at an optimal level. Thus new entrants will initially only capture a small share of the market. To get a bigger share they must obviously set their price on a par with, or below that, of established rivals, which will imply either minimal profits or actual losses, due to the fact that their costs will be relatively high until full advantage can be taken of scale economies.

Eventually however this barrier could theoretically be overcome. Given this fact, we must investigate what established

[1] R. G. Lipsey, *An Introduction to Positive Economics*, pp. 272–3.

[2] This topic is dealt with in J. S. Bain, *Barriers to New Competition* (Harvard University Press, 1956). P. Sylos-Labini, *Oligopoly and Technical Progress* (Harvard University Press, 1962). F. Modligiani 'New Developments on the Oligopoly Front', *Journal of Political Economy* (June 1958).

[3] A dissenting view is however expressed in P. W. S. Andrews, *On Competition in Economic Theory* (Macmillan, 1964).

firms do to make life tougher for new entrants. There are basically two possibilities here.

If the product is one such that consumers switch brands frequently, then increasing the number of brands sold by existing firms will reduce the expected sales of a new entrant. Where brand switching is important there will be a large floating population of brand switchers who constitute potential customers for the new firm. The greater the number of brands sold by existing firms the more diffused will be this brand-switching effect, and the lower will be the percentage of the brand switchers gained by a *single* brand of the new firm. The proliferation of brands by existing firms is thus seen to constitute a defensive reaction, making it harder for a new firm to pick up brand switchers.

Finally we find that if there is a vast amount of brand-name advertising then a new firm will have to spend a great deal on advertising its product in order to bring it to the public's attention. Where the firm's sales are initially small then advertising costs per unit sold will be very heavy.

This explains a phenomenon which many readers will have observed applies especially to the markets for tobacco products and detergents, where a very few companies play off brands not merely against those of competing companies but also against their own brands. This results from the fact that technological barriers to entry are weak in these markets, and economies of scale are exhausted at low output levels. Hence market domination can only be retained via heavy advertising expenditures and brand proliferation.

The Theory of Games[1]

As we have already indicated above, when a firm is planning its future strategy it must make allowances for the reactions of its competitors to that strategy. This implies of course that it must also have available a set of counter-moves which, if brought into operation after its competitors have reacted to its original strategy, will once again enable the firm to attain its

[1] The original exposition of this theory is to be found in J. von Neumann and O. Morgenstern, *Theory of Games and Economic Behaviour* (Princeton University Press, 1947).

objectives. It is obvious however that such a line of reasoning will also apply to its competitors, who will have made contingency plans to counter whatever counter-move is introduced by the first firm, and so forth. This then presents a picture of a never-ending series of strategies with no firm ever being satisfied with its existing position.

This problem of conflict of interest is, for each participant, a problem of individual decision making under a mixture of risk and uncertainty, the uncertainty arising from his ignorance as to what the others will do.

Game Theory is an attempt to postulate precepts of strategy which, if followed by the participants in a competitive situation, will enable them to reduce the degree of uncertainty surrounding their actions. This is not accomplished directly by assuming knowledge of what an opponent will do, but indirectly by assuming that the opponent has certain information and that he is motivated in certain ways, or, in other words, that he behaves rationally.

More specifically a game is defined as follows. A game is a decision situation involving conflict of interest between two or more interacting decision makers in which the following conditions hold:

(1) Each decision maker has available to him a set of two or more well-specified choices or sequences of choices called 'plays'.

(2) Every possible combination of plays available to the players leads to a well-defined end state, e.g. win, lose or draw, which terminates the game.

(3) A specified pay-off for each player is associated with each end state.

These conditions are represented in a pay-off matrix in which the pay-off associated with each possible combination of choices is shown:

		Player B's possible plays				
		b_1	b_2	b_3	b_4	b_n
Player A's	a_1	X_{11}	X_{12}	X_{13}	X_{14}	X_{1n}
possible	a_2	X_{21}	X_{22}	X_{23}	X_{24}	X_{2n}
plays	a_3	X_{31}	X_{32}	X_{33}	X_{34}	X_{3n}
	a_4	X_{41}	X_{42}	X_{43}	X_{44}	X_{4n}
	a_n	X_{n1}	X_{n2}	X_{n3}	X_{n4}	X_{nn}

Now where each participant knows the value of the X pay-offs in the table, and also that his competitors are aware of the strategic principles (as set out below) underlying competitive behaviour, his pursuit of a rational objective (to maximise his pay-off) will be undertaken in effect under circumstances of certainty about the outcome of the strategy.

The above paragraph can most easily be clarified by setting out some illustrative examples of competitive games. In so doing we are not concerning ourselves with situations in which it is impossible to reduce the uncertainty of the outcome, known frequently as 'games against nature'. The outcome of a farmer's crop strategy will depend very much upon the weather. From the farmer's point of view however, he can hardly treat the weather as a competitor whose actions can be assumed to be rational. Hence the outcome of his strategy can never be known with certainty. Although this problem is interesting in its own right, and is referred to again in Chapter 5, we are concerned here purely with the industrial sector where players are all assumed to behave rationally.

Let us consider a two-person game (duopoly) in which whatever one player loses the other gains. This is called a *two-person zero-sum game*. Suppose the following pay-offs apply to A, the pay-offs to B being the negative of those to A.

		Player B (losses)	
		b_1	b_2
Player A	a_1	2	8
(gains)	a_2	4	6

Now if A knows that B will choose b_1, he should select a_2 for a gain of 4. If on the other hand he knows that B will choose b_2 he should select a_1 for a gain of 8.

But which choice of strategy will be made by B? A will reason as follows: 'B will observe that if he selects b_1 the most that he can lose is 4, whereas strategy b_2 can potentially lose him 8. B will as a consequence choose strategy b_1, in which case I want to pursue strategy a_2 for a pay-off of 4.' This reasoning is based upon the MINIMAX principle which assumes that B will act so as *to minimise his maximum possible loss* (and hence to minimise A's maximum possible gain).

At the same time B will have been attempting to rationalise

A's most likely course of action. His reasoning is as follows: 'A observes that if he selects a_1 the least he can gain is 2, whereas if he selects a_2 the least he can gain is 4. Therefore he will select a_2 and I should select b_1.' This reasoning assumes that A will be acting so as to *maximise his minimum possible gain*, known as the MAXIMIN principle.

In the above situation we thus find that *both* competitors reach the same conclusion, namely that a_2b_1 will be the optimal strategic combination. Notice further that neither A nor B can improve his pay-off *where his competitor does not also change his strategy*.

This then is a solution to the game, since both players are satisfied with the outcome and neither is tempted to further change his strategy.

However not all two-person zero-sum games have such a solution. This solution exists only if the pay-off matrix has an entry which is the *highest in its column and the lowest in its row*. Such an entry is known as a *saddle point*. Several or more such entries may be found. An example of a matrix containing no saddle point is set out below.

| | | Player B (losses) | |
		b_1	b_2
Player A	a_1	4	8
(gains)	a_2	6	2

B is assumed to choose his strategy based upon the minimax principle. This suggests a choice of strategy b_1. A is assumed to choose his strategy based upon the maximin principle. This suggests a choice of strategy a_1.

A combination of strategies a_1b_1 will however satisfy neither party. A will see the opportunity to improve his position by moving to strategy a_2 which will improve his pay-off *where B does not alter his strategy*. On the other hand B will not turn a blind eye to such a change of strategy, and will respond by himself moving to strategy b_2, which will in turn cause A once again to alter his strategy. Thus there is no equilibrium combination of strategies in the above matrix.

To resolve such a matrix we must turn to a technique known as *mixed strategies*, as set out below, which can be used in the absence of a saddle point.

A few further points are however worth noting at this point.

Where a matrix contains a large number of entries, implying that each participant has open to him a wide range of choice of strategies, it is generally possible to eliminate many of the entries from consideration using the principle of *dominance*. Consider the following situation in which a manufacturer is in conflict with his supplier with respect to prices paid for products bought by the manufacturer.

		Manufacturer's strategies (costs)			
		M_1	M_2	M_3	M_4
Supplier's	S_1	20	14	10	25
strategies	S_2	30	12	6	10
(gains)	S_3	19	3	18	4
	S_4	−3	9	5	1

The pay-offs represent gains to the supplier and costs to the manufacturer. Some of the supplier's strategies are obviously more forceful than others (e.g. S_1) and the same is true for the manufacturer (e.g. M_2).

There is no saddle point, and hence no immediately obvious solution. Not all the above entries will however be important to the participants.

No matter what strategy is chosen by the manufacturer, the supplier stands in all cases to gain more by adopting S_1 in preference to S_4 since all the pay-offs are greater. S_1 is thus said to dominate S_4, and S_4 will be dropped from the matrix.

In the *residual* matrix the manufacturer stands to concede less to the supplier by adopting either M_2 or M_3 rather than M_1 since all the pay-offs are lower. M_1 is thus dominated by M_2 and M_3 and will be dropped from the matrix. This leaves 9 entries.

But S_2 is dominated by S_1 and will be dropped from the matrix, leaving 6 entries. Furthermore in the residual matrix M_4 is dominated by M_2. This leaves us with only 4 entries as follows.

		Manufacturer's strategies	
		M_2	M_3
Supplier's	S_1	14	10
strategies	S_3	3	18

C

A matrix may not always reduce down to only 4 entries, but any reduction in its size is inevitably beneficial for the application of mathematical techniques. Where a matrix has no saddle point we utilise the *mixed strategy* approach to arrive at a solution. We can illustrate this approach by using the above matrix of manufacturer's and supplier's strategies.

If the manufacturer adopts the minimax principle he will choose M_2. If the supplier adopts maximin he will choose S_1. The combination S_1-M_2 is not however a saddle point, for the manufacturer will react to the supplier's choice of S_1 by himself altering strategy to M_3. Thus the question arises as to whether it is possible to find a solution preferable from the manufacturer's point of view to the combination S_1-M_2 – that is one with a pay-off of less than 14 – but at the same time preferable from the supplier's point of view to the combination S_1-M_3 where the pay-off is only 10. Such a solution, where it exists, will automatically fall somewhere between the pay-offs for combinations S_1-M_2 and S_1-M_3 respectively.

Firstly let us consider the manufacturer's optimum mixed strategy. Fig. 2.10 shows the gains to the supplier where he adopts strategy S_1 for various combinations of strategies by the manufacturer. The pay-offs are measured on the vertical axis. On the left-hand axis where the probability of the manufacturer adopting strategy M_2 is 1 ($M_2\ p = 1$) and that of adopting M_3 is zero ($M_3\ p = 0$) the pay-off will be 14 as we can see from the matrix ($S_1 M_2 = 14$).

Where the probability of the manufacturer adopting M_2 is zero ($M_2\ p = 0$) and of adopting M_3 is 1 ($M_3\ p = 1$) the pay-off to the supplier adopting strategy S_1 will be 10.

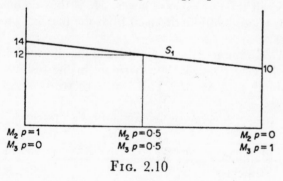

Fɪɢ. 2.10

But let us suppose that the manufacturer adopted both strategy M_2 and M_3 in equal measure ($M_2 p = 0.5$, $M_3 p = 0.5$). This will give a pay-off of 12 since $12 = 0.5 \times 14 + 0.5 \times 10$.

By combining its strategies M_2 and M_3 in different ways the manufacturer can select any desired pay-off to the supplier having a value between 10 and 14, provided the supplier adopts strategy S_1.

However, exactly the same approach can be adopted to analyse the expected pay-offs to the supplier were he to adopt strategy S_3, which in Fig. 2.11 has been superimposed upon

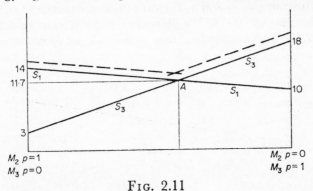

Fig. 2.11

our previous diagram. The double line now defines the *set of maximum gains to the supplier*, assuming that the supplier always adopts the most favourable strategy in response to any mixed strategy adopted by the manufacturer. Hence where the manufacturer is trying to minimise the maximum payment to the supplier, he will choose the combination of strategies indicated by point A above.

At point A the pay-off to the supplier is the same whatever strategy he adopts. Hence if A represents the manufacturer's mixed strategy M_2 with probability p and M_3 with probability $(1-p)$ then:

$$14p + 10(1-p) = 3p + 18(1-p)$$

Therefore
$$14p - 3p = 18 - 18p - 10 + 10p$$
$$11p = -8p + 8$$
$$19p = 8$$

Therefore $\qquad p = 0.42 \quad$ and $\quad (1+p) = 0.58$

The pay-off to the supplier is then either

$$14 \times 0.42 + 10 \times 0.58 = 11.7$$
or
$$3 \times 0.42 + 18 \times 0.58 = 11.7$$

The value of the pay-off thus lies within the previously ordained limits of 10 to 14.

Thus we have found that, bearing in mind the supplier's potential choice of strategy, the manufacturer will be willing to make a conciliatory offer of 11·7. But will the supplier find the offer acceptable? To answer this question we reverse the above process to show the gains to the supplier where he adopts strategies S_1 and S_3 for various combinations of strategy by the manufacturer. We thus derive a diagram as seen in Fig. 2.12. The double line now defines *the set of minimum rises*

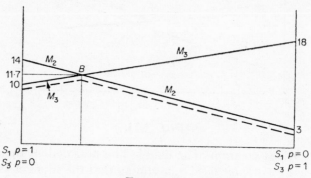

FIG. 2.12

which the supplier can expect to achieve assuming the manufacturer always adopts the most adverse strategy for the supplier in response to any mixed strategy adopted by the supplier. Logically the supplier will want to choose the combination represented by point B above.

The pay-off at B will be determined by the formula below.

$$14p + 3(1-p) = 10p + 18(1-p)$$
$$14p + 3 - 3p = 10p + 18 - 18p$$
$$11p + 8p = 15$$
$$19p = 15$$

Therefore $p = 0.79$ and $(1-p) = 0.21$

The pay-off to the supplier is then either

$$14 \times 0\cdot79 + 3 \times 0\cdot21 = 11\cdot7$$
or
$$10 \times 0\cdot79 + 18 \times 0\cdot21 = 11\cdot7$$

This solution exactly matches that derived for the previous formula. In other words the sum which the supplier will find acceptable matches the sum which the manufacturer is willing to pay, and the solution falls somewhere between the manufacturer's previous offer of 10 and the supplier's previous demand for 14. In fact the bargaining process has come out marginally in favour of the manufacturer.

The above technique can be adapted to the particular characteristics of all other two-person zero sum games.

It can be shown that any two-person zero-sum game, regardless of the number of strategies available to the two players, has a unique equilibrium value. Unfortunately this is the only part of game theory that is essentially complete.[1]

Some of the reasons why game theory has not been found to be of greater usefulness in competitive decision problems are as follows. Firstly, in a real-life situation the number of competitors is often greater than two. This leads to significant difficulties for analytical purposes. As soon as three or more players are involved it becomes possible for coalitions of players to form. In a game with three players for example two may form a coalition against the third, and by agreeing to their own selection of strategies may be able to guarantee themselves pay-offs greater than those which would result from the maximin principle. Thus the situation may become too complex for analysis.[2]

Also, in the real world, the conditions are not usually of the zero-sum type, such that the competitors' gains are identical

---

[1] Some interesting developments can however be found in, for example, G. W. Nutter, 'Duopoly, Oligopoly, and Emerging Competition', *Southern Economic Journal* (Apr 1964). R. D. Luce and H. Raiffa, *Games and Decisions* (John H. Wiley, 1957). L. B. Lave 'An Empirical Approach to the Prisoner's Dilemma Game', *Quarterly Journal of Economics* (Aug 1962) pp. 424–36.

[2] A sophisticated attempt to apply the principles of game theory appears in M. Shubik, *Strategy and Market Structure, Competition, Oligopoly and the Theory of Games* (New York: Wiley, 1959).

with another competitor's losses. Even where it is a zero-sum game, there is no generally accepted theory. Difficulties arise here because one player may be able to inflict heavy losses upon an opponent at the cost of small losses to himself, and hence by threats be able to force his opponent to adopt strategies to the advantage of the first player.

In conclusion we may note that none of the above three approaches to the oligopoly problem is at all satisfactory. This is one area in economic theory where the student can quickly reach the limits of what is known, which must be considered an unsatisfactory state of affairs where a large number of industries within the United Kingdom fall within the scope of the oligopolistic structure.

BIBLIOGRAPHY

K. G. COHEN and R. M. CYERT, *Theory of the Firm* (Prentice-Hall, 1965).

R. L. HALL and C. J. HITCH, 'Price Theory and Business Behaviour', *Oxford Economic Papers* (May 1939).

J. HARVEY, *Modern Economics* (Macmillan, 1969).

K. LANCASTER, *Introduction to Modern Micro-Economics* (Rand McNally, 1969).

R. G. LIPSEY, *An Introduction to Positive Economics* 3rd edn (Weidenfeld & Nicolson, 1971).

F. LIVESEY, *Economics* (Polytech Publishers, 1972).

G. MEANS, 'The Administered Price Thesis Reconfirmed', *American Economic Review* (June 1972) pp. 292–306.

M. MOORE, 'Stigler on Inflexible Prices', *Canadian Journal of Economics* (Nov 1972) pp. 486–94.

G. J. STIGLER, 'The Kinky Oligopoly Demand Curve and Rigid Prices', *Journal of Political Economy* (Oct 1947).

P. SWEEZY, 'Demand under Conditions of Oligopoly', *Journal of Political Economy* (Oct 1947).

3

Alternative Theories of
the Firm

We have previously developed the traditional models of perfect competition and monopoly, the nature of which were first expounded in the nineteenth century in order to describe the way in which firms actually behaved at that time. We also discussed the fact that the modern theory of oligopoly is not at present readily utilisable for the purpose of analysing the behaviour of firms. Thus the traditional models are the only generally accepted ways of describing how firms behave even today, a century or so after they were first formulated. Nevertheless the models are both limiting cases of competition, either describing markets where no one firm has any control over price, or markets completely dominated by a single firm. The most cursory study of the post-war structure of industry reveals that there are very few such markets to be found. Hence one cannot help but conclude that the traditional models no longer reflect reality. It is our intention in the pages which follow to consider attempts which have been made to make the theory of the firm more realistic, in order to discover whether any alternative theory to the classical models can justifiably be adopted in their place.

We have discussed in some detail the hypotheses underlying the traditional models. In looking critically at these models it is appropriate to single out the assumptions common to them all for closer scrutiny because we are seeking to piece together a general theory of the firm which can be used to predict the behaviour of all firms irrespective of market circumstances. We do not thus intend to cover all potential areas of criticism of traditional theories but rather to single out those which are most significant from the point of view of constructing a new theory.

Very broadly we can sum up the traditional theories of the firm as describing a situation in which the owner-manager of a firm (known as the entrepreneur), possessed of perfect knowledge about the internal workings of his firm and about its environment, sets out to maximise profits by equating marginal cost with marginal revenue. The entrepreneur has no objectives other than to make as much profit as possible, all of which accrues solely to himself, and he is able to achieve his objective at all times because he acts in full knowledge both of his own cost and revenue curves and also of those of his competitors (where such exist).

As a description of the way in which firms behave today the above is hardly accurate. That much at least appears intuitively obvious. But when we come to try to describe how firms do behave in reality we find that this is by no means an easy question to resolve. Obviously a new theory must take full account of all the changes in the industrial structure which have taken place over the last century. Many people would probably point to the rise of the conglomerates or corporations as being the main factor here, not so much because of their numbers since there are many more small businesses even today than large corporations, but because of the proportion of Gross National Product which originates from them. It is, as we shall see, largely the appearance of the corporation which has led economists to believe that many firms today no longer behave in the way that most firms behaved a century ago, and we shall discover further that this is often ascribed to the gradual separation of ownership from control in the large corporation.

THE SEPARATION OF OWNERSHIP FROM CONTROL

The hypothesis of the separation of ownership from control broadly states that for any one of a number of reasons (but most often because of the inability of any one individual to raise enough funds to ensure his company's long-term growth) most large private companies are eventually forced to go public and hence to issue shares. Furthermore it becomes impossible for one individual to control a large firm by himself, and he is obliged to hire professional managers. Over a period of years the number both of shareholders and of managers tends to grow. The managers must be left to their own devices on a day to day basis, although they are theoretically responsible, when all is said and done, to the shareholders, who express their wishes through the Board of Directors of the company.

In an ideal world the managers, being in effect the employees of the shareholders, desire only to do the best they are able for their employers. This requires that their sole objective be to maximise profits. On the other hand the managers, if left to their own devices, will want to maximise their own welfare, which is often reflected in a desire to maximise their salaries, their leisure, or their progress up through the firm. The presumption however is that they cannot maximise both their own welfare and that of the shareholders simultaneously, and hence, in most firms, profits are not maximised. The shareholders are either unaware that this is happening or unable to do anything about it. This is because there are supposedly a very large number of small shareholders, most of whom take no active interest in the firm. Hence very few shareholders attend the Annual General Meeting of the firm when management present the accounts for the previous year. With the help of a few friendly shareholders at the A.G.M. the accounts are always accepted, provided that dividends paid out are not inexcusably low. But even where the shareholders are disturbed by the poor performance of the firm, and turn up in force to question management at the A.G.M., it is almost impossible for the shareholders to demand that all responsible management be dismissed because of the huge disruption to the firm were such an eventuality to come to pass. Thus in essence managers and owners are two distinct groups, having different aims, with those of the management predominating subject to the need to keep the shareholders in a reasonable state of contentment.

There are however two broad areas of contention in the above discussion. Firstly we must ask the question 'Is shareholder control as non-existent as is popularly supposed?', and secondly we must ask 'Are managers motivated towards goals other than profit maximisation?' The latter question will be

discussed at a later point in the chapter, and we will now
turn to answer the former question.

The classical statement regarding shareholder control
appears in Berle and Means[1] to the effect that 'ownership is
so widely distributed that no one individual or small group
has even a minority interest large enough to dominate the
affairs of the company'. Their case is however legalistic
rather than economic – that is they set out to demonstrate that
shareholders have no legally enforceable rights over the
managers, who are therefore freed from the only major constraint upon their behaviour. According to Berle and Means
any other constraints such as exist are not sufficiently important
to alter the behaviour of management.

Berle and Means's study was updated by Larner,[2] who concluded that 'it would appear that Berle and Means in 1929
were observing a "managerial revolution" in process. Now,
30 years later, that revolution seems close to complete, at
least within the range of the 200 largest financial corporations.'

Now midway between the shareholders and managers is
to be found the Board of Directors. Directors may or may not
themselves be shareholders. In either event are we to suppose
that they will support primarily the shareholders to whom
they are legally responsible, or the managers, with whom they
have close personal links? Berle and Means consider that
management can for the most part pursue their own objectives
without interference by the Directors.[3] Since many director-

[1] A. A. Berle and G. Means, *The Modern Corporation and Private
Property* (New York, 1932; revised edition, New York: Harcourt,
Brace & World, 1968).

[2] R. J. Larner, 'Ownership and Control in the 200 Largest
Non-financial Corporations 1929 and 1963', *American Economic
Review* (Sep 1966) pp. 777–87.

[3] A view with which Hindley concurs: see 'Separation of Ownership and Control in the Modern Corporation', *Journal of Law and
Economics*, p. 186, but for an example L. R. Desfosses and P. Smith
in 'Interlocking Directorates. A Study of Influence', *Mississippi
Valley Journal* (June 1972), pp. 57–69 conclude as a result of analysing the 500 largest industrial companies in the U.S.A. in terms of
interlocking directorates that 'banks in particular were shown to
have considerable power'. On the other hand we do not know if they
exercised it.

ships are regarded as a sinecure, it would be rash to suppose that Directors can be relied upon to prevent management pursuing goals other than profit maximisation. On the other hand it would be equally rash to suppose that the Board of Directors would turn a blind eye to proposed operations clearly intended to be of no advantage to the shareholders, especially where the Directors are themselves shareholders. Managers may in principle be able to appoint the Directors they so wish, but the standing of a company is often reflected in the supposed integrity of the members of its Board. Where public figures are voted off the Board or resign because they disapprove of management policies, a proxy fight might quickly develop. Thus it is appropriate to regard the Board of Directors as a constraint upon free management action.

Viewed in retrospect other aspects of the post-war world appear to belie the above contention. Periods of furious merger activity and a whole host of successful or otherwise take-over bids litter the past quarter century. Threat of a take-over, which, if successful, often leads to the dismissal of several managers in the company taken over, thus seems to Hindley[1] to be a significant constraint upon the behaviour of managers, a factor dismissed by Berle and Means as unimportant. Beed[2] however does not accept that it requires a take-over bid to get shareholders together with a view to considering the performance of the existing management. He feels that Berle and Means never adequately proved their statement[3] that 'clearly no individual or small group was in a position to dominate the company through stock ownership'. Berle and Means looked at ownership registers in an attempt to determine whether or not there were any sufficiently large shareholder interests to dominate the company concerned in the legalistic sense. But as Beed points out[4] the fact that one cannot detect a majority of shares registered in one person's name can

[1] B. Hindley, 'Capitalism and the Corporation', *Economica* (Nov 1969), pp. 428–9. See also H. Manne, 'Mergers and the Market for Corporation Control', *Journal of Political Economy* (1965).

[2] C. Beed, 'The Separation of Ownership From Control', *Journal of Economic Studies* (University of Aberdeen) vol. 1, no. 2 (1966).

[3] Berle and Means, *Modern Corporation and Private Property*, p. 84.

[4] Beed, *Journal of Economic Studies*, vol. 1, no. 2, p. 31.

be interpreted in two ways, 'either it could mean, with Berle and Means, that no one individual, or small group could gain sufficient votes for control, *or*, contradicting Berle and Means, that only a few per cent of votes was required for control'. Beed quotes evidence gathered in Australia to indicate that a small number of minority interests of the order of 1 to 5 per cent of the voting shares could determine the structure of control. It is difficult to find substantive data for the United Kingdom but several attempts have been made to quantify the minority control issue in the U.S.A.[1] Such large minority shareholders would obviously lose a proxy fight under circumstances in which the very small shareholders banded together against them, but such a circumstance is unlikely, and it is widely accepted that in practice a small minority of shareholders exercise such control as exists over management. It is as well to remember in addition to the above that ultimate control over the way in which a voting share is exercised should not always be presumed to be in the hands of the person in whose name the share is registered. By regrouping the largest shareholders and tracing their interrelationships the picture of minority share interests can change drastically.[2] Such relationships are often difficult to pin down for obvious reasons, and they also tend to lead to too great an emphasis being placed upon the actual exercise of voting rights as a means of controlling management. Berle and Means themselves listed thirteen ways in which directors can be selected, guided and influenced. We cannot look at all of these in detail at this point, but it is perhaps appropriate to examine one of the thirteen, namely the implications of changes in the source of capital.

The extreme view is to the effect that 'major Corporations in most instances do not seek capital. They form it themselves.'[3] If this is true it frees companies from the constraint of scrutiny

[1] See for example: Temporary National Economic Committee (T.N.E.C.) Monograph No. 29, *The Distribution of Ownership in the 100 Largest Non-financial Corporations* (Washington, 1940). R. A. Gordon, *Business Leadership in the Large Corporation* (Washington, 1945). V. Perlo, *The Empire of High Finance* (New York, 1957).

[2] See for example V. Perlo, ibid.

[3] A. A. Berle, *The 20th Century Capitalist Revolution* (New York, 1954).

by bodies from whom outside capital has to be raised. Dooley[1] however points out that in the U.S.A. 'the total liabilities of non-financial business approach one half trillion dollars, that about one third of the assets of the 100 largest non-financial corporations are financed on credit, and that these 100 corporations interlock (directors) 616 times with the 50 largest banks and life insurance companies alone'. But do these figures present a prima facie case for the proposition that management is subject to the control of external sources of finance? Dooley concludes that this must be true, but Beed[2] and Hindley[3] are not sure. Hindley points out that the need to raise new capital will enter into managerial calculations 'only in so far as the managers wish to achieve objectives for which the flow of capital available from retained earnings or the issue of bonds will not suffice'.

It is interesting to note that the strongest critics of modern capitalism do not see any real distinction between management and control. Baran and Sweezy[4] point out that

> there is no justification for concluding from [the apparent freedom of management from stockholder control] that managements in general are divorced from ownership in general. Quite the contrary, managers are among the biggest owners; and because of the strategic positions they occupy they function as the protectors and spokesmen for all large scale property. Far from being a separate class, they constitute in reality the leading echelon of the property owning class.

With respect to dividend policy they point out that

> Most managers are themselves big owners of stock...and as such have the same interest in dividends as other big stockholders. This interest is neither in a minimum nor a maximum pay-out rate but somewhere in-between; stock-

[1] P. C. Dooley, 'The Interlocking Directorate', *American Economic Review* (June, 1969).

[2] Beed, *Journal of Economic Studies*, vol. 1, no. 2, pp. 39–40.

[3] Hindley, *Economica* (Nov 1969) pp. 430–4 and *Journal of Law and Economics* (Apr 1970) p. 186.

[4] P. Baran and P. Sweezy, *Monopoly Capital* (Pelican, 1968) p. 46.

holdings should yield a reasonable cash income...; on the other hand they should also steadily appreciate in value.

They suggest that pressure for low dividends arises because of the lower rate of taxation in the U.S.A. on capital gains as against dividends, and that pressure for high dividends comes from small shareholders whose political support is needed by the leaders of big business.

Further exploration of the issues involved in the alleged separation of ownership from control bring us no nearer to a conclusive answer. The whole issue, as Beed points out, is far from resolved 'mainly because passive control may never exhibit itself in an active manner. That such exhibition is lacking does not disprove its existence, but quantification of it becomes impossible.'[1, 2]

THE THEORY OF THE FIRM RECONSIDERED

With the above discussion firmly in mind we can now turn to consider the most important respects in which the traditional theory of the firm is thought to diverge from reality. Hoogstraat[3] suggests a sixfold categorisation as follows:

(1) Firms are assumed to seek profits, but the firm is not regarded as pursuing a profit objective alone. Firms are assumed to have a number of goals, and the profit goal is not even necessarily the most important among them.

(2) Firms are assumed to seek profits, but this objective plays a very subsidiary role because managers are above all seeking to satisfy their own personal objectives.

(3) Firms are assumed to regard the pursuit of profits as their primary objective. They do not however seek to maximise profits but rather to earn 'satisfactory' profits.

[1] Beed, *Journal of Economic Studies*, vol. 1, no. 2, pp. 39–40.

[2] It is worth bearing in mind at this point that even if one accepts that ownership is effectively separated from control, a firm's performance may remain wholly, or in good part, unaffected by such changes in control.

[3] E. E. Hoogstraat, 'Attacks on the Value of the Profit Motive in Theories of Business Behaviour', in *Interdisciplinary Studies in Business Behaviour,* ed. J. W. McGuire (Southwestern, 1962) p. 18.

(4) Firms are assumed to regard profit maximisation as their sole or dominant objective, but are unable to achieve this objective because they cannot in practice implement marginal analysis in decision making.

(5) Firms are assumed to regard profit maximisation as their sole or dominant objective, but are prevented from achieving it because of uncertainty or lack of knowledge.

(6) Firms may regard profit maximisation as their dominant objective, but the structure of large organisations militates against the achievement of this objective.

Categories (1) and (2) above clearly overlap to a considerable extent because one cannot readily treat the 'firm' as having objectives separate from those of the individuals who comprise it. As we shall discover the notion of 'satisficing' (achievement of satisfactory profits) will have relevance to most of the above categories.

ALTERNATIVE OBJECTIVES TO PROFIT MAXIMISATION

Managers who go away on courses to play business games invariably decide that the objective towards which they are to strive should be the maximisation of profits. Buried deep in the subconscious of most businessmen is the belief that they should be making as much money as possible for the owners of their firm even if in practice they know full well that they either cannot do so or that they want to achieve other conflicting objectives at the same time. Nevertheless it is not hard to understand why the objective of profit maximisation has become a sacred cow of capitalist societies. Economists themselves must shoulder part of the blame because they have tended to concentrate upon teaching the precepts of the traditional theories of the firm to the relative exclusion of modern theories such as are discussed below. This is possibly because of the intellectual appeal of the traditional models,[1] which enable us to predict with absolute assurance how a firm

[1] See for example: B. J. Loasby, 'Hypothesis and Paradigm in the Theory of the Firm', *Economic Journal* (Dec 1971) p. 167 or R. N. Anthony, 'The Trouble with Profit Maximisation', *Harvard Business Review* (1960) pp. 127–8 or Hoogstraat in *Interdisciplinary Studies in Business Behaviour*, for a discussion on this point.

will behave when for example its costs rise or there is a slacken-ing off of demand for its product. Furthermore the perfectly competitive model, as we have suggested in a previous chapter, allegedly maximises the welfare of the community, and therefore holds out the promise of a kind of Utopia not to be found in modern theories of the firm.[1] To admit that the traditional models bear no relationship to the real world is to accept that much of economic theory is an irrelevance. Nevertheless most economists have now faced up to this unpalatable fact, and are attempting to produce theories based upon empirical studies. It is therefore now the time to examine some of the more interesting and important of these ideas.

In practice we must first clear up a problem which arises concerning time. The traditional theory of the firm is based upon the assumption that firms maximise profits both in the short and in the long run, however defined. All the theories discussed below conflict sharply with the desire to maximise profits in the short run. It is however possible to argue that in the long run they will all lead to profit maximisation. It can be argued, for example, that a firm which holds back on a proposed price rise, resulting initially in satisfactory rather than maximum profits, will reap long-term benefits. This is because it will have avoided alienating any of its customers, and thus will have maximised goodwill, an essential ingredient in the pursuit of long-run profit maximisation. Unfortunately the 'long run' is a hazy concept which is never pinned down in quantitative terms in the literature. This implies that the firm can always justify its short-term policies as expedient in the light of its desire to maximise long-run profits, safe in the knowledge that it will never in practice have to look back from some point in the future and justify its past policies in the light of its avowed long-run goals.

For the purposes of our analysis we shall however assume

[1] It is interesting to note that several commentators make express allowance for social responsibility, which implies a decline in profits in the short run at least, although in the longer term anti-pollution drives, etc. may prove a good way for firms to develop consumer loyalty. See for example K. R. Andrews, 'Public Responsibility in the Private Corporation', *Journal of Industrial Economics* (Apr 1972) pp. 135–45, for a discussion on this point.

that the alternative theories of the firm discussed below are intended to demonstrate conflict with the goal of profit maximisation both in the short run and in the long run. One widely quoted theory is that postulated by Baumol.[1] He puts forward the idea that the firm has as its objective the maximisation of sales revenue subject to a profit constraint. Firms prefer to pursue sales revenue rather than profit because managers believe that their salaries, power and standing, both within their own company and the business community as a whole, will be enhanced by the pursuit of the former objective rather than the latter. Pursuit of sales revenue requires that ownership be separated from control, a matter we have already discussed in detail, but it is fair to say that managers are never entirely free from shareholder influence. They must at all times earn sufficient profits to enable the firm to pay out dividends sufficiently great as to keep shareholders in a contented state. Hence Baumol postulates a profit constraint.

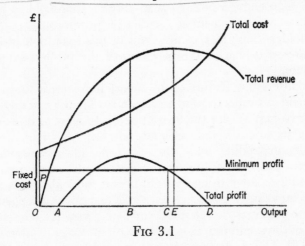

FIG 3.1

Profit consists of revenues less costs. Hence we can draw the profit curve by measuring the distance between the total revenue and total cost curves (Fig. 3.1). No profits will be earned for outputs less than OA or greater than OD because profits are only earned where revenues exceed costs. Profits are maximised where the two curves are furthest apart, which is

[1] W. J. Baumol, 'On a Theory of Oligopoly', *Economica* (1958).

at output OB. On the other hand sales revenue will be maximised at the highest point of the total revenue curve given by output OE.

But the firm is required to produce profits to the tune of £OP to satisfy shareholders. Hence it will not be possible to produce OE units which do not yield sufficient profits to satisfy the profit constraint. The highest level of sales revenue commensurate with the profit constraint is to be found at output OC.

This theory can also be placed within the group of 'satisficing' theories of business behaviour. This is because the firm is under obligation to provide a satisfactory level of profits for its shareholders, but, once having done so, it may pursue any other objectives it so wishes. The major drawback of this, as indeed is true of all satisficing theories, is that the meaning of the term 'satisfactory profits' is never pinned down with any accuracy. In the Baumol model it simply refers to a level of profits high enough both to keep existing shareholders happy and to make the firm an attractive prospect to would-be shareholders. The lack of precision of this definition however compares poorly with the precision of the profit-maximising postulate.

One interesting feature of the theory however, is that it can be extended to incorporate an argument for the extensive role of advertising. Where the firm attempts to expand its sales by cutting its prices it may or may not achieve an increase in revenue, depending upon the elasticity of demand for the product. But where the firm expands sales as a result of increasing its advertising expenditures it must always increase its revenues, since price per unit sold remains unchanged but sales have increased. The total cost curve now includes advertising, outlays, and thus rises in line with increases in advertising (Fig. 3.2). The profits curve is once again the difference between the total revenue and total cost curves. The level of advertising expenditures which would maximise profits is £OB, and the level which would maximise sales revenue is £OC. Where, however, the firm is seeking to maximise sales revenue subject to a profit constraint of £OP it will spend £OA on advertising, a level of expenditure which might in practice be reasonably considered somewhat excessive.

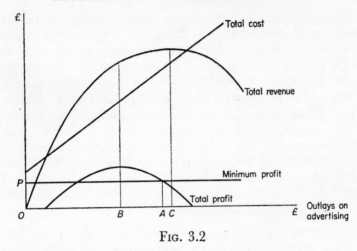

FIG. 3.2

Several features of the model have aroused considerable comment. On a theoretical level Shepherd[1] set out to prove that 'the more there is of oligopolistic interdependence, the less will sales-maximisation effect or explain output decisions'. Hawkins however[2] concludes that 'wherever advertising and/or other non-price forms of competition are possible (almost everywhere in oligopoly?) the sales revenue maximiser will choose to produce a greater output and, in order to gain demand for it, will advertise more than the profit maximiser. Both firms will charge the same price.' Hence the sales revenue maximiser and profit maximiser only choose the same output where 'advertising and all other forms of non-price competition are either completely ineffective or impossible'.

Alchian[3] further considers that the model is open to the objection 'that it implies the firm will not make any sacrifice in sales, no matter how large an increment in wealth would thereby be achievable'.

[1] W. G. Shepherd, 'On Sales Maximising and Oligopoly Behaviour', *Economica* (1962) pp. 420–4.

[2] C. J. Hawkins, 'The Sales Revenue Maximisation Hypothesis', *Journal of Industrial Economics* (Apr 1970) pp. 135 and 138.

[3] A. A. Alchian, 'The Basis of Some Recent Advances in the Theory of Management of the Firm', *Journal of Industrial Economics* (Nov 1965) pp. 30–41.

Baumol stated that[1] 'Executive salaries appear to be far more closely correlated with the scale of operations of the firm than with its profitability'. As a result commentators have sought most often not to refine the theory itself but to test the above postulated correlation between sales and executive incomes. Patton[2] concluded that executive pay is directly related to company size and that above average pay leads to above average profits. Roberts[3] found that the relationship between executive pay and sales was apparently stronger than that between pay and profits. Chiu, Elbing and McGuire[4] investigated correlations between executive incomes, sales, and profits for 45 of the largest 100 corporations in the U.S.A. from 1953 to 1959. They found that

> the line of apparent causation runs from sales to incomes rather than incomes to sales. In other words when the Board of Directors of an enterprise...determines executive compensation this decision is affected significantly by current or past sales or by realized changes in sales. Executive compensation is primarily a reward for past sales results and is not necessarily an incentive to future sales efforts... for these 45 firms for the period examined in the study.

Hall, however,[5] hypothesising that 'positive departures from the profit constraint should set in motion forces that will lead to increases in sales revenue', found no evidence to support this supposition.

Masson, furthermore,[6] finds all these studies wholly unpalatable, particularly the way in which they ignore executive

[1] W. J. Baumol, *Business Behaviour, Value and Growth* (New York, 1959) p. 46.

[2] A. Patton, *Men, Money, and Motivation* (New York, 1961).

[3] D. R. Roberts, *Executive Compensation* (Glencoe, 1959).

[4] J. W. McGuire, J. S. Y. Chiu and A. O. Elbing, 'Executive Incomes, Sales and Profits', *American Economic Review* (Sep 1962) pp. 753–61.

[5] M. Hall, 'Sales Revenue Maximisation. An Empirical Examination', *Journal of Industrial Economics* (Apr 1967) pp. 143–56.

[6] R. T. Masson, 'Executive Motivations, Earnings, and Consequent Equity Performance', *Journal of Political Economy* (Dec 1971) pp. 1278–92.

ownership of stock in their own companies,[1] 'all of these studies have omitted a full definition of executive compensation, including present value aspects of stock options and retirement benefits, and they have excluded executive return from stock ownership as well'.[2] Llewellen[3] had previously found that a ratio of compensation based on executive stock and stock options to other compensation was of the order of 5 to 1. Hence Masson feels that

> Executive financial incentives are found to be primarily related to firm stock market performance. The sales performance of the firm has no consistent positive or negative effect on executive financial return.... It was found that firms with executives whose financial rewards more closely paralleled stockholders' interests performed better in the stock market over the post-war period. For this sample of firms it was concluded that the hypothesis of present value maximisation better explains firm's behaviour than the hypothesis of sales maximisation.

The evidence is therefore inconclusive.

Growth

In a later study[4] Baumol himself grew dissatisfied with his previously quoted static analysis.

> Though I remain firmly convinced of the merit of the hypothesis as a static characterization of the current facts of oligopolistic business operations, in the present context – a growth equilibrium analysis – it is desirable to modify the hypothesis in two respects.

First maximisation of *rate of growth* of sales revenue seems a

---

[1] As originally evidenced by F. W. Taussig and W. S. Barker, 'American Corporations and their Executives', *Quarterly Journal of Economics* (Nov 1925).

[2] Masson, *Journal of Political Economy* (Dec 1971) p. 1281.

[3] W. G. Llewellen, 'Management and Ownership in the Large Firm', *Journal of Finance* (May 1969) pp. 299–323.

[4] W. J. Baumol, 'On a Theory of Expansion of the Firm', *American Economic Review* (1962) pp. 1078–87.

somewhat better approximation to the goals of many
management groups in large firms than is maximisation of
the current *level* of sales.

The second modification deals with the nature of the profit
constraint which in a static model may have seemed to be
arbitrarily imposed from the outside. In the later model
the profit constraint becomes the 'means for obtaining
capital needed to finance expansion plans'. But beyond
some point profits compete with sales. Thus 'the optimal
profit stream will be that intermediate stream which is
consistent with the largest flow of output (or rate of growth of
output) over the firm's lifetime.' ´

Williamson[1] extends Baumol's model, but concludes that
'growth is never limited by lack of finance as such...but by
the fear of takeover'. In other respects he is strongly in favour
of a growth maximising hypothesis, and sets out in detail the
differences between the behaviour of a growth maximiser and
a profit maximiser.

Mueller[2] points out that the problem with the growth
hypothesis is not its theoretical justification but 'the failure of
both its defenders and its critics to recognize that its validity
probably varies depending on the age of the firm and its
investment opportunities'. He begins by postulating the separation of ownership from control and goes on to argue that
managers' non-pecuniary rewards are 'directly associated with
size and growth and not with profitability'. For this reason, even
though a growing firm will be subject eventually to managerial
diseconomies of scale and a declining rate of return on its
investments, managers' pursuit of growth is not limited by a
desire to maximise stockholder welfare but by limited availability of investment funds (a factor which Mueller largely
discounts, as does Williamson above), threat of takeover and
compassion for stockholders. Mueller thus expects the growth
maximising firm to 'undertake more investment than a
stockholder–welfare maximiser, pay equivalently smaller divi-

[1] J. H. Williamson, 'Profit, Growth and Sales Maximisation',
Economica (Feb 1966).

[2] D. C. Mueller, 'A Life Cycle Theory of the Firm', *Journal of
Industrial Economics*, vol. xx, no. 3 (July 1972) pp. 199–219.

dends, grow at a faster rate, and have a lower market value for its firm'.

Mueller expects, however, that the freedom to pursue growth and the accompanying conflict between owners and managers will only appear over time as the firm expands and matures. 'At the firm's creation the stockholders have complete control over the amount of investment undertaken since they supply all of the initial capital.' Over time the capital shortage disappears, firstly because its internal fund flows eventually outpace its new investment opportunities, and secondly because the reduction in uncertainty regarding the future following its early success lowers the cost of outside capital. Gradually, however, managers' interests supercede those of the stock-holders who are powerless to prevent this happening.

Unfortunately, after surveying the literature,[1] Mueller can find no direct evidence to support the growth maximisation hypothesis. On the other hand he detects favourable evidence to the extent that 'the returns mature firms earned by reinvesting their internal cash flows appear to be substantially below their stockholder's outside investment opportunities'.[2]

Wealth Maximisation

One obvious advantage of the above model is that it incorporates a discussion of dynamic changes over time. It is to be presumed that the firm's principal interest is its continued existence over long periods of time, and this fact suggests that static models of the firm are of limited validity. An alternative dynamic model incorporates the concept of wealth maximisation which postulates that firms seek to maximise the present value of expected net revenues over all periods within the forecastable future. The derivation of present value appears on pp. 49–50, and need not be covered in detail at this point other than to bear in mind that among its advantages is the fact that it both expressly recognises that a pound today is worth more than a pound at some future date, and also that it can be

[1] Ibid., pp. 210–16.

[2] See also M. Hall and L. Weiss, 'Firm Size and Profitability', *Review of Economics and Statistics* (Aug 1967) p. 329 for some supportive evidence.

adjusted to incorporate an allowance for uncertainty by varying the discount factor. Despite this, however, Gordon[1] remains unconvinced as to the validity of wealth maximising concepts because he does not feel that a firm can adequately measure the effects of uncertainty upon future returns.

Managerial Discretion and Growth

Marris[2] has produced a model of managerial discretion which takes as its starting point the separation of ownership from control. He suggests a model based on the hypothesis that managers are particularly concerned with the growth rate of the firm, subject to minimum constraints on security.[3] He points out that if managers were simply concerned with size *per se* they would move from smaller firms to larger firms, and then to even larger firms. But most managers prefer to stay put in their existing firms. Consequently 'managements are likely to see the growth of their own organization as one of the best methods for satisfying personal needs and ambitions'.[4] Salary, power and prestige result from policies of rapid growth, so the manager is motivated to pursue such policies. Growth and security are, however, competing objectives, since security demands conservative financial policies such as excess liquidity, whereas growth requires the undertaking of relatively risky investments and risky methods of obtaining capital. In particular security is sought from the threat of take-over, which Marris considers will tend to become more likely where the firm has an

'(I) internal rate of return on productive assets substantially lower than could be obtained with a complete
change of management;

[1] R. A. Gordon, 'Short Period Price Determination in Theory and Practice', *American Economic Review* (June 1948) pp. 280–1.

[2] R. Marris, 'Why Economics Needs a Theory of the Firm', *Economic Journal* (Mar 1972; special issue) pp. 321–52; *The Economic Theory of 'Managerial Capitalism'* (Macmillan, 1964); 'A Model of the "Managerial" Enterprise', *Quarterly Journal of Economics* (May 1963) pp. 185–210.

[3] Marris, *Quarterly Journal of Economics* (May 1963) p. 186.

[4] Ibid., pp. 187–8.

(II) excessive retention ratio, especially but not only in firms suffering from (I) with little prospect of early change;

(III) excessive liquidity.'

On the other hand he points out that 'A minimum-profit restraint inhibits the firm's ability to stimulate growth of demand for its products while a restraint on retentions affects its ability to obtain capital to meet the demand.' Thus he suggests that it is possible to envisage a trade-off relationship between growth and security. This relationship will be such that the extent of the trade-off cannot be altered in favour of shareholders. 'The best the stockholders can get is the position of over-all optimum for the managers, since the managers in choosing this point, take just that much account of the stockholder's bargaining position that they, the managers, regard as optimal.'[1]

One consequence of successful growth maximising is a greater share of the market. Total concentration is, however, avoided 'because the most successful maximizers of today are not the most successful tomorrow'. In practice Marris considers that his theory predicts accurately the existing size distribution of industry.[2]

Marris's model provides us with a testable hypothesis because it follows from the above that owner-controlled firms will achieve on average lower growth rates and higher profit rates than management-controlled firms. Radice[3] set out to test this hypothesis with respect to 89 firms in the food, electrical engineering, and textile industries in the United Kingdom from 1957–67. 'In general, companies in which there was a definable interest group holding more than 15% of the voting shares were classified as owner-controlled, and where the proportion was less than 5% as management-controlled.'[4] He concluded that

---

[1] Ibid., pp. 206–7.

[2] See for example H. Simon and C. Bonini, *American Economic Review* (Sep 1958) and Marris, *Theory of 'Managerial Capitalism'*, chap. 7.

[3] H. K. Radice, 'Control Type, Profitability and Growth in Large Firms', *Economic Journal* (Sep 1971) pp. 547–62.

[4] Ibid., p. 551.

differences in performance do appear to exist between the two control types in profitability. But whereas we might have expected the higher profit rates of owner-controlled firms to be associated with lower growth rates than those of management-controlled firms the former are in fact superior in both respects. In addition they show greater variability in the relationship between profit and growth rates.

Monsen, Chiu, and Cooley[1] conclude that[2]

An analysis of the data reveals that the owner-controlled group of firms outperformed the management-controlled firms by a considerable margin. The net income to net worth ratio was 75% higher for owner-controlled firms than the management-controlled ones over the twelve year period. This result indicates that the owner-controlled firm provides a much better return on the original investment and suggests a better managed capital structure and more efficient allocation of the owners' resources.

On the other hand Kamerschen[3] is of the opinion that the type of control does not appear to explain very much of the variation in profit rates among the 200 largest non-financial companies included in the study by Larner referred to previously. Hindley[4] also considers that the control status of firms does not crucially affect firm performance, a view which is shared by Llewellen,[5] who concludes that a significant separation of the pecuniary interests of ownership and management does not exist because of extensive executive shareholdings in their own companies.

The Marris model is not well received by Solow,[6] who points out firstly that

[1] J. S. Chiu, D. E. Cooley and R. J. Monsen, 'The Effect of Separation of Ownership and Control on the Performance of the Large Firm', *Quarterly Journal of Economics* (1968) pp. 435–51.

[2] Ibid., p. 442.

[3] D. R. Kamerschen, 'A Theory of Conglomerate Mergers. Comment', *Quarterly Journal of Economics* (Nov 1970) pp. 668–73.

[4] Hindley, *Journal of Law and Economics*, pp. 185–221.

[5] Llewellen, *Journal of Finance* (May 1969) pp. 299–323.

[6] R. M. Solow, 'The Truth Further Refined. A Comment on Marris', *The Public Interest* (Spring 1968) pp. 47–52.

the alternative theory – that corporations maximise long run profits, more or less, and expand whenever they earn more than a target rate of return – also entails that successful companies will be growing most of the time, and will no doubt be talking about it [and secondly that] devotion to growth is quite consistent with profit maximisation if profit is interpreted as the after-tax return to the stockholder because long term capital gains are not taxed as heavily as dividends.

Survival

Several other theories revolve around the question of the firm's long-run survival.[1] Survival, security and conservatism are all part and parcel of the same approach to decision taking. This approach has been expressed by Rothschild[2] as follows: 'But there is another motive which cannot be so lightly dismissed, and which is probably of a similar order of magnitude as the desire for maximum profits, the desire for secure profits.' Security implies risk-avoidance whereas high profits will for the most part arise out of medium- or high-risk projects. Hence a desire for security is unlikely to be synonymous with long-run profit maximisation. As Rothschild points out, a firm bent on maximising profits will put money into the projects offering the greatest returns whether internal or external to the firm whereas a firm bent on security will always reinvest the bulk of its profits.

On much the same lines is Fellner's[3] objective of a 'safety margin' which is the difference between the sales price of a commodity and the average unit cost incurred in its production. The safety margin then allows for unexpected price falls or increases in costs for which the firm cannot compensate in the short term, thus suffering a decline in profits.

The output offering the greatest degree of safety will not

[1] For example P. Drucker, 'Business Objectives and Survival Needs', *Journal of Business* (Apr 1958).

[2] K. W. Rothschild, 'Price Theory and Oligopoly', *Economic Journal* (Sep 1947) pp. 308–9.

[3] W. Fellner, *Competition among the Few* (New York: Alfred A. Knopf, 1949) p. 153–4.

provide the greatest level of profits except under perfectly competitive conditions. But as Hoogstraat points out,[1]

> if the unfavourable cost and price changes are more than just feared – if they are actually anticipated – then the cost and revenue data on which the firm bases its output and pricing decisions will be changed correspondingly, and the level of output selected actually will be the most profitable level under the changed cost and revenue assumptions.

According to Gordon[2] a businessman operates in such a degree of uncertainty that 'he may well take the sort of action which yields a substantial margin of safety and particularly the sort of action which promises to stabilize one or more of the variables with which he has to deal'.

Day, Aigner and Smith[3] investigated the possibility of determining a compromise between expected profit maximisation and high safety margins. They concluded that

> the desire to cover overheads and hence to avoid losses in the presence of uncertainty about price or the position of the monopolist's demand curve result in various output policies which can be most simply characterized as full cost pricing or safety margin pricing. In some cases behaviour satisfies conventional $MC = MR$ rules so long as it does not violate a bound placed by the desire for safety first. However, in general a concern for safety margins will lead to a departure from conventional rules.

Internal Finance

The desire for security as we have suggested will tend to lead to re-invested profits. This can be viewed from another angle as the desire by the firm to avoid a liquidity crisis. Reder[4] argues that management may have to accept some form of trade-off

[1] Hoogstraat, in *Studies in Business Behaviour*, p. 21.

[2] Gordon, *American Economic Review* (June 1948) p. 270.

[3] D. J. Aigner, R. H. Day and K. R. Smith, 'Safety Margins and Profit Maximisation in the Theory of the Firm', *Journal of Political Economy* (Dec 1971) pp. 1293–301.

[4] M. W. Reder, 'A Reconsideration of the Marginal Productivity Theory', *Journal of Political Economy* (1947).

between liquidity and profitability where the firm seeks to finance its expansion out of retained earnings. Dean[1] points out that a firm may prefer a less profitable but more liquid investment. We have already noted in discussing the separation of ownership from control that the need to go public will act as a constraint upon the management of a firm, so that one would expect this to be allowed for in some way in any theory of the firm.[2] Gordon[3] suggests that 'economists tend to underrate the importance of what may be called the liquidity-solvency motive in business. The fear of bankruptcy and the even more widespread fear of temporary financial embarrassment are probably more powerful drives than the desire for the absolute maximum in profits.' He refers to the 'banker mentality' which in large firms leads to the sacrifice of probable profits for the sake of an impregnable financial position.

Homeostasis

Several theories are based upon the physical sciences, particularly biology. Firms, like organisms, start small, mature, produce offspring, and eventually die. Such theories can be divided into two groups, 'viability' theories which emphasise long-run changes, and theories of 'homeostasis' which emphasise short-run changes.[4] Homeostasis is a synonym for stability. It is alleged that physical organisms always attempt to lead stable lives[5] because change is threatening and requires the

[1] J. Dean, *Managerial Economics* (Englewood Cliffs, N.J.: Prentice-Hall, 1951).

[2] See also K. B. Boulding, 'Implications for General Economics of More Realistic Theories of the Firm', *American Economic Review* (May 1952) p. 40; or W. W. Cooper, 'A Proposal for Extending the Theory of the Firm', *Quarterly Journal of Economics* (Feb 1951).

[3] Gordon, *American Economic Review* (June 1948) p. 271.

[4] For further details of both 'viability' and 'homeostasis' see L. S. Burns, 'Recent Theories of the Behaviour of Business Firms', *University of Washington Business Review* (Oct 1959) pp. 30–40; also A. G. Papandreou, 'Some Basic Problems of the Theory of the Firm', in *Survey of Contemporary Economics*, ed. B. Haley (1952) p. 212, for a discussion of the hypothesis of 'selection of the fittest'.

[5] Walter B. Cannon, *The Wisdom of the Body* (New York: W. W. Norton, 1932) p. 317.

organism to go to great lengths to adapt to its changed circumstances. Boulding[1] has suggested that 'there is some "state" of the organism which it is organised to maintain, and any disturbance from this state sets in motion behaviour on the part of the organism which tends to re-establish the desired state'. In Boulding's scheme the notion of equilibrium is more general than that of maximisation, although there will always be firms seeking to maximise profits even where most other firms are pursuing what Boulding calls the 'line of least resistance'. Where a firm pursues the objective of homeostasis it requires only to decide a set of norms for its behaviour. Once such norms have been established any deviation from the norms will automatically set up forces within the firm which will correct the deviations and re-establish the norm. The original set of norms may either be unique to the individual firm or may be borrowed from another firm which is considered to have achieved great success. The set of norms may thus come in a variety of guises. Typically, however, it will involve a set relationship between some of the variables to be found in the firm's balance sheet, or, as we shall be discussing in more detail further on, a set relationship between costs and price. Where, however, a firm employs any form of inflexible relationship between operating variables it is most unlikely that this will result in profit maximisation, which requires the firm to continuously vary its operating procedures to take advantage of small changes in market circumstances.

Viability

Alchian's[2] suggested approach embodies 'the principles of biological evolution and natural selection by interpreting the economic system as an adaptive mechanism which chooses among exploratory actions generated by the adaptive pursuit of "success" or "profits".' He begins by accepting Tintner's[3]

[1] K. Boulding, *A Reconstruction of Economics* (New York: John Wiley, 1950) pp. 26–7.

[2] A. Alchian, 'Uncertainty, Evolution and Economic Theory', *Journal of Political Economy* (1950) pp. 211–21.

[3] G. Tintner, 'The Theory of Choice under Subjective Risk and Uncertainty', *Econometrica*, ix (1941) 298–304.

postulate that in an uncertain world profit maximisation is a meaningless guide to specifiable action because he feels that 'realized positive profits, not maximum profits are the mark of success and viability'. Further, 'it does not matter through what process of reasoning or motivation such success was achieved. The fact of its accomplishment is sufficient.'

Now 'Positive profits accrue to those who are better than their actual competitors' irrespective of how good or bad those competitors may be. Also 'the greater the uncertainties of the world, the greater is the possibility that profits would go to venturesome and lucky rather than to logical, careful, fact-gathering individuals'. This suggests that relatively superior firms survive, but also that it is as much a matter of luck as good judgement as to which firms are relatively superior at any given time.

It is usually assumed that surviving firms must have adapted themselves to their environment. On the other hand there may have been no motivated adapting, in which case surviving firms must have been adopted by their environment. Alchian does not regard the survival of certain firms over long periods of time as prima facie proof of their adaptability.

Firstly one needs to know how many firms started off together and the size, risk and frequency of each commitment. Rather than there being 'too many firms with long lives in the real world to admit an important role to chance...one might insist that there are actually too few'.[1]

Two forms of adaptive behaviour are, however, emphasised. Firstly firms tend to imitate the successful behaviour of other firms. This, Alchian claims, has led to the widespread introduction of conventional mark-ups, price leadership, accounting ratios, etc. In an uncertain world imitation appears less risky than the introduction of untried concepts. Imitative behaviour, however, cannot guarantee success, which often requires the willingness to abandon it when the time is ripe.

Secondly firms can adapt through a process of 'trial and error', selecting those policies which appear to have moved the firm to some extent nearer its optimal operating position.

[1] Alchian, *Journal of Political Economy* (1950) p. 215.

This is however a short-term process since the firm cannot in a world of uncertainty foresee the whole sequence of policies which will eventually lead to profit maximisation.

Firms are therefore regarded as relatively passive. Despite this lack of motivation many firms are adopted by the environment and survive. Other firms are able to successfully adapt through imitation or trial and error, but here again long-run survival requires that they are relatively lucky in moving away from established patterns of behaviour at exactly the right time. The correct policy at the wrong time will of course cause the firm to disappear.

Biological analogies are severely criticised by Penrose.[1] She points out that 'the development of firms does not proceed according to the same "grim" laws as does that of living organisms', and also that to abandon the development of firms to 'the laws of nature' diverts attention from the importance of human decisions and motives, and from problems of ethics and public policy, and surrounds the whole question of the growth of the firm with an aura of 'naturalness' and even 'inevitably'. She feels that mankind, unlike other species, has the ability to adapt his environment to suit himself, or to become independent of it, whereas biological theories allow only that man can adapt to his environment. Thus she feels that any analogy which passes over the ability of an organism to consciously deliberate should be discarded.

PERSONAL MOTIVES OF MANAGERS

The personal motives of managers, unlike certain of the objectives discussed above, will always conflict with profit maximisation even in the long run. It is often suggested that, for example, managers will try to maximise their own incomes rather than the incomes of the shareholders. There is, however, a good deal of evidence that managers do not regard their work simply as a source of income. The rather amorphous concept of job satisfaction often relates to non-monetary objectives. An interesting classification of non-profit maximising

[1] E. Penrose, 'Biological Analogies in the Theory of the Firm', *American Economic Review* (Dec 1952) pp. 804–20.

objectives (which encompasses all those mentioned so far) has been put forward by Higgins,[1] who divides them into three categories: those which induce a firm to produce less than the profit maximising output; those which induce a firm to produce more than the profit maximising output; and those which induce the firm to stay put irrespective of whether or not the output in question is greater than or less than the profit maximising output.

The main objective of managers which falls within the first category above will be a desire for leisure. Into the second category fall the desire for growth, power or prestige, and into the third category any forces making for conservatism. Of those objectives in the first category one deserves further mention, as follows:

Leisure

Hicks[2] has stated that 'the best of all monopoly profits is a quiet life'. This suggestion has subsequently been picked up by Scitovsky,[3] Nettl[4] and Reder,[5] and incorporated into their theories of business behaviour. Managers are assumed to be continuously faced by a choice between more profit or more leisure. In general managers will find the attractions of more leisure growing stronger as the firm's profits rise, and it is suggested that managers will not always work hard enough to actually maximise profits. This would only happen where a manager's desire for greater profits is unaffected by the level of profits so far earned. No quantification of how often this is true in practice is, however, forthcoming. Again it would obviously depend upon the extent of the separation of ownership

---

[1] B. Higgins, 'Elements of Indeterminancy in the Theory of Non-Perfect Competition', *American Economic Review* (Sep 1939) pp. 468–79.

[2] J. R. Hicks, 'Annual Survey of Economic Theory. The Theory of Monopoly', *Econometrica*, III (Jan 1935) pp. 1–20.

[3] T. Scitovsky, 'A Note on Profit Maximisation and its Implications', *Review of Economic Studies* (1943).

[4] J. P. Nettl, 'A Note on Entrepreneurial Behaviour', *Review of Economic Studies* (Feb 1957) pp. 87–94.

[5] Reder, *Journal of Political Economy* (1947).

from control, although there is some controversy[1] as to whether it is the entrepreneur or the salaried manager who is the more likely to forgo profits in favour of an easier life. The entrepreneur has more to gain than the manager if he maximises profits. On the other hand a manager's income is not so readily substitutable with leisure.

Management Discretion

Into Higgins's second category above falls Williamson's model of management discretion.[2] In this model he postulates the existence of 'expense preference'. 'That is the management does not have a neutral attitude towards costs. Directly or indirectly certain classes of expenditure have positive values associated with them. In particular staff expense, expenditure for emoluments, and funds available for discretionary investment have value additional to that which derives from their productivity.'[3] Staff expansion is particularly hard to resist because 'not only is it an indirect means to the attainment of salary but it is a source of security, power, status, prestige and professional achievement as well'. By 'emoluments' he means discretionary pay and perquisites, which thus constitute part of 'organisational slack' as defined below. For various reasons staff may prefer to obtain this slack in non-pecuniary form.

However, 'the existence of satisfactory profits is necessary to assure the interference-free operation of the firm to the management'. Furthermore, management 'will find it desirable to earn profits that exceed the acceptable level. For one thing, managers derive satisfaction from self-fulfilment and organizational achievement and profits are one measure of this success. In addition profits are a source of discretion.'[4] Williamson

---

[1] Nettl, *Review of Economic Studies* (Feb 1957) pp. 87–94, suggests that the salaried manager will work harder.

[2] O. E. Williamson, *The Economics of Discretionary Behaviour. Managerial Objectives in a Theory of the Firm* (Englewood Cliffs, N.J.: Prentice-Hall, 1964).

[3] Ibid., p. 1034.

[4] Ibid., p. 1035.

combines the various managerial goals into a utility function and postulates that the objective of utility-maximisation will override that of profit-maximisation. This provides him with the hypothesis that 'those expenditures that promote managerial satisfactions should show a positive correlation with opportunities for discretion and tastes'. His conclusion was that the evidence

> generally supports the implications of the utility-maximisation approach. Although it is not strong enough to provide a discrimination between the utility and profits-maximising theories, it does suggest that either firms are operated as indicated by the managerial model or, if 'actual' profits era maximised, that reported profits are reduced by absorbing some fraction of actual profits in executive salaries and possibly in perquisites of a variety of sorts.

In similar vein Monsen and Downs[1] suggest that owners seek maximum profits whereas managers 'act so as to maximise their own lifetime incomes'.[2] Stockholders are in general considered unlikely to switch from holding shares in one company to holding them in another because of uncertainty about the outcome of the switch and because capital gains are taxed. Thus they tend to accept 'satisfactory' profit levels without much fuss. Nevertheless, managers are aware of the likelihood of an uprising among shareholders if they perform very badly. On the other hand managers do not expect optimum performance to be commensurately rewarded. Hence 'the punishment for grievous error is greater than the reward for outstanding success'.[3] Thus, subject to the necessity to earn satisfactory profits for shareholders, managers seek to maximise 'the present value of their lifetime incomes in dollar terms' (where such incomes include both monetary and non-monetary elements). Unfortunately no empirical justification of the theory is provided.

The above sentiments are also reflected in Papandreou's

[1] A. Downs and R. J. Monsen, 'A Theory of Large Managerial Firms', *Journal of Political Economy* (June 1965) pp. 221–36.
[2] Ibid., p. 225.
[3] Ibid., p. 226.

concept of the maximisation of a preference function.[1] He conceives of a 'peak co-ordinator' who formulates the firm's operating budget or strategy. The selection of the strategy requires the specification of some value premises (preference system) and factual premises. The preference system is 'regarded as being a resultant of all the influences which affect the value premises of enterprise strategy selection'.[2] Over a period of time the peak co-ordinator is subject to 'a changing structure of conscious influence' which largely arises out of the separation of ownership from control and from the rise of the trade unions.

The firm is thus seeking to maximise its general preference function rather than profits.

The sort of factors which tend to enter a firm's preference function are a desire for a quiet life, for power, control or prestige. But as Papandreou himself points out, the difficulties of quantifying a preference function are considerable so that 'we must always take pains to impart empirical meaningfulness to our model'.[3]

Several of the ideas referred to above were neatly juxtaposed by Earley when he wrote that

The major goals of modern large scale business are high managerial incomes, good profit, a strong competitive position, and growth. Modern management does not view these goals as seriously inconsistent, but rather, indeed, as necessary, one to the other. Competitive strength, and even survival, management believes, require large innovative and substantial growth expenditures in the rapidly changing technical and market conditions of the present day. Since growth by merger is hazardous and frequently impossible, large, and more or less continuous capital expenditures are necessary. For well recognized reasons management wishes to minimize outside financing, so the funds for most of these

---

[1] Papandreou, in *Survey of Contemporary Economics*. See also M. Silver, 'Managerial Discretion and Profit Maximising Behaviour. Some Further Comments', *Journal of Industrial Economics* (Apr 1967) p. 159.

[2] Papandreou, in *Survey of Contemporary Economics*, p. 204.

[3] Ibid., p. 213.

expenditures must be internally generated. This requires high and growing profits above dividend levels. As too, do high managerial rewards. High and rising profits are hence an instrument as well as a direct goal of great importance.[1]

THEORIES OF SATISFICING BEHAVIOUR

We have already mentioned several times the suggestion that a firm seeks 'satisfactory' rather than maximum profits. In fact it is logically feasible to include all the above objectives under the heading of 'satisficing' theories, since if a firm is not maximising profits the term 'satisfactory' profits must describe at any rate one aspect of its objectives. Nevertheless, there are basically few theories which regard the achievement of satisfactory profit levels as the firm's primary objective rather than as an objective which runs alongside, but is subsidiary to, other objectives.

The first of these theories has already been discussed under the heading of 'homeostasis'. Boulding's theory relies, as we have seen, upon inflexible operating relationships between variables such as cost, price, and hence profit. The level of profits which results from these relationships can fairly be described as satisfactory for the firm concerned, and, once a profit norm has been established, this will be the firm's only major objective.

Satisficing theory is, however, most often associated with Simon.[2] He has expressed his viewpoint as follows.[3] 'We must expect the firm's goals to be not maximising profits, but attaining a certain level or rate of profit, holding a certain share of the market or a certain level of sales. Firms would try to "satisfice" rather than to maximise.'

He carries on to point out that[4] 'Models of satisficing behaviour are richer than models of maximising behaviour, because they treat not only of equilibrium but of the method of

[1] Baran and Sweezy, ibid., p. 51 strongly support Earley's viewpoint.

[2] Simon, 'New Developments in the Theory of the Firm' and 'Theories of Decision Making in Economics and Behavioural Science', *American Economic Review* (May 1962; June 1959).

[3] Simon, *American Economic Review* (June 1959).

[4] Ibid.

reaching it as well.' He concludes that there is some empirical evidence that business goals are in fact stated in satisficing terms. This he suggests is to be found in studies (which are discussed in Chapter 4) which indicate that businessmen often set prices by applying a standard markup to costs. He also refers to Cyert and March,[1] who found in one industry some evidence that firms with a declining share of market strove more vigorously to increase their sales than firms whose shares of the market were steady or increasing.

Gordon[2] is inclined to agree.

In an important sense, the primary aim of a businessman is to stay in business. Given the fog of uncertainty within which he must operate, the limited number of variables his mind can juggle at one time, and his desire to play safe, it would not be at all surprising if he adopted a set of yardsticks that promised reasonably satisfactory profits in the long run and a maximum of stability in his relations with customers, suppliers and competitors. These conditions suggest that many businessmen are likely, as we have already noted, to substitute the principle of satisfactory profits for that of profit maximisation. These considerations also suggest... that businessmen may seek to use average total rather than marginal cost as a guide in pricing in order to achieve satisfactory profits.

Margolis[3] starts off with the premise that a firm is faced with uncertainty. As a result a firm may often deliberately ignore an opportunity which offers the prospect of greater profitability than the opportunity which the firm adopts instead. This is because

The firm has adopted a pattern of behaviour which will

[1] R. M. Cyert and J. G. March, 'Organisational Factors in the Theory of the Firm', *Quarterly Journal of Economics*, 70 (Feb 1956) pp. 44–64.

[2] Gordon, *American Economic Review* (June 1948) pp. 270–1.

[3] J. Margolis, 'The Analysis of the Firm, Rationalism, Conventionalism and Behaviorism', *Journal of Business* (July 1958) pp. 187–99.

protect itself from the unknown while seeking ever growing profits. This does not mean that the theorist should feel free to conceive of the firm as acting randomly or imitatively. Instead of assuming either extreme of a complete absence of rational efforts of maximisation or the presence of perfect foresight, it would be preferable to assume realistically that the management hopes to achieve more and more profits; that, operating as they must under conditions of uncertainty the rules and tools they adopt must be quite different from those appropriate to conditions of perfect foresight. The managers, rather than being either omniscient at one extreme or mechanically random at the other extreme, are deliberating leaders of a firm who adopt procedures and rules because of the lack of information necessary to be fully 'rational'.

As compared to traditional theories Margolis's model of the 'deliberative' firm (a term he prefers to satisficing or behavioural) 'imposes far fewer demands on necessary knowledge'. Despite this the theory is structured. The firm is motivated to seek better solutions to problems through the adoption of aspiration levels[1] which must (a) 'be high enough to ensure the long-run survival of the firm' and (b) 'must be equal to or greater than current normal profits'. The firm treats decisions sequentially, selecting a policy which, on the basis largely of current information (itself the outcome of information gathered as a result of implementing previous policies) rather than upon guesses about the future, satisfies the aspiration level then in existence. The firm is thus inefficient according to the criteria of the traditional models, but this inefficiency is simply the 'cost paid to reduce uncertainty'. Provided the firm bases decisions upon 'current information supplemented by strategical rules based upon past experience' then rational decisions will be forthcoming.[2]

Lee has aptly summed up the present state of satisficing

[1] See also the section on Behavioural Theories pp. 102–3.
[2] D. Bodenhorn, 'A Note on the Theory of the Firm', *Journal of Business* (Apr 1959) p. 172, argues that Margolis's theory will lead to essentially the same predictions as traditional theory. Margolis disagrees. *Journal of Business* (Apr 1959).

theories as follows.[1] 'However the vagueness of satisficing as the goal of a firm presents serious problems in building a predictive model of business organisations.' Thus the theories cannot at present be subjected to meaningful statistical testing.

THE MARGINALISM CONTROVERSY

According to the traditional models of competition, the firm determines its optimum output by equating marginal cost with marginal revenue. But if the firm is unable to determine its marginal cost and revenue curves with any accuracy, it will logically be unable to determine its optimal price–output combination. Difficulties concerning the determination of the marginal curves arise from the existence of uncertainty and lack of knowledge (such as are discussed in the following section).

The case against marginalism has been expressed by Newbury as follows:[2] 'The top management of a plant or corporation usually deals with total revenue, total cost, and total profit. Policy decisions concerning production volumes, employment, control of overhead expenses and similar problems are based on total operating figures, on financial accounting statements and not on detail cost accounting figures.'

Acceptance or rejection of this postulate is, however, only one half of the controversy, since some economists who accept the postulate then go on to suggest that a firm does not need to employ marginal analysis in order to maximise profits in the first place. The best known proposition of this viewpoint is to be found in the work of Hall and Hitch,[3] who discovered that many firms used 'full-cost pricing' techniques, which involve the computation of fixed and variable costs, to which is

[1] C. A. Lee, 'Organisation Theory and Business Behaviour', in *Interdisciplinary Studies in Business Behaviour*, ed. J. W. McGuire (Southwestern, 1962) p. 62.

[2] F. D. Newbury. *A Businessman's Reaction to the Theory of Monopolistic Competition*, as quoted in W. W. Cooper, 'Theory of the Firm – Some Suggestions for Revision', *American Economic Review* (1949) p. 87.

[3] R. L. Hall and C. T. Hitch, 'Price Theory and Business Behaviour', *Oxford Economic Papers* (May 1939) pp. 12–45.

added a certain profit margin. If the profit mark-up is fixed then price is determined by factors of cost rather than market factors. This directly contradicts the traditional theory in principle. Where, however, the mark-up is flexible, which is to say that it varies according to the state of the market, this comes closer to the traditional concept of marginal analysis, but is still too insensitive a method of price setting to ensure maximum profits in conventional terms. Hall and Hitch, however,[1] noted that many of the firms which they interviewed believed themselves to be following policies which could reasonably be expected to lead to maximum profits, on the grounds that too frequent adjustment of prices would alienate their customers and spur their competitors into retaliatory behaviour.

Earley[2] set out to reconcile full-cost pricing with marginalist principles, noting that 'Marginal analysis may well be very useful in describing actual or rational behaviour, even if nobody fashions his actual or potential behaviour in these exact terms.' In other words, if a firm is maximising profits, irrespective of the means by which they are achieved, the resultant output can be described as that output which results from the equating of marginal cost and marginal revenue.

Earley sent questionnaires to 217 manufacturing companies rated as 'excellently managed' by the American Institute of Management, of whom 110 replied. He concluded[3] that 'short views, innovative sensitivity, marginal costing and marginal pricing are all predominant among the responding companies'. As he himself points out, however,[4] his study relies upon inference from indirect evidence, and several commentators[5] have accused him of asking leading questions.

Rules of thumb, such as full-cost pricing, are in practice consistent with a maximisation approach in areas of decision

---

[1] Hall and Hitch, *Oxford Economic Papers* (May 1939) pp. 36–40.

[2] J. S. Earley, 'Marginal Policies of "Excellently Managed" Companies', *American Economic Review* (Mar 1956) as reprinted in *Readings in Economics*, ed. H. Kohler, no. 47, p. 402 (New York: Holt, Rinehart & Winston, 2nd edn, 1969).

[3] Ibid., p. 410.

[4] Ibid., p. 403.

[5] E.g. Simon, *American Economic Review* (June 1959).

making which are particularly costly or where information is particularly poor, since it is quite possible at the margin for a firm to spend more money discovering information which enables it to adjust exactly to changing market conditions than it accrues in additional profit from so doing. It has also been noted that[1] in many ways firms are in a much better position to maximise profits today than say two decades ago because of the proliferation of, for example, market research and computer departments which exist to diminish the uncertainty surrounding a firm's decisions, and this process is likely to continue, perhaps at an increasing rate, into the future. This point has been most clearly expressed by Earley.[2] He contends that management literature is strongly biased towards cost reduction, revenue expansion, and profit growth; that the use of business specialists is likely to lead to profit-oriented rationality; and that the rapid development of analytical and managerial techniques both stimulate and assist the search for the least costly ways of doing things and the most profitable things to do. He recognises the limited informational and computational resources of the firm and accepts the concept of aspiration levels, but develops the objective of 'a systematic temporal search for highest practicable profits'. Unfortunately lack of empirical evidence makes it difficult to say anything meaningful about the marginalism controversy in the context of the United Kingdom.

IMPERFECTIONS OF INFORMATION

The crux of the argument has been expressed by Margolis as follows[3]

> The information and calculability necessary for the management of a firm to move to its equilibrium profit-maximising price–output combination are clearly not available. Uncertainty and ignorance are omni-present. No matter how

[1] See for example W. Baumol and M. Stewart, 'On the Behavioural Theory of the Firm', in *The Corporate Economy*, ed. R. Marris and A. Wood (Macmillan, 1971) chap. 5.

[2] Earley, *American Economic Review*, Papers and Proceedings (1956).

[3] J. Margolis, *Journal of Business* (July 1958) p. 189.

pleasing may be the prospect of an activity with the greatest possible profits, the choice for management is rarely on the agenda.

Uncertainty arises simply because the outcome of a decision will only become known at some time in the future, so that a policy chosen by a firm because it appears to offer the prospect of maximum profits may turn out in practice to earn very little profit or even no profit at all.

But even where no uncertainty attaches to the outcome of a project there are grounds for questioning whether the project will be optimal where the choice between competing projects is based upon imperfect information.

The acquisition of detailed information is a costly business for the firm. Furthermore the process of information retrieval often turns out to be more expensive than is necessary because the wrong information is obtained, and is subsequently stored away never to be used again. The firm thus has to trade-off the increased costs of obtaining information against the hoped-for additional benefits which it expects one project to yield over and above the benefits obtainable from the next best project. In many cases, given the uncertainty surrounding the outcome of most projects, the trade-off will come down in favour of not searching out information.

There are further difficulties where the data appear in an unsuitable form for comparisons to be made between projects. The economist's view of relevant costs differs from that of the accountant,[1] whereas cost information will always be supplied by the latter. Reliance upon accounting data may give a distorted view of the costs and benefits of individual projects. But even where the data comes in the most suitable form for project selection, the manager must himself be both capable of recognising this fact and of placing the correct interpretation upon the data.

We may note that information will always relate to previous time periods rather than to the present. It takes time to collect information, to process it, and to set in motion decisions based upon it. Such delays may at times result in a decision being taken in circumstances which no longer correspond to reality.

[1] This is discussed in detail in Chapter 1, pp. 12-16.

The extent to which this criticism applies will obviously depend upon the variability of the firm's environment.

Uncertainty and lack of knowledge can thus help account for such practices as full-cost pricing mentioned above, since this technique requires relatively unsophisticated and readily available information.

Gordon[1] summarised many of the difficulties when he wrote:

> Most of my criticisms centre around the fact that the tool box of formal marginalism is not very useful in a business world characterized by as much ignorance and uncertainty as do in fact prevail. These characteristics in turn stem primarily from two conditions; unending and unpredictable change and the existence of more 'directions of Adjustment' (variables to be manipulated) than the businessman can possibly handle in the manner assumed in formal theory. If adjustments could be made once and for all, or if conditions would change only at long intervals, the businessman might be able to adjust marginally among alternatives theoretically available. But uninterrupted change makes physically impossible the continuous manipulation of all the relevant variables, even if the results of all alternative lines of action could be known with certainty. Uncertainty compounds this ignorance and adds the complication of future contingencies, independent of present action that must be prepared for.

THE BEHAVIOURAL THEORY OF THE FIRM

Dissatisfaction with the traditional theory of the firm for all of the reasons so far discussed has led certain commentators to branch out in a new direction, borrowing heavily from the behavioural sciences.

Classical economic theory is normative in the sense of postulating how a firm *should* behave if it is to go about maximising its profits. Traditional organisation theory is also normative in the sense of postulating the ideal structure for different sorts of organisation. Ideas on organisation structure tended to originate from the analysis of existing institutions such as the Church and Army. In the traditional model the individual

[1] R. A. Gordon, *American Economic Review* (June 1948) p. 287.

is subordinate to the organisation, and his functions are spelled out for him as part of the overall scheme of relationships between individuals within the company. This allocation of roles is not, however, acceptable to modern behavioural theorists, who emphasise the fact that people do not fit into neat little slots, but have needs and objectives which do not tally exactly with those of the firm. Their approach is therefore positive rather than normative, and involves an attempt to find ways of describing how firms actually operate in practice.

Behavioural theorists set out to determine the process by which firms decide upon their objectives (which will be multiple rather than single). In any situation where a firm has more than one objective, however, it must be undertaking a continuous process of balancing one objective against another, which implies the existence of conflict. The behavioural theorists are therefore interested to discover how such conflict arises, what form it takes, and how it gets resolved. Furthermore we can treat every objective as a constraint upon the firm's behaviour in the sense that the firm must achieve all of its objectives at the same time. Where it fails to do so the firm will feel obliged to set in motion search behaviour to discover what has gone wrong and how it can be remedied. The most comprehensive behavioural theory is that postulated by Cyert and March[1] and this section will be broadly based upon their ideas.

Once again our starting point is the separation of ownership from control. In the large corporation the entrepreneur is replaced by a large number of salaried managers. These managers have, as we indicated above, certain personal objectives which they pursue in their day-to-day work. Their loyalties will not, however, be simply directed to do the best they can for themselves. They will associate themselves both with the firm as a whole and with that part of it to which they specifically belong. Their personal motivations and their desire to put their own department before other departments within the firm will inevitably create conflicts both between individuals and between departments. Unless such conflicts become resolved in some way, however, the firm will obviously be in a state of anarchy, with different sections going their own way

[1] R. M. Cyert and J. G. March, *A Behavioural Theory of the Firm* (Englewood Cliffs, N.J.: Prentice-Hall, 1965).

without regard to the interests of the rest of the firm. This is unacceptable, and therefore the conflict must somehow be resolved more or less to everyone's satisfaction. In practice the conflict situation will encompass more than just the managers, who, as we have seen in an earlier chapter, are not freed from all external constraints upon their behaviour. Cyert and March accordingly introduce the concept of the 'coalition' which will include everyone who has reason to expect anything from the firm at any given time. The composition of the coalition will be variable, but will in general incorporate the managers, shareholders, customers, workers and creditors. The question then immediately arises as to how such a divergent group of interests can agree upon the objectives of the firm. Cyert and March suggest that in general the various groups will lose interest in the detailed objectives of the firm provided they receive a satisfactory level of 'side-payments' from the firm. The concept of 'side-payments' was implicit in the traditional theory of the firm, where the entrepreneur is the sole decision taker. He bought off interference by outside groups by paying a sufficiently high level of wages to his workers and dividends to his shareholders; by producing a product which satisfied his customers; and by paying off his creditors in good time. Cyert and March believe that this argument can be extended to the corporation. Shareholders continue to remain passive so long as they earn a satisfactory dividend stream, as do workers who earn a satisfactory wage level, and so forth. The passivity of the majority of coalition members does not, however, by itself resolve the conflict because we are still left with the managerial group split up into departments and also on an individual basis. The idea of side-payments is useful here also in the sense that certain managers can be rewarded with higher salaries or greater prestige, etc., in return for not participating in the decision making process, but most of the management group will by pushing for specific policy commitments for their own area of the firm. Such pressures will particularly manifest themselves when the firm is discussing its annual budget plans or where the firm is considering branching out in new directions. Cyert and March consider that two broad areas of objectives will transpire from the bargaining process which can be labelled 'qualitative' and 'quantitative'. In the former case we are referring to objectives which have no operational content. Managers can be led to believe that they are pursuing such an objective to the best of their ability and hence that they all share a communal goal, thus eliminating a major source of conflict. Such goals are typified by the slogans 'our aim is to satisfy the customer' or 'our aim is to produce products of the highest quality'. It is evident that almost any managerial decision can be justified under such apparently impressive headings as those above.

Nevertheless the firm will still need to have some set of quantifiable objectives. For reasons discussed below these do not need to be fully consistent one with the other, and Cyert and March suggest that the following five goals will be the most important.

(1) *The Production Goal*. The production department is most concerned with questions of output and employment. Its members want all their machinery to be fully utilised so that they can retain their workforce, and they also want the fewest possible changeovers from making one product to making another because of the disruptive effects of such changeovers upon the smooth running of their department. Long production runs also make production scheduling much easier and keep down costs. If sales are poor their interests will coincide with those of the advocates of the inventory goal.

(2) *The Inventory Goal*. This expresses a desire to avoid running out of stocks, both of raw materials (which would annoy the production department) and of finished goods (which would annoy the sales force and its customers). Holding inventories therefore pleases both production and sales departments, but conflicts with the interests of the financial managers, who regard the holding of excessive inventory as unprofitable and as tying up valuable working capital.

(3) *The Level of Sales Goal*. This can be defined in terms of revenues or of output, but in either case implies the possibility that the sales force will attempt to increase sales without paying due regard to the profitability of these sales.

(4) *The Market Share Goal*. This reflects an interest in the firm's standing in its various markets vis-à-vis its competitors, and is therefore an important reference point when the firm is planning its future strategy.

(5) *The Profit Goal*. Profit is obviously necessary for the firm's continued existence in the sense of the continued need to pay dividends and to fund the future growth of the firm. Despite the considerable difficulties in calculating profit, it is often taken as a guide to the firm's performance because no better index of efficiency exists. Furthermore it is possible to make inter-firm profit comparisons.

In a sense all members of the coalition are interested in the profit goal, but it is particularly important to shareholders and to managers who regard the efficacy of their performance as being reflected in the profit figures.

Associated with all of the above quantifiable objectives will be an 'aspiration' level. An aspiration level signifies a desire on the part of the firm to do rather better, or worse, or the same in the future as compared to the present in each area of its operations. Aspiration levels will obviously be related to the balance of power within the management group, and we have already suggested that this will tend to fluctuate over time. Despite this fact Cyert and March expect aspiration levels to fluctuate comparatively little. The main reason for this stability of aspirations arises from the way in which decisions are taken in large firms. There is an observed tendency for large firms to become bureaucratic and to establish sets of rules for the conduct of significant areas of the firm's operations. These rules are laid down after lengthy discussions by committees and, once established, tend to be treated with some reverence, despite the fact that the firm's environment is possibly undergoing rapid changes. The rules are often financial in nature, appearing in the form of budgets and operating standards, which greatly constrain the scope of the individual manager for unorthodox behaviour. It is possible for any level of the firm's managerial hierarchy to keep a very close eye upon the performance of subordinate managers since there is provision for this to be compared at regular intervals against the previously agreed budgets. Where a manager fails to meet his targets he will be expected to explain his failure. On the other hand each department can reasonably expect to be provided with all the resources allocated to it when the available resources for the forthcoming year were shared out. Failure to do this will create further frustration and conflict when the next allocation of resources falls due, and it is therefore to be avoided wherever possible.

There will be a tendency for aspirations to be realistic. A department will not want to set its objectives too high because failure to achieve them invites censure. Setting objectives at too low a level will, however, present no challenge and will also invite pressure from the hierarchy to achieve the department's full potential.

Rigid modes of behaviour may well also reflect the fact that it is a good deal easier for all concerned to keep to what is established by precedent than to try to upset the apple-cart through continual questioning of the relevance of yesterday's rules to today's environment. Managers do not anyway have the time to reconsider precedents at frequent intervals. Hence whenever a situation occurs which has arisen on previous occasions a solution is found by reference to what was successful in the past. The use of precedents will exert a significant stabilising effect upon the firm's objectives and will also stifle a major source of conflict which would arise were a department to question the established order.

Aspirations thus change but slowly, and this can reasonably be defined as 'satisficing' behaviour. Profit maximising behaviour would require a much more flexible *modus operandi* where the firm's environment is changeable. In general aspirations will be moving in an upwards direction, but not of necessity. Every now and again the firm will fall a long way short of achieving one or more of its objectives. When this happens search behaviour will be instigated in order to discover the cause of the failure. Where the failure is human in origin the remedy is clear. Where, however, the failure arises out of an unfavourable alteration in the firm's environment it will be necessary to adjust aspirations downwards in certain areas to keep them in line with reality. This sort of search operation, however, only results from appreciable failure to meet targets. The firm does not search out ways of improving its efficiency as long as targets are more or less being met, despite the fact, as is suggested above, that aspirations may fall considerably below what could potentially be achieved were the firm to respond to every variation in market conditions.

From the management's point of view this approach saves a

great deal of stress and strain. It must also, however, lead to inconsistencies between objectives. Assuming that once upon a time the firm began with a consistent set of objectives, it has adjusted them one by one whenever a crisis situation has arisen. No real attempt has, however, been made to alter the objectives which are being satisfactorily met to keep them consistent with the objective which has been significantly altered. Given a sufficient period of time one must conclude that the original coherent structure of objectives will have fallen by the wayside. If so the firm cannot be maximising profits. This is why, when the firm's possible quantitative goals were listed above, the reader was referred to the ways in which they conflicted one with the other.

Organisational Slack

In circumstances in which aspirations change slowly but the firm's environment fluctuates a good deal one would expect the firm to often perform considerably better or worse than it had anticipated. If it does much better than expected, how does the firm absorb the excess receipts without corresponding changes in aspirations? And from where can the firm obtain unused resources to make up the shortfall when performance falls short of aspirations? The answer to both of these questions is to be found in the concept of 'organisational slack'. Cyert and March argue that the members of the coalition are often paid in excess of their opportunity costs. Wages, salaries and profits will be higher than they need to be to keep workers, managers and shareholders happy. Creditors are paid too quickly and prices are kept below what the market will bear. This is due in part to the difficulties inherent in trying to obtain accurate information about the magnitude of these variables, but it may also reflect an indifference on the part of the firm to maximising profits.

There are thus several unutilised sources of profits; firstly in the surplus payments to coalition members; secondly where factor inputs of all types are not being fully utilised; and thirdly where the firm pursues non-optimal pricing, production or marketing strategies, etc.

Now at times when the firm does much better than it had

anticipated it allows slack to develop which will absorb most of the difference between aspiration and actuality. For example, wages and salaries are allowed to rise and unprofitable investments are undertaken. Where, however, the firm later falls upon hard times, it can eliminate the slack without creating the sort of major disturbances, such as large-scale movements of labour to firms offering relatively better rewards, which would result from attempts to cut wages in circumstances where no slack had previously been accumulated. Prices might also be raised and a drive to increase productivity set in hand.

The firm therefore tends to find itself in an ambivalent situation when slack arises. On the one hand slack implies that the firm is operating at an unnecessarily high level of costs, but on the other hand it cannot afford to eliminate the slack for fear of what might happen in less satisfactory trading conditions. Some form of trade-off between the two extremes is therefore called for.

Turning once again to our five quantitative goals enumerated above, we can apply to them the logic of the preceding discussion. The firm has aspiration levels with regard to each individual goal. Although the goals are inconsistent, it is possible for all to be satisfied at the same time where the firm is not trying hard to be efficient in all areas simultaneously. The holding of inventories in excess of those strictly necessary does not conflict *per se* with a desire for profit or liquidity. It will only do so where the profit goal is not being met. This in turn leads to search behaviour, which will cease when some form of slack has been identified and eliminated, thus increasing profits into line with aspirations. No real attempt is, however, likely to be made to eliminate slack beyond the extent required if the firm is to meet the profit aspiration level. The firm sub-optimises at all times.

It can reasonably be said that behavioural theories are in principle the most realistic of the theories outlined above. Unfortunately, however, it cannot be said that there is *a* behavioural theory. Furthermore a behavioural model needs to encompass a very wide range of variables, which makes it difficult to test against reality. Another drawback appears to be that the emphasis upon internal decision-making processes detracts from the relationship of a firm with its environment,[1] a relationship which, as we have seen above in our discussion of homeostasis and viability, is in the forefront of current economic theories of the firm. Perhaps, however, these problems will eventually be overcome.

Defence of Traditional Theory

It is worth observing as a tailpiece to this chapter that several attempts[2] have been made to defend the traditional theory of the firm. These are for the most part rather esoteric[3] although the nub of the Friedman position[4] appears to be a claim that the theory of the firm is not intended to describe how firms reach internal decisions but is rather an attempt to develop predictions about how firms in the aggregate will behave in a changing environment.

It is also often pointed out by commentators that none of the suggested alternatives to profit maximisation is any more acceptable than the original theories. Hence it is logical to continue to utilise the traditional assumptions. This defence, which is based in effect on a claim that there is nothing much to defend against, is not, however, very satisfactory when so many firms can be observed to be pursuing multiple goals. Nevertheless one is inevitably led to conclude that a good deal more empirical research into the behaviour of firms will be necessary before a replacement for the traditional theory can be deemed preferable to it.

[1] See for example Lee, in *Studies in Business Behaviour*, pp. 65–6.

[2] See for example M. Friedman, *Essays in Positive Economics* (University of Chicago Press, 1953); E. Nagel, *Assumptions in Economic Theory*, plus discussion by P. Samuelson and H. Simon, *American Economic Review*, vol. 53 (May 1963); F. Machlup, 'Marginal Analysis and Empirical Research', *American Economic Review* (Sep 1946) and 'Rejoinder to an Anti-Marginalist', *American Economic Review* (1947); or Bodenhorn, *Journal of Business* (Apr 1959).

[3] A useful summary can be found in S. G. Winter jr, 'Economic Natural Selection and the Theory of the Firm', *Yale Economic Essays* (Spring 1964) pp. 231–6. See also some comments in C. I. Savage and J. R. Small, *Introduction to Managerial Economics*, pp. 18–20.

[4] See footnote 2, above.

Conclusion

Any relatively short summary of modern theories of the firm cannot do justice to the vast range of the literature. What has been attempted in this chapter is to indicate the broad areas of interest to writers on this subject, and to provide a résumé of some of the most interesting ideas so far proposed. The state of the theory of the firm remains in constant flux so that we can expect in the future both modifications of the theories discussed above and also completely new theories of the firm. It is perhaps unfortunate that, although most economists are agreed upon the inapplicability of the traditional theories, no alternative so far suggested has the same theoretical appeal. The question of how to deal with uncertainty has not so far been satisfactorily resolved, nor has the question as to how to satisfactorily predict the outcome of decisions taken by committees. Many theories which appeal at first glance have not as yet been adequately tested against reality, and the process of accumulating empirical evidence on the behaviour of firms will occupy researchers for many years to come. Because of the indeterminacy of the present state of the theory of the firm the author has preferred to set out the ideas without commenting extensively upon their validity. The reader will be able, either intuitively or upon the basis of personal experience, to select those theories which seem to him to be the most satisfactory, but it will be as difficult for the reader as for the author to predict which approach will prove most fruitful in the long term. The reader is reminded in conclusion that what we are seeking is a generalisation of economic theory which expands upon the range of empirical data which is satisfactorily explained by traditional theory rather than simply some theory which explains only or primarily those events which traditional theory cannot explain. Such a generalisation will clearly take a long time to appear.

BIBLIOGRAPHY

D. J. AIGNER, R. H. DAY and K. R. SMITH, 'Safety Margins and Profit Maximisation in the Theory of the Firm', *Journal of Political Economy* (Dec 1971) pp. 1293–301.

A. A. ALCHIAN, 'Uncertainty, Evolution and Economic Theory', *Journal of Political Economy* (1950) pp. 211–21.

——, 'The Basis of Some Recent Advances in the Theory of Management of the Firm', *Journal of Industrial Economics* (Nov 1965) pp. 30–41.

K. R. ANDREWS, 'Public Responsibility in the Private Corporation', *Journal of Industrial Economics* (Apr 1972) pp. 135–45.

R. N. ANTHONY, 'The Trouble with Profit Maximisation', *Harvard Business Review* (1960) pp. 126-34.

W. L. BALDWIN, 'The Motives of Managers, Environmental Restraints, and the Theory of Managerial Enterprise', *Quarterly Journal of Economics* (May 1964).

W. J. BAUMOL, *Economic Theory and Operations Analysis* (Englewood Cliffs, N.J.: Prentice-Hall, 1965).

——, 'On a Theory of Expansion of the Firm', *American Economic Review* (1962) pp. 1078–87.

——, 'On a Theory of Oligopoly', *Economica* (1958).

W. J. BAUMOL and M. STEWART, 'On the Behavioural Theory of the Firm', in *The Corporate Economy*, ed. R. Marris and A. Wood (Macmillan, 1971) chap. 5.

C. BEED, 'The Separation of Ownership from Control', *Journal of Economic Studies*, vol. 1, no. 2 (University of Aberdeen) (1966).

D. BODENHORN, 'A Note on the Theory of the Firm', *Journal of Business* (Apr 1959) pp. 164–75.

K. E. BOULDING, 'Implications for General Economics of More Realistic Theories of the Firm', *American Economic Review* (May 1952) pp. 35–44.

J. S. CHIU, D. E. COOLEY and R. J. MONSEN, 'The Effect of Separation of Ownership and Control on the Performance of the Large Firm', *Quarterly Journal of Economics* (1968) pp. 435–51.

J. S. CHIU, A. O. ELBING and J. W. MCGUIRE, 'Executive Incomes, Sales and Profits', *American Economic Review* (Sep 1962) pp. 753–61.

W. W. COOPER, 'A Proposal for Extending the Theory of The Firm', *Quarterly Journal of Economics* (Feb 1951).

——, 'Theory of the Firm – Some Suggestions for Revision', *American Economic Review* (1949).

R. M. CYERT and K. J. COHEN, *Theory of the Firm. Resource Allocation In a Market Economy (Part III)* (Englewood Cliffs, N.J.: Prentice-Hall, 1965).

R. M. CYERT and C. L. HEDRICK, 'Theory of the Firm; Past, Present and Future. An Interpretation', *Journal of Economic Literature* (June 1972) pp. 392–412.

R. M. CYERT and J. G. MARCH, 'Organisation, Structure and Pricing Behaviour in an Oligopolistic Market', *American Economic Review* (Mar 1955).

——, *A Behavioural Theory of the Firm* (Englewood Cliffs, N.J.: Prentice-Hall, 1963).

L. R. DESFOSSES and P. SMITH, 'Interlocking Directorates. A Study of Influence', *Mississippi Valley Journal* (June 1972) pp. 57–69.

P. C. DOOLEY, 'The Interlocking Directorate', *American Economic Review* (June 1969).

A. DOWNS and R. J. MONSEN, 'A Theory of Large Managerial Firms', *Journal of Political Economy* (June 1965) pp. 221–36.

J. S. EARLEY, 'Marginal Policies of "Excellently Managed" Companies', *American Economic Review* (Mar 1956).

R. A. GORDON, 'Short Period Price Determination in Theory and Practice', *American Economic Review* (June 1948) pp. 265–88.

M. HALL, 'Sales Revenue Maximisation. An Empirical Examination', *Journal of Industrial Economics* (April 1967) pp. 143–56.

M. HALL and L. WEISS, 'Firm Size and Profitability', *Review of Economics and Statistics* (Aug 1967) pp. 319–32.

R. L. HALL and C. J. HITCH, 'Price Theory and Business Behaviour', *Oxford Economic Papers* (May 1939) pp. 12–45.

C. J. HAWKINS, 'The Sales Revenue Maximisation Hypothesis', *Journal of Industrial Economics* (Apr 1970) pp. 129–40.

B. HINDLEY, 'Capitalism and the Corporation', *Economica* (Nov 1969) pp. 426–38.

——, 'Separation of Ownership and Control in the Modern Corporation', *Journal of Law and Economics* (Apr 1970) pp. 185–221.

E. E. HOOGSTRAAT, 'Attacks on the Value of the Profit Motive in Theories of Business Behaviour', in *Interdisciplinary Studies in Business Behaviour*, ed. J. W. McGuire (Southwestern, 1962).

D. R. KAMERSCHEN, 'A Theory of Conglomerate Mergers. Comment', *Quarterly Journal of Economics* (Nov 1970) pp. 668–73.

——, 'The Influence of Ownership and Control on Profit Rates', *American Economic Review* (June 1968) pp. 432–47.

C. A. LEE, 'Organisation Theory and Business Behaviour', in *Interdisciplinary Studies in Business Behaviour*, ed. J. W. McGuire (Southwestern, 1962).

R. A. LESTER, 'Marginalism, Minimum Wages, and Labour Markets', *American Economic Review* (1947) pp. 135–48.

W. G. LLEWELLEN, 'Management and Ownership in the Large Firm', *Journal of Finance* (May 1969) pp. 299–323.

B. J. LOASBY, 'Management Economics and the Theory of the Firm', *Journal of Industrial Relations* (1966/7) pp. 165–77.

——, 'Hypothesis and Paradigm in the Theory of the Firm', *Economic Journal* (Dec 1971) pp. 863–85.

F. MACHLUP, 'Marginal Analysis and Empirical Research', *American Economic Review* (Sep 1946) pp. 519–44.

——, 'Rejoinder to an Anti-Marginalist', *American Economic Review* (Mar 1947) pp. 148–54.

——, 'Theories of the Firm, Marginalist, Behavioural, Managerial', *American Economic Review* (Mar 1967) pp. 1–33.

J. MARGOLIS, 'The Analysis of the Firm, Rationalism, Conventionalism and Behaviourism', *Journal of Business* (July 1958) pp. 187–99.

——, 'Traditional and Revisionist Theories of the Firm. A Comment', *Journal of Business* (Apr 1959) pp. 178–83.

R. MARRIS, 'The Modern Corporation and Economic Theory', in *The Corporate Economy*, ed. R. Marris and A. Wood (Macmillan, 1971) chap. 9.

——, 'Why Economics Needs a Theory of the Firm', *Economic Journal* (Mar 1972; special issue) pp. 321–52.

——, *The Economic Theory of 'Managerial Capitalism'* (Macmillan, 1964).

——, 'A Model of the "Managerial" Enterprise', *Quarterly Journal of Economics* (May 1963) pp. 185–210.

R. T. MASSON, 'Executive Motivations, Earnings, and Consequent Equity Performance', *Journal of Political Economy* (Dec 1971) pp. 1278–92.

D. C. MUELLER, 'A Life Cycle Theory of the Firm', *Journal of Industrial Economics*, vol. xx, no. 3 (July 1972) pp. 199–219.

J. P. NETTL, 'A Note on Entrepreneurial Behaviour', *Review of Economic Studies* (Feb 1957) pp. 87–94.

A. G. PAPANDREOU, 'Some Basic Problems of the Theory of the Firm', in *A Survey of Contemporary Economics*, vol. ii, ed. B. Haley (Homewood, Ill.: Irwin, 1952).

E. T. PENROSE, 'Biological Analogies in the Theory of the Firm', *American Economic Review* (Dec 1952) pp. 804–20.

H. K. RADICE, 'Control Type, Profitability and Growth in Large Firms', *Economic Journal* (Sep 1971) pp. 547–62.

M. W. REDER, 'A Reconsideration of the Marginal Productivity Theory', *Journal of Political Economy* (1947).

K. W. ROTHSCHILD, 'Price Theory and Oligopoly', *Economic Journal* (Sep 1947).

T. SCITOVSKY, 'A Note on Profit Maximisation and its Implications', *Review of Economic Studies*, vol. xi, no. 1 (1943) pp. 57–60.

W. G. SHEPHERD, 'On Sales Maximising and Oligopoly Behaviour', *Economica*, (Nov 1962) pp. 420–4.

M. SILVER, 'Managerial Discretion and Profit Maximising Behaviour. Some Further Comments', *Journal of Industrial Economics* (Apr 1967) pp. 157–62.

H. A. SIMON, 'New Developments in the Theory of the Firm', *American Economic Review*, Papers and Proceedings (May 1962).

——, 'Theories of Decision Making in Economics and Behavioural Science', *American Economic Review* (June 1959).

——, 'A Behavioural Theory of Rational Choice', *Quarterly Journal of Economics* (Feb 1955).

E. P. SMITH, 'Interlocking Directorates among the "Fortune 500" ', *Anti-trust Law and Economics Review* (Summer 1970) pp. 47–53.

R. M. Solow, 'The Truth Further Refined. A Comment on Marris', *The Public Interest* (Spring 1963) pp. 47–52.

D. Villarejo, 'Stock Ownership and the Control of Corpotions', *New University Thought* (Autumn 1961) pp. 33–61. Also (Feb 1962) pp. 47–65.

J. H. Williamson, 'Profit, Growth and Sales Maximisation', *Economica* (Feb 1966).

O. E. Williamson, *The Economics of Discretionary Behaviour. Managerial Objectives in a Theory of the Firm* (Englewood Cliffs, N.J.: Prentice-Hall, 1964).

——, 'Managerial Discretion and Business Behaviour', *American Economic Review* (1963) pp. 1032–57.

S. G. Winter, jnr, 'Economic Natural Selection and the Theory of the Firm', *Yale Economic Essays* (Spring 1964).

A. Wood, 'Economic Analysis of the Corporate Economy. A Survey and Critique', in *The Corporate Economy,* ed. R. Marris and A. Wood (Macmillan, 1971) chap. 2.

4
Pricing Behaviour

The success, or lack thereof, of a firm's attempts to attain its chosen objective, depends upon the firm's ability to correctly assess the various parameters of the markets in which it operates. Above all the firm, unless operating in a perfectly competitive environment, has got to decide upon that price which will maximise either its profits, sales, revenues or whatever. Sales, revenues and profits all depend upon the extent to which the market responds to the price at which a good is being put on offer by the firm. Consequently it is far from surprising that a sizeable part of traditional economic analysis is given over to a consideration of prices under various market circumstances. Nevertheless it is not necessarily true to say that in practice its pricing policy is a matter of the greatest concern to a firm. In any market for example which even approximates to that described in the theory of perfect competition (into which category fall many food markets) a firm has little latitude over prices. This fact is borne out in a wider sense by a study in which Udell[1] sent out questionnaires to a sample of 200 producers of industrial and consumer goods in the U.S.A., asking them to pinpoint those areas of their policies which they considered to be most vital to their company's marketing success. Udell concluded as follows.[2] 'It appears that business management did not agree with the economic views of the importance of pricing – one half of the respondents did not select pricing as one of the five most important policy areas in the firm's marketing success.'

[1] J. G. Udell, 'How Important is Pricing in Competitive Strategy?', *Journal of Marketing*, vol. 30 (Apr 1966).
[2] Ibid., p. 44.

Furthermore pricing policy is closely linked to a firm's overall objectives. The pursuit of certain objectives, as we shall see, requires that prices be set according to a set formula which relieves management of the need to formulate discretionary pricing policies. We may note further that in many industries competition is on a non-price basis, with the stress laid instead upon quality or service. Where this holds true pricing decisions will be treated as routine adjustments based upon general industry movements.

The above is not, however, meant to suggest that a firm will be better off were it to cease to employ some form of pricing policy. There are many situations in which pricing decisions will require considerable skill and experience. Any firm which seeks to maximise profits must constantly vary prices in line with changes in demand conditions. Where firms compete closely with one another, especially where they are tendering for contracts, pricing rules will not prove satisfactory. Careful pricing will also be a question of survival for firms in an industry characterised by over-capacity, or where the nature of the marketing process is undergoing change (e.g. where established retail businesses are suddenly confronted by mail-order concerns).

APPROACHES TO PRICING

There are two broad methods of price determination.

(1) *The Prescriptive Approach.* This encompasses all the traditional economic models in which pricing rules are postulated for a firm seeking to maximise profits (in which case the firm should equate marginal cost with marginal revenue to determine how much to sell; and read off from the demand curve the highest price at which that output can be sold) in addition to more modern theories which also incorporate pricing rules.

(2) *The Descriptive Approach.* This encompasses all attempts to determine through empirical research how firms actually price their products.

THE PRESCRIPTIVE APPROACH

Perfect competition

The original market model applies to a perfectly competitive industry. In such an industry each firm is treated as a price-taker. The interaction of market demand and supply curves determines the price at which each firm can sell its products, and the firm does not therefore have any pricing decisions to make. Although examples of firms which have no apparent pricing policy as such are relatively few and far between, it is not altogether uncommon in industries associated with primary products, or where there is a central trading area in which almost perfect information exists (e.g. the Stock Market, the Baltic Exchange, or the Covent Garden). It is perhaps true to say that where firms are unable to meaningfully differentiate their products, the forces of competition will allow of very little scope for pricing policy.

Monopoly

The monopolist is treated as a price-maker, having complete discretion over the price which he charges. Where the monopolist is taken to be a profit-maximiser, he is assumed to equate marginal cost with marginal revenue in order to determine his profit-maximising output, and the use of marginal analysis provides the underlying rationale of his pricing policy. But no matter what the monopolist's chosen objective, he is free to make marginal price adjustments such as to move him ever nearer to the attainment of that objective.

Oligopoly

As noted in our earlier discussion of oligopoly, all firms in an oligopolistic industry are to a greater or lesser extent interdependent. Any attempt by such a firm to alter its pricing policy is therefore an unpredictable move in the sense that the firm cannot be sure as to the reactions of its competitors. The firm will not be wholly ignorant of likely competitive reactions because it will know what has happened when a similar move was tried on a past occasion, and knowledge of relative market shares and cost structures will help shorten the odds on guessing correctly. Nevertheless several imponderables remain, especially with respect to attitudes to risk-taking, and this obviously provides an incentive for any individual firm to avoid taking any actions likely to upset its competitors.

We have analysed oligopoly behaviour in some detail in an earlier chapter. We noted that there was some tendency for oligopolistic markets to be characterised by rigid prices. We found that where the market is depressed it will hardly ever profit a single firm to raise prices, and further that it will only rarely be profitable for a single firm to cut prices, in the former case because competitors do *not* respond (by raising their own prices) and in the latter case because competitors *do* respond (by lowering their prices). Only in circumstances in which the market is buoyant will there be a definite tendency for all firms to raise their prices, often to an extent dictated by a price leader. This will be especially true where there is little excess capacity within the industry as a whole or where costs are rising. Competitive strategy will therefore depend not upon differentiation of products by price, but upon non-price competition.

We also took note of the theory of joint profit maximisation; which suggests that firms either overtly or tacitly agree upon that strategy which will maximise their joint profits. Presumably the negotiation of such a strategy must be preceded by some sort of trial of strength since we cannot expect every firm to have an absolutely equal say in the choice of strategy. Those firms which fare badly during such a trial soon learn that it is in their best interests to go along with the wishes of the dominant firms in return for a guarantee by the latter that the profit levels of their weaker brethren will be protected.

Price discrimination

According to traditional theory there are specific pricing rules for firms wishing to discriminate between markets. As previously demonstrated a discriminatory firm will maximise its profits by firstly equating marginal costs with aggregate marginal revenue, and secondly by allocating its optimal output level amongst the various markets which it serves such as to equalise marginal revenue in all markets.

Price leadership

One inference to be drawn from our above analysis of oligopoly is that there is a strong likelihood that one or more firms (or different firms at different times) will adopt the role of price leader. Price leadership may or may not be a function of firm size, but it is unlikely that a small firm will play a dominant role in price setting. Unfortunately it is not possible to draw any meaningful inferences about the role of the price leader, or to discuss the underlying principles of price setting in detail because of a lack of empirical data in this area. There is of course no reason to suppose that any two oligopolistic markets will share common characteristics in this respect. Two factors are, however, particularly important here; firstly the number of firms within the industry, and secondly the type and height of entry barriers. It is to be presumed that the greater the number of firms within the industry, the more difficult it will be for any one firm to dictate pricing policy to the group as a whole. Barriers to entry are probably a more important factor, however, and there is rather more evidence to draw on in this respect.[1] In its original formulation[2] Bain's theory was that firms in an oligopolistic industry would act in collusion in order to determine the highest price acceptable to all negotiating parties which could be set without tempting other firms to set up within the same industry (known as the 'limit' price). The 'limit price' would vary from one time period to another, and would depend upon a wide range of factors. Much would of course depend upon the elasticity of demand for the product and upon the relative cost efficiency both of firms within the industry and also of those outside the industry who might be

[1] See for example J. S. Bain, 'Conditions of Entry and Emergence of Monopoly' in *Monopoly and Competition and their Regulation*, ed. E. H. Chamberlain (Macmillan, 1954). J. S. Bain, 'Economies of Scale, Concentration and the Condition of Entry in Twenty Manufacturing Industries', *American Economic Review* (1954) pp. 15–39. J. S. Bain, *Barriers to New Competition* (Harvard University Press, 1956). P. Sylos-Labini, *Oligopoly and Technical Progress* (Harvard University Press, 1962; revised 1969).

[2] Bain, 'A Note on Pricing in Monopoly and Oligopoly', *American Economic Review* (Mar 1949).

tempted to enter it. Bain's general conclusion was that there
was a clear relationship between barriers to entry and the level
of abnormal profits within the oligopoly group. He went on
to determine empirically those factors most likely to constitute
barriers to entry. He concluded one study as follows:[1]

> A significant corollary of these findings is that the following
> popular horseback observations are apparently not true:
> that economies of scale are never or almost never important
> in encouraging oligopoly or impeding entry, and that such
> economies always or almost always are important in these
> ways. . . . The economies of large plants frequently erect
> formidable barriers to entry in the shape of absolute capital
> requirements. . . . The height of such barriers is not clearly
> correlated with percentage of the market supplied by a single
> plant so that a relatively independent influence on entry is
> discovered.

In other studies Bain emphasises the role of product differentiation and absolute cost advantages. Cost advantages
typically arise from control of scarce resources, superior
methods of production, or better management. This implies
that the entry forestalling price will vary according to the cost
level of the most efficient potential entrant. If the potential
entrant is low cost in relation to firms already within the
industry, then they presumably have to let it in since the
alternative is to forestall entry by the introduction of heavy
loss-making prices. Bain thus draws a distinction between
'effectively impeded' and 'ineffectively impeded' entry, and
also refers to the possibility of the existing firms being low-cost
producers and therefore able to make considerable profit while
still preventing entry (which he calls 'blockaded entry').

Product differentiation provides a barrier to entry because
it induces brand loyalty, and the provision of servicing facilities
by existing firms, which takes time and a good deal of capital
to set up, puts potential competitors at a more or less severe
disadvantage. Hence it is not sufficient to relate market power
purely to the number of firms within the industry. A small
group with low entry barriers would probably set prices at a

[1] Bain, *American Economic Review* (1954) p. 81.

lower level than a large group with high entry barriers and so forth.

Sylos-Labini, whose work has been discussed by other commentators,[1] based his notion of barriers to entry upon the premise that existing firms within the oligopoly group could effectively deter entry by refusing to cut down on production irrespective of whether or not other firms entered the industry. They would agree amongst themselves to set a price which would not be profitable in relation to a prospective entrant's cost structure were prices to fall any lower than the agreed price as the result of the new firm's entry into the industry. But if existing firms do not intend to reduce output, and the potential entrant knows this to be true, it must expect price to fall once it has entered the industry, because total supply will have been increased by the extent of its own production. This will make entry an unprofitable proposition, at least in the short term. Sylos goes on to conclude that 'price tends to settle at a level immediately above the entry – preventing price of the least efficient firms which it is to the advantage of the largest and most efficient firms to let live'.

Drawbacks to Traditional Pricing Policy

Imperfect knowledge of cost and revenue conditions

In analysing perfect competition and monopoly, economic theorists assume that every firm has perfect knowledge of the cost and revenue functions of all firms producing for a particular market. In the monopoly model the sole producer clearly only requires knowledge of his own cost and revenue curves, although in the competitive model there has to be some arrangement for the dissemination of cost and revenue information between all firms. Criticisms of the perfect knowledge postulate are dealt with at length elsewhere, but it is appropriate at this point to reconsider these criticisms in a different guise, in the context of a firm's pricing behaviour.

Obviously one would in principle expect the estimation of

[1] E.g. W. A. Silberston, 'Surveys of Applied Economics. Price Behaviour of Firms', *The Economic Journal* (Sep 1970) pp. 521–3. F. Modligiani, 'New Developments on the Oligopoly Front', *Journal of Political Economy*, vol. LXVI (June 1958) pp. 215–32.

E

cost and revenue functions to get progressively easier the longer a given product has been on the market. The estimation of these functions with respect to new products must rely to a good degree upon guesswork for want of adequate quantitative data. Over a period of years it should be possible for the firm to develop fairly accurate cost curves unless there are large elements of common costs (i.e. common to the production of several products over the initial stages of their manufacture); but even in the latter case the firm can apportion the costs up according to a set formula which makes it possible to draw cost curves in practice even if they are to some extent arbitrary.

The estimation of revenue or demand curves is, however, a much less tractable problem. This is firstly because the level of demand is functionally dependent upon many unquantifiable variables, such as tastes, and secondly because many of the independent variables which determine the level of demand are highly intercorrelated. In other words demand depends upon, for example, both the incomes and the tastes of consumers, while at the same time tastes are dependent upon incomes. This implies that the level of demand can only be derived through the solution of a set of simultaneous equations. But even where past data are available, it is not appropriate to employ them for the purposes of demand estimation unless the postulated relationships can reasonably be expected to remain constant over time.

Given the likelihood of errors arising for the reasons outlined above, it is possible in practice to postulate the shape of cost and revenue curves only subject to a certain degree of error. Further analysis of this problem takes us into the area of operations research and hence lies outside the scope of the present discussion, although it may be worth noting that one of the most important tasks of managers concerned with pricing policy under conditions of imperfect knowledge is to assess the significance for the shape of the demand function of small changes in the value of the independent variables on which it depends (known as 'sensitivity analysis').

Inflexibility of pricing policy

According to traditional theories of competitive behaviour firms do not have a flexible pricing policy. The perfectly competitive firm is at all times a price-taker, and the monopolist, once he has selected that price which will maximise profits in the short term, has no need to take any further action with respect to price, because it is assumed that the firm's cost and revenue conditions do not alter in the long run (all potential competitors being excluded from the industry).

But in practice, no matter what the competitive nature of any market, we would expect both cost and demand conditions to change either gradually or markedly over the life span of a product. The parameters of demand, such as incomes and tastes, are not constant, nor are the parameters of cost such as factor prices and technical efficiency. In a dynamic world therefore we would expect a firm's pricing policy to be to a greater or lesser extent adaptive, especially in markets characterised as oligopolistic. In particular we must consider the likely response of managers to such changes in the market environment with respect to the pricing of a product over different stages of its life span.

(a) *Market penetration*. Where a firm wishes to establish a new product with a view to obtaining for it a significant share of the available market, it is most likely to be successful where it adopts an initially low penetration price. Much depends, however, upon a variety of market factors, such as those set out below.

Where the market is readily responsive to price alterations any given fall in price will produce a more than proportionate increase in demand. Hence the greater the price elasticity the more successful will be a low pricing policy. Secondly, a low price will be beneficial where there are other firms anxious to enter the market, since they will themselves then have to price down their products if they wish to appear competitive, and this may not be considered an attractive proposition. Thirdly, if a low price ensures a high level of demand, and the firm's operations are subject to economies of scale (falling costs per unit produced) higher profits per unit may be obtained in this way as compared to the profits obtainable through the imposition of a higher initial price taken in conjunction with a higher level of costs.

(b) *Market skimming*. Market skimming is analogous to price discrimination over time. When new products are brought out there will always be people willing to buy at any price simply in order to be one of the first to possess the product. The firm thus seeks to obtain a very high profit per unit on a relatively small output to begin with, and to obtain a successively lower profit per unit over successively greater outputs as time goes on. Such a policy will be beneficial when the following market circumstances are too be found:

(1) Where economies of scale are not significant.
(2) Where the product can be given a quality image.
(3) Where the number of status buyers is fairly large.
(4) Where high prices are unlikely to stimulate competition.

In both of the two examples of new product pricing discussed above the precise movement of price over time depends upon the overall objective of the firm. Where a firm seeks satisfactory rather than maximum profits it will be less inclined either to skim the market or to calculate with the greatest possible accuracy that penetration price which is most profitable. Nor will the firm be concerned to adjust the price downwards to take full advantage of changes in demand elasticity. Alternative objectives of the firm will have different implications for pricing policy. If liquidity is a firm's major objective it will seek to set prices such as will recover its outlays on product development as quickly as possible, irrespective of the effects of such a policy upon sales in the long term. Likewise firms whose objective is either a certain market share, growth, or sales revenue maximisation, will vary their pricing policies in order to best achieve these goals.

In the longer term, unless the firm has monopoly power, the onset of competition will require price adjustments, generally in a downward direction. Much will depend here upon competitors' pricing policies, in which case the oligopoly analysis explored in Chapter 2 might apply, but there will also be general market factors, such as the likelihood of market saturation, to consider.

Alternative Methods of Price-Setting

It is useful to distinguish those circumstances in which firms base their prices either upon the level of costs, upon the state of demand, or upon the degree of competition within the industry.

Pricing Based on Costs

Cost oriented methods generally adhere to the same principles despite some divergence in their nomenclature. The commonest terms are 'full-cost', 'cost-plus', and 'mark-up' pricing and it is easiest to treat the first two terms as synonymous, although the difference between the former two methods and mark-up pricing can be explained as follows.

In mark-up pricing the mark-up is generally added to fixed costs without any attempt being made to allocate overhead expenses to individual items, often because of the difficulties involved in an accurate allocation of overheads. Thus price is determined solely by taking the invoiced price and adding to it a certain percentage mark-up according to the nature of the product. Such mark-ups may simply be of long standing or may reflect the manufacturer's recommended retail prices. Different retailers may, however, apply different mark-ups to identical products.

Cost-plus pricing is rather commoner in manufacturing. The pricing formula will then require the adding together of fixed costs, an allowance for overheads, and for marketing expenses where appropriate. The mark-up will then be applied to the sum total of all costs as defined above.

The mark-up can itself be either fixed or flexible. If it is fixed then price will itself only remain constant where unit costs remain constant. Where costs vary a fixed mark-up will produce variable prices. Where a firm requires price to remain constant irrespective of cost conditions, because, for example, competitors follow such a procedure, it will have to employ flexible margins which vary inversely with costs. This will of course imply variable profits. Although there are severe drawbacks to these naive models, they remain relatively popular because:

(1) They have the advantage of simplicity as compared to demand oriented approaches, which imply the necessity to constantly reassess the prevailing demand elasticity. Data on cost will anyway be forthcoming from the firm's normal

124   MANAGERIAL ECONOMICS

accounting procedures so that it is an easy step from costs to prices.

There are also added benefits from the flexible mark-up procedure which keeps prices constant. The firm's marketing division will find it much easier to operate where prices are stable and this will be welcomed by customers who will be able to calculate their own buying prices in advance.

(2) It is unlikely for reasons set out below that full-cost pricing will lead to maximum profits. On the other hand the firm's customers will probably regard what is in essence a satisficing approach as being preferable to a profit maximising approach which requires constant adjustments of price as demand elasticity varies in order to charge what the market will bear. Where the firm produces a large number of products the latter process will anyway be both time consuming and expensive. In this respect at least the cost-plus approach may move the firm fairly close to a position of maximising profits. Given the difficulties of obtaining information and the risks inherent in basing prices upon demand information which may prove out of date or inaccurate in practice, prices based upon costs will firstly provide the firm with a relatively stable environment in which to operate, and secondly relieve it of the necessity of heavy outlays expended in searching out information about market conditions. Nevertheless there are drawbacks to prices based upon costs. To begin with it will in general be fair to suggest that pricing policies which totally ignore the current state of demand are unlikely to lead to profit maximisation (assuming that this is anyway the firm's objective). In many markets demand may vary considerably on either a seasonal or cyclical basis, and we have already noted the necessity to vary prices over the life span of a product.

In addition, the allocation of costs to a product is frequently a difficult process, and several cost definitions are to be found in practice. These may include the use of historic costs, expected costs (i.e. past or present cost levels extrapolated into the future) or standard costs (i.e. the costs which the firm expects to be associated with a 'normal' output level). No cost convention typically utilised by the firm's accountants may, however, be appropriate. It may, for example, be more profitable for a firm to operate in the short run at a price sufficient only to cover variable costs in the hope of utilising spare capacity or deterring prospective competitors.

Target Pricing

Closely allied to full-cost pricing is pricing in order to achieve a target rate of return on investment, which was found by the Brookings Study[1] to be the commonest pricing policy employed by very large firms in the U.S.A. In effect these firms set out to achieve a target return in the long-run by calculating the appropriate mark-up on full costs according to the formula below

Percentage mark-up =

$$\text{Target return on investment} \times \frac{\text{Av. capital employed}}{\text{Cost of sales}}$$

The cost of sales is calculated on a 'standard' or 'normal' level of output, which will be set at a given percentage of available capacity. Let us suppose such a normal output level to be 20 units, and that the following data has also been quantified.

Total costs of producing 20 units = £100
Capital employed = £200
Target rate of return on capital = 10 per cent

The desired profit figure is then 10 per cent of £200 or £20. This must be added to total costs in order to determine the total revenues which will yield such a profit figure. Hence desired total revenue = £120.

Average cost per unit = £100 ÷ 20 = £5
Average revenue per unit = £120 ÷ 20 = £6
The profit mark up is therefore £1 on £5 = 20 per cent

We can check that solution by substitution into the above formula. We then find that

$$20\% = 10\% \times \frac{£200}{£100}$$

[1] J. B. Dirlam, A. D. H. Kaplan and R. F. Lanzillotti, *Pricing in Big Business* (Washington, D.C.: The Brookings Institution, 1958).

which verifies the previous calculation. There is some controversy as to whether the achievement of target rate of return should be regarded as a managerial tool or as an objective of the firm. Baldwin,[1] Chamberlain[2] and Kahn[3] prefer to treat it as the former rather than as the latter. According to Baldwin 'it seems far more reasonable to assume that a target rate of return is a tool, used to assist in the attainment of other goals'. Chamberlain regards it as one of several 'useful instruments in its (the firm's) objective of making a profit'. One suggestion as to how target pricing can be used as a managerial tool comes from Means[4] whereby 'the price-maker starts with an estimate of the highest rate of profits which will not induce new entrants and then works back to determine the prices which will just yield this rate of profit when operating at a reasonable proportion of capacity'. The inclusion of a discussion of target rate of return pricing in this chapter rather than elsewhere reflects a general acceptance of the viewpoints expressed above.

Break-Even Analysis and Target Return Pricing

The above discussion can be linked with break-even analysis, which purports to indicate the level of output which a firm must produce at different prices for it to cover all its costs, both fixed and variable. It is not, however, of itself a method of determining price unless linked to a target rate of return as explained below. A break-even chart simply consists of total cost and total revenue curves, superimposed one upon the other. Where they cross is the break-even point (i.e. the minimum output producible such that the firm is enabled to cover all its costs). With price set at £6 per unit the total revenue curve will have the shape as shown in Fig. 4.1 (linear because price does not alter

[1] W. L. Baldwin, 'The Motives of Managers, Environmental Restraints and the Theory of Managerial Enterprise', *Quarterly Journal of Economics* (May 1964) pp. 244–8.

[2] N. W. Chamberlain, *The Firm. Micro-Economic Planning and Action* (New York: McGraw-Hill, 1962) chap. 4, p. 207.

[3] A. E. Kahn, 'Pricing Objectives in Large Companies. Comment', *American Economic Review*, vol. 39 (Sep 1959) pp. 670–8.

[4] G. C. Means, *Pricing, Power and the Public Interest* (New York: Harper, 1962) p. 236.

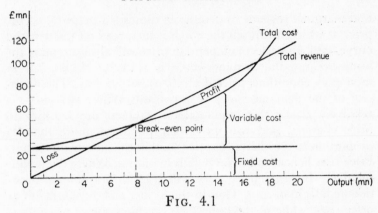

FIG. 4.1

as output varies). The firm will thus cover all of its costs at an output of 7·8 million units. Different break-even points will of course result from price alterations, but this does not provide management with a very satisfactory way of determining its optimal price, although it may give some indication where there are specific limitations on the potential level of output produceable. Break-even analysis can be extended to illustrate the basic approach to target return pricing.[1] But both break-even charts and target pricing are subject to one major drawback. No consideration is given to demand conditions. In target pricing the firm calculates its 'normal' output and the costs associated with it, and applies whatever is the appropriate mark-up in order to achieve its chosen target return. The price–output combination thrown up by this procedure may not, however, lie anywhere along the demand curve for the product. The price set by the firm is itself a determinant of demand, and there is no reason for the firm to presume that the price it fixed will be at exactly that level which will enable it to sell its 'normal' output. Hence it may well in practice find itself unable to achieve its desired target return.

Pricing Based Upon Demand or Competition

All the traditional methods of price setting are linked to demand factors. The profit maximising firm equates its marginal cost

[1] See for example P. Kotler, *Marketing Decision Making* (Holt, Rinehart & Winston, 1971) pp. 342–3.

and marginal revenue to determine its desired output, and the
price at which it can sell the goods is then read off the demand
curve itself. In perfect competition price will always remain the
same because the demand curve is perfectly elastic, but in
monopoly conditions price declines as output rises. The elasticity of the demand curve is important. Where the curve is
relatively elastic this implies that customers are sensitive to
price changes, and will vary their purchases more than in
proportion to the change in price (and in the inverse direction).
Price rises hence lead to large falls in output. Where demand is
relatively inelastic price rises will lead to less than proportionate falls in output. Thus in the former case revenues fall as
price rises, while in the latter case revenues rise as price rises.
The effect upon profits cannot, however, be determined
independently of the shape of the relevant cost curves. Where a
firm operates only along the horizontal section of its average
cost curve, the fact that average costs do not vary as output
varies implies that revenues and profits rise or fall together.
Where, however, the firm is subject to economies of scale,
implying a falling average cost curve, falling output is accompanied by rising average production costs per unit, so that
profit may or may not move in the same direction as revenues.
Empirical evidence suggests that constant average costs are
commonly to be found over a firm's normal operating outputs,
so that where a firm considers itself to be operating over a
relatively inelastic section of its demand curve it can increase
both sales revenue and profits by raising its prices. Obviously
the firm must be able to identify the shape of its demand curve
in order to determine that part of it over which it is operating,
a procedure which as indicated above is not without difficulties.
Nevertheless prices based upon demand elasticity are in principle at least those most likely to lead to profit maximisation.

    The importance of demand elasticity in price setting is
brought out in particular in the two extensions of the traditional
theory discussed in Chapter 2, namely oligopoly and price
discrimination. In one variant of the oligopoly model the firm
is predicted to operate along a kinked demand curve. In
depressed conditions an individual firm will not raise price
because it will find itself on the relatively elastic part of its
demand curve, implying losses of both revenue and profits

where other firms do not follow suit in raising prices. Where the individual firm cuts its prices competitive firms will, however, follow suit, hence taking every firm on to a relatively inelastic part of its demand curve, since aggregate market demand is unlikely to increase very much. Where demand is relatively inelastic, however, price falls will lead to falls in revenue and profits (accentuated by the increased costs of the higher output level). Thus there is a tendency for prices to be rigid where demand is depressed. In terms of cost-oriented pricing this implies as mentioned above that mark-ups must be flexible so that as costs vary prices can be kept stable. Where demand is booming firms will in general expect to operate over the relatively inelastic part of their demand curve even where prices are pushed up, because in such circumstances customers are unlikely to be price-conscious. Thus there will be no great advantage to a firm which finds itself charging rather less than its competitors, since there is unlikely to be a significant switch of consumer loyalties from the more expensive to the relatively cheap products. A price increase by one firm (the price leader) will therefore be duplicated by other firms within the industry, especially where it is a response, in whole or in part, to an increase in costs. This implies that mark-ups are inflexible in such circumstances with cost increases always producing an increase in price determined by the agreed rate of mark-up. It is still, however, necessary for the firm to assess the elasticity of demand since this will determine the extent to which it is profitable to continue pushing up prices. Differences in demand elasticity also lead to price differences in cases of price discrimination. The market circumstances under which a firm is enabled to discriminate are set out in Chapter 2. The firm apportions its optimum output among the various markets which it serves according to the principle of the equality of marginal revenue in each market. The price which it can then charge depends upon the elasticity of demand in each market.

Going-Rate Pricing

The oligopoly situation described above can be taken as illustrative of what is known generally as 'going-rate' or 'imitative' pricing, whereby a firm seeks to set prices at the average level charged by the industry. The rationale for such pricing is that firstly, as we have seen, accurate estimation of costs and particularly of demand is beyond the scope of most firms, and secondly it makes for an easy life because competitive pressures are minimised, and it is also cheap to utilise.

Going-rate pricing does not, however, describe what happens in perfect competition since in the latter case the firm is obligated to follow the industry price, otherwise it will not earn normal profits in the long run. Going-rate pricing describes a situation where a firm is able to set prices at various levels, all of them profitable, but chooses to adopt the price common to the other firms. Usually the common price will be established by a price leader, with all other firms moving their prices into line with the price leader within a short space of time.

This procedure has specific implications where a firm seeks to achieve a given profit level. Because prices are not based upon costs but upon market and competitive forces, the only way that a firm can achieve its profits target is by subtracting such profits from expected revenues and keeping within the cost constraint so defined. In other words the firm will have to keep costs below a certain figure for its 'normal' output level where both prices (revenues) and profits are predetermined for that output. When the products are identical there will be only one price at which they are sold. Product differentiation, whatever its form, will tend to lead to a series of prices set at discrete intervals, with all firms producing broadly similar products opting for the same price in the series. There might, for example, be three basic prices, each associated with a product of a given quality. There is a tendency for car manufacturers to produce models in the price range in which their main competitors have existing models for sale. And when a price leader in each price category alters his price, all other firms within that category will tend to follow suit.

Pricing Other Than to Maximise Profits

We have so far been largely concerned with profit-maximising behaviour by firms. It is, however, worthwhile to briefly consider the implications of more modern theories of the firm for pricing policy.

We have already noted in passing that prices based upon costs are unlikely to lead to maximum profits. This conclusion does not necessarily hold true since many firms appear to believe that if they, like their competitors, adhere to a simple pricing rule based upon costs, they will in the long run be maximising their profits. The underlying rationale here is that this will avoid the possibility of price wars and the like and thus eliminate an important source of uncertainty surrounding the firm's future actions. As the long run is an amorphous concept at best we cannot determine empirically whether the above is or is not correct. Therefore it is probably fair to say that pricing based upon costs is analogous to satisficing behaviour as described in the previous chapter.

Baumol's theory of sales revenue maximisation implies that prices must be set with intent to produce the greatest possible level of sales (subject to a profit constraint). Thus price must be set well below that which would produce maximum profits, but not so low as to make the profit constraint difficult of achievement. The further point made to the effect that it will pay the firm to undertake heavy advertising outlays in order to push up the level of sales (largely at the expense of profits but subject to a profit constraint) perhaps suggests that where brand loyalty can be aroused in customers, price can be raised as a consequence, with beneficial results for revenues. Much, however, would then depend upon the elasticity of demand for the product.

There is unfortunately little which can usefully be said about the implication for pricing policy of theories either based upon managers' pursuit of their own objectives or upon growth maximisation. This fact is openly acknowledged by the authors of some of the best known of these models, but they contend that they are trying above all to draw useful inferences about economic efficiency and equity, and that therefore it is relatively unimportant to try to specify the exact nature of price determination. Presumably it is to be expected that firms will adopt some simple pricing rule, possibly full-cost pricing, which will not interfere with the pursuit of their chosen objectives.

It is equally difficult to extract any precise implications for pricing policy from behavioural theories of the firm, because every firm is assumed to react somewhat differently to all others in much the same circumstances. Cyert and March were aware of this shortcoming and built up a simplified simulation model incorporating three organisational goals, aspiration levels, and organisational slack. They found that price depended mainly upon the potential for cutting back on sales promotion, upon factors causing changes in the amount of organisational slack, and upon changes in desired profits consequent upon profits earned in the previous time period. The inference here is clearly that the firm's ability to raise or lower price is largely dependent upon its ability to manipulate its costs, and this is clearly related to the extent of slack and the level of promotional expenditure.

THE DESCRIPTIVE APPROACH

There is not much available evidence on how firms actually price in practice. This is not altogether surprising in view of the continued popularity of the traditional models of the firm, which postulate prices based exclusively upon the equating of marginal cost and marginal revenue. Furthermore many firms are not able to pinpoint precisely how they go about setting prices. Hall and Hitch[1] point out that 'most of our informants were vague about anything so precise as elasticity....In addition many, perhaps most, apparently made no effort, even implicitly, to estimate elasticities of demand...and of those who do the majority considered the information of little or no relevance to the pricing process save perhaps in very exceptional conditions'. Hall and Hitch's work was one of a number which set out to specifically refute the axioms of marginal analysis, and was largely paralleled by Sweezy[2] in the U.S.A. Sweezy postulated that competitors in an oligopolistic market would respond quickly to a price cut by an individual firm but either slowly or not at all to a price rise (thus leading to a kink in the demand curve). Alternatively he suggested either that a price cut might take place secretly, enabling the price cutter to remain on a relatively elastic part of his demand

[1] R. L. Hall and C. J. Hitch, 'Price Theory and Business Behaviour', *Oxford Economic Papers* (May 1939) p. 18.

[2] P. M. Sweezy, 'Demand under Conditions of Oligopoly', *Journal of Political Economy*, vol. 47 (1939).

curve, or that a price rise by a major firm would be followed by all other firms (price leadership). Hence overall, except where price cuts can be conducted in secret or where there is price leadership, oligopoly prices rise in boom conditions and remain constant in slumps.

Hall and Hitch interviewed thirty-eight entrepreneurs running firms which can be described as oligopolistic. They concluded that most of the entrepreneurs were unfamiliar with marginal analysis, and that they were not anyway seeking to maximise profits in the short run. They mostly relied upon some variant of full-cost pricing, although they were of the opinion that in the long run this would take them reasonably near to maximising their profits, given the need to make allowances for competitive reactions. They felt that it was fairer to all concerned not to try and maximise short-run profits. Now and again certain entrepreneurs lowered or raised their prices when demand conditions were significantly altered, but for the most part prices were kept constant, implying flexible mark-ups on costs. As we have seen, rigid prices imply a good degree of tacit or open collusion.

Hall and Hitch were trying to combine the full-cost pricing principle with the kinked demand model, unlike Sweezy who did not develop the full-cost postulate. As Stigler[1] points out, however, the two theories of price setting are incompatible in several respects, and are therefore best treated as separate models by the reader.

As indicated in Chapter 3 attempts were made to produce evidence to refute the conclusions of Hall and Hitch. The best known refutation was produced by Earley.[2] Earley set out to infer from indirect evidence whether or not two non-marginalist hypotheses were true; firstly one which claimed that a firm has 'predominantly a long-run and defensive viewpoint in its pricing, production and investment policies (rather than an alert attitude toward its near at hand profit opportunities)', and secondly that it uses 'in the main a full-cost rather than incremental cost calculus in its pricing, production and investment decisions'. He considered as a result of his survey that

[1] G. J. Stigler, 'The Kinky Oligopoly Demand Curve and Rigid Prices', *Journal of Political Economy*, vol. 55 (1947) pp. 432–47.

[2] Earley, *American Economic Review* (Mar 1956).

'judged either by responses to individual questions or the foregoing component indexes, the evidence of overall marginalism among companies is very strong. . . . Approximately 60 per cent of them show what can be considered from "substantial" to "very strong" Marginalism.' His conclusions were that 'Short views, innovative sensitivity, marginal costing and marginal pricing are all preponderant among the responding companies', that 'where considerable segmented variable cost data are brought to management's attention the companies short-range policies are consistent with their longer-range costing, pricing and other product related policies' and finally that 'with such companies marginalism is apparently not dependent upon – though it is increased by – a short time perspective'.

Hague,[1] however, points out that the results of this kind of study 'depend too much on inferences and implications read into personal opinions expressed verbally by businessmen and too little on authentic written statements and statistical data'. This objection applies of course to his own study[2] in which he interviewed eight large and twelve small firms in the Black Country. He found that the firms were less interested in profit maximisation than in 'a comfortable and secure income'. Two distinct types of output policy were found. 'In small firms output was rarely fixed so as to equate marginal cost and marginal revenue, but by rule of thumb methods.' 'In large firms on the other hand there was a greater desire to earn maximum profits . . . but again there was no attempt at careful balancing of marginal revenue and marginal cost. In general these firms seemed to be satisfied that long-run profits were maximised, but they had no scientific policy for ensuring this.'

Where there was no conventional or controlled price for the article firms based price upon what appeared in general to be the accountant's estimate of 'total unit cost' (which is much the same thing as Hall and Hitch's notion of 'full cost') to which was added a profit margin based largely on convention.

Skinner[3] sent out a postal questionnaire to all members of

[1] D. C. Hague, 'Economic Theory and Business Behaviour', *Review of Economic Studies*, vol. XVI, p. 144.

[2] Ibid.

[3] R. C. Skinner, 'The Determination of Selling Prices', *Journal of Industrial Economics* (July 1970) pp. 201–17.

the Merseyside Chamber of Commerce in early 1968. His main conclusion[1] was that 'although 70 per cent of the respondents in the survey claim to use cost-plus pricing, great weight is given in fixing prices to competition and demand, although not quite as much weight as to a firm's own cost and profits'.

Unfortunately in reading through various published studies one can at times be left feeling awash in a sea of semantics. In his study Skinner asked firms whether they divided their costs into fixed and variable elements, and if so, whether the distinction provided the basis for price setting. Seventy-three per cent claimed to make the distinction and 69 per cent to use it for price setting. Skinner then goes on to argue, much as does Earley,[2] that a firm which makes this distinction is employing variable (otherwise known as direct or marginal) costing. Sizer,[3] however, thinks that 'A more reasonable interpretation of Skinner's results may be that firms analyse costs into fixed and variable elements as part of the procedure for establishing overhead recovery rates and mark up on cost percentages.'

A brief summary of other studies is to be found in Silberston.[4] He concludes, not surprisingly in the light of the above analysis, that

full cost can be given a mark of beta query plus, but no more than this, since there are so many marginalist and behavioural qualifications. It seems clear that the procedure of calculating prices very often starts with an average cost type of calculation but the qualifications that arise are concerned with the next stage of the process, including the exact method by which full costs are calculated. An important point to remember is that the studies mentioned concentrate mainly on home market prices, and that there is abundant evidence that in export pricing, marginal calculations figure much more prominently.

An attempt has occasionally been made, invariably in the United States, to specifically collect information on pricing

[1] Ibid., p. 202.

[2] Earley, *American Economic Review* (Mar 1956).

[3] J. Sizer, 'Note on the Determination of Selling Prices', *Journal of Industrial Economics* (Nov 1971) p. 88.

[4] A. Silberston, *Economic Journal* (Sep 1970) pp. 542–6.

policies, which one would expect to throw up more extensive and useful information than the above. This has been done both for large[1] and for small[2] businesses.

The findings of the Brookings study, originally conducted between 1948 and 1951 but subsequently updated, were primarily based upon the pricing practices as reported by representative firms in all sectors of big business, including primary production, distribution and manufacturing. The basic technique used was the interview, which, as was pointed out in the study, is not the most reliable way of obtaining information. However, this is unlikely to have seriously affected the validity of the results, which in general indicated that the firms concerned invariably sought to earn satisfactory profits, and that they often felt themselves to be approximating to profit maximising behaviour in the long run. The firms did not consider that profit maximisation as a goal had any operational implications for pricing policy, although it was not necessarily incorrect to suppose that they would not achieve it in the end. The authors observed that 'for the most part the companies doubted that by changing their pricing policies they could raise their profits in the long run'.[3]

The authors found it appropriate to cluster the respondents' avowed pricing policies into five groups, into one of which each firm could be slotted, although most firms did not keep rigidly to only one approach to pricing irrespective of market circumstances. The first of these groups was referred to as:

Pricing to Achieve a Target Return on Investment

Over one-third of the interviewed companies claimed to use this method, in particular General Motors Corporation. For the most part they adopted the basic cost-plus formula described earlier in the chapter although 'the discussions of policy also disclosed that among those that could be characterized in

[1] Dirlam, Kaplan and Lanzillotti, *Pricing in Big Business* and Lanzillotti, 'Pricing Objectives in Large Companies', *American Economic Review*, vol. 48 (Dec 1958) pp. 921–40.

[2] W. W. Haynes, *Pricing Decisions in Small Business* (Lexington: University of Kentucky Press, 1962).

[3] Dirlam, Kaplan and Lanzillotti, *Pricing in Big Business*, p. 130.

general as following an administered, stabilized, cost-plus system of pricing, the degree of precision and of compliance ranged too widely to make target return a master key to pricing'.[1]

Target return pricing was particularly popular with firms which either operated in industries characterised by entry barriers or which were introducing new products, because in neither case was much competition to be expected. This is borne out by other studies. The evidence has been assessed by Baldwin[2] as follows. 'Very crudely we should expect to find a positive correlation between the height of barriers to entry and use of target rate of return pricing unless entry is blockaded', where 'blockaded' entry results when the price that would attract new entrants is above the profit maximising price of the most favoured firms now in the industry.

Lanzillotti calculated that for the twenty companies he investigated average target return was above 14 per cent of invested capital, net of taxes; also that in only one case was it below 10 per cent while in no case was it above 20 per cent. He noted a wide range of explanations for the choice of a specific target return as follows:[3]

The most frequently mentioned rationalizations included (a) fair or reasonable return, (b) the traditional industry concept of fair return in relation to risk factors, (c) desire to equal or better the corporation average return over a recent period, (d) what the company felt it could get as a long run matter and (e) use of a specific profit target as a means of stabilising industry prices.

Lanzillotti went on to conclude that

This reinforces the observation made earlier that no one single objective or policy rules all price making in any given company. In fact in many companies a close inter-

[1] Ibid., p. 284.
[2] Baldwin, *Quarterly Journal of Economics* (May 1964) p. 247.
[3] Lanzillotti, *American Economic Review,* vol. 48 (Dec 1958).

relationship exists among target return pricing, desire to stabilise prices and target market share (either a minimum or maximum objective).

Stabilisation of Price and Margin

Not surprisingly most companies regarded this as a desirable policy in principle, even if in practice it has to be relegated to a subordinate role. It is part and parcel of cost-plus pricing as previously defined. As we noted in our discussion of cost-plus pricing both price and profit per unit can only be kept stable at the same time if cost per unit is also constant. In other circumstances either the price is held constant and the mark-up is flexible or vice versa. The ability to hold prices steady is generally dependent upon price leadership within the industry and implies a desire not to maximise profits in the short run. Thus the United States Steel Corporation summed up its policy as selling 'at the lowest price consistent with cost and a reasonable profit'. Lanzillotti[1] found that

> The distinction between target return on investment as a pricing philosophy and cost-plus pricing in the companies surveyed is difficult to define....The difference between the two rationalizations lies in the extent to which the company is willing to push beyond the limits of a pricing method to some average return philosophy....Cost-plus, therefore, may be viewed as one step on the road to return on investment as a guide, or precept for price policy. But some firms never go any further. The standard can be accepted as self-sufficient.

Pricing and Product Differentiation

Some firms in the study placed considerable emphasis upon product differentiation. Successful product differentiation reduces the need for an active pricing policy since there will be fewer goods with which the customer can compare prices.

[1] Ibid., p. 932.

Pricing to Meet or Match Competition

This objective reflects our previous discussion of going-rate pricing, with its implicit disregard for cost factors.[1] In many cases the policy of meeting competition appeared to Lanzillotti 'to be materially influenced by market share psychology'.

Pricing to Maintain or Improve Market Share

This policy is not consistent with target return pricing. Attempts to maintain or improve market share in the face of competition will in general mean that prices need to be held down, which will in turn have detrimental implications for the target return. It is, however, possible for a firm to wish to maximise its market share subject to the necessity of achieving a given target return. Obviously the strength of competition is very important for this policy which is by definition irrelevant in a pure monopoly situation. Share of the market was ordinarily thought of as a maximum, bearing witness to the power of the corporations interviewed. Hence, according to Lanzillotti[2] the target share of the market as a guide to pricing tended to be used for those products in which the firm did not, at the outset, enjoy a patent or innovative monopoly because 'they apparently did not wish to gobble up any market they entered unless it was one which they had created.'

Not surprisingly, few firms have only one major pricing policy, and for the most part several policies are pursued at the same time. Overall the authors of the Brookings study concluded that

(1) Most firms set themselves some sort of long-run profit goal and introduce or vary pricing methods with a view to the attainment of that goal.
(2) Most of the firms produced a whole range of products, and thus tended to have an overall pricing policy rather than one specially geared to different products.
(3) To some extent the pursuit of certain pricing policies would be constrained by the need to pursue subsidiary policies simultaneously.

[1] See for example G. Maxey and A. Silberston, *The Motor Industry*, Cambridge Studies in Industry (Allen & Unwin, 1959).

[2] Lanzillotti, *American Economic Review*, vol. 48 (Dec 1958) p. 933.

This according to Lanzillotti implies that no single theory of the firm 'is likely to impose an unambiguous course of action for the firm for any given situation; nor will it provide a satisfactory basis for valid and useful predictions of price behaviour'.

PRICING AND DECISIONS IN SMALL BUSINESS

A few years after the Brookings study of pricing in large firms, Haynes conducted a parallel investigation for small firms employing for the most part fewer than 200 employees. Eighty-eight firms were investigated, predominantly from the manufacturing, retailing and service sectors of the U.S. economy, and the conclusions were broadly as follows

(1) Prices were more often based upon costs rather than upon demand.
(2) 'Mark-up' pricing was common, particularly in retailing firms.
(3) Mark-ups were set at different levels for different groups of products.
(4) Price leadership by large firms made many small firms price followers.
(5) Information on costs and demand was often poor making it difficult for the firms to apply pricing rules.

CONCLUSIONS

It is difficult to draw any hard and fast conclusions from the above analysis except with reference to markets characterised by either perfect competition or monopoly, and even in the latter case only where the firm is attempting to maximise profit. No generally accepted theory of oligopolistic price setting is at present available, so that we must expect there to be a wide range of pricing policies in practice. This is borne out by our brief reference to the pricing implications of objectives other than profit maximisation.

The main controversy as we have seen relates to the validity of marginal as against full-cost theories of price determination. In support of marginalism we have referred to price discrimination which requires the equating of marginal cost and aggregated marginal revenue; to market skimming, which requires that price be responsive to the elasticity of demand as it changes over the lifetime of the product; and to various empirical studies such as that of Earley. We have also, on the other hand, referred to several studies which indicate that prices are based upon some variant of cost-plus. In particular we have noted that price leadership and going-rate pricing, which often require flexible mark-ups, typify established firms' behaviour in circumstances in which a quiet life is preferred to cut-throat competition. In the short run we must expect prices to remain for the most part unchanged. As Silberston points out this may be due either to administrative problems of changing and publishing price lists; or to uncertainty with respect to competitive reactions to price alterations; to a desire for a quiet life; or to a desire to avoid anti-monopoly investigations or loss of customer goodwill. Over the long period, however, everything is subject to change and pricing behaviour will have to adapt to the requirements of a changing environment.

Perhaps, therefore, as some economists appear to believe,[1] we must set off in a completely new direction in order to resolve questions relating to pricing policy, although it is necessary to absorb the ideas discussed above for use as a basis for such a departure.

BIBLIOGRAPHY

N. W. CHAMBERLAIN, *The Firm. Micro-Economic Planning and Action* (New York: McGraw-Hill, 1962) chap. 4.

J. DEAN, 'Problems of Product Line Pricing', *Journal of Marketing*, vol. 14 (Jan 1950).

——, *Managerial Economics* (Prentice-Hall, 1951).

J. B. DIRLAM, A. D. H. KAPLAN and R. F. LANZILLOTTI, *Pricing in Big Business* (Washington, D.C.: The Brookings Institution, 1958).

J. S. EARLEY, 'Marginal Policies of "Excellently Managed" Companies', *American Economic Review* (Mar 1956).

W. A. H. GODLEY and C. GILLION, 'Pricing Behaviour in Manufacturing Industry', *N.I.E.S.R. Review* (Aug 1965).

[1] See for example J. F. Weston, 'Pricing Behaviour of Large Firms', *Western Economic Journal*, vol. 10, no. 1 (1972) pp. 1–18.

R. A. GORDON, 'Short-period Price Determination in Theory and Practice', *American Economic Review* (June 1948) pp. 265–88.

D. C. HAGUE, 'Economic Theory and Business Behaviour', *Review of Economic Studies*, vol. XVI, pp. 144–59.

R. L. HALL and C. J. HITCH, 'Price Theory and Business Behaviour', *Oxford Economic Papers* (May 1939) pp. 12–45.

W. W. HAYNES, *Pricing Decisions in Small Business* (Lexington: University of Kentucky Press, 1962).

A. E. KAHN, 'Pricing Objectives in Large Companies. Comment', *American Economic Review*, vol. 39 (Sep 1959) pp. 670–8.

R. F. LANZILLOTTI, 'Pricing Objectives in Large Companies', *American Economic Review*, vol. 48 (Dec 1958) pp. 921–40.

P. J. LUND and F. RUSHDY, 'The Effect of Demand on Prices in British Manufacturing Industry', *Review of Economic Studies* (Oct 1967).

R. A. LYNN, *Price Policies and Marketing Management* (Irwin, 1967).

J. MARKHAM, 'The Nature and Significance of Price Leadership', *American Economic Review* (Dec 1951).

A. R. OXENFELDT, *Pricing for Marketing Executives* (Wadsworth, 1961).

I. F. PEARCE, 'A Study in Price Policy', *Economica*, new series (May 1956).

K. W. ROTHSCHILD, 'Price Theory and Oligopoly', *Economic Journal* (Sep 1947).

A. W. SILBERSTON, 'The Pricing of Manufactured Products. A Comment', *Economic Journal* (June 1951).

——, 'Surveys of Applied Economics. Price Behaviour of Firms', *Economic Journal* (Sep 1970) pp. 511–82.

J. SIZER, 'Note on the Determination of Selling Prices', *Journal of Industrial Economics* (Nov 1971) pp. 85–9.

R. C. SKINNER, 'The Determination of Selling Prices', *Journal of Industrial Economics* (July 1970) pp. 201–17.

J. G. UDELL, 'How Important is Pricing in Competitive Strategy?', *Journal of Marketing* (Jan 1964) pp. 44–8.

T. E. WENTZ, 'Realism in Pricing Analyses', *Journal of Marketing*, vol. 30 (April 1966).

J. F. WESTON, 'Pricing Behaviour of Large Firms', *Western Economic Journal*, vol. 10, no. 1 (1972) pp. 1–18.

5

Capital Investment Appraisal

An efficient and accurate means of appraising the worth-whileness of prospective investment is obviously essential for a firm which seeks to maximise profits, where all investments manifestly do not yield the same returns over the same period of time. The substitution of other objectives for that of profit maximisation does not, however, negate the need for accurate investment appraisal, since it is virtually impossible to justify an intended investment subjectively except in circumstances where the potential economic returns are immaterial, whereas most firms in practice do couch their objectives in some sort of economic terms.

It is curious therefore to discover how little attention has been paid to this area of a firm's operations within the United Kingdom. This has led several commentators[1] to postulate a connection between the unscientific approach to investment appraisal and the slow rate of growth of the British economy post-war, during which period the vast bulk of published data on this subject has appeared. The evidence suggests that most firms have concentrated exclusively upon what we shall call below the traditional methods of appraisal, namely variants of the pay-back method or of the rate of return on capital employed method. These two approaches to investment appraisal have been viewed in an unfavourable light by virtually all post-war commentators, principally on the grounds that they are either inaccurate, too conservative, or both, when compared with modern techniques such as Internal Rate

[1] See for example A. M. Alfred, 'Discounted Cash Flow and Corporate Planning', *Woolwich Economic Papers*, no. 3 (Woolwich Polytechnic, 1964), or C. J. Hawkins and D. W. Pearce, *Capital Investment Appraisal* (Macmillan, 1971).

of Return or Net Present Value. However, it is not our intention in this chapter to come down heavily in favour of either traditional or modern techniques, but rather to try to set out their basic advantages and disadvantages in such a way as to enable the reader to draw his own conclusions.

TRADITIONAL METHODS OF APPRAISAL

The Pay-Back Method

The principle of this method is extremely simple. The firm decides on the longest permissible period over which a project will be allowed to repay the original investment outlay, known as the pay-back period. The firm then calculates the expected returns for different projects on, say, an annual basis, and if over the required pay-back period the returns add up to more than the capital outlay, the project will be accepted, whereas if the returns add up to less than the capital outlay over the pay-back period the project will be rejected.

Thus, assuming a desired pay-back period of 4 years, and a stream of expected future profits as follows:

Year:	0	1	2	3	4
£ project A	−100	40	30	20	20
£ project B	−100	30	20	20	20

then project A will satisfy the pay-back criterion since the capital outlay is £100 (usually expressed as a negative figure under Year 0) but expected returns are £110 over 4 years. Project B on the other hand will not satisfy the criterion since expected returns on an original outlay of £100 are only £90 over 4 years.

The most obvious advantage of such a method is its simplicity, which requires no further comment. A second advantage is that it tends to minimise risk, since most firms require their money back over a comparatively short space of time, and the near future is obviously less uncertain than periods further into the future.

The disadvantages are, however, many. That most frequently quoted alludes to the fact that this method ignores any profits stream beyond the pay-back period, which is much the same thing as saying that the method is too conservative.

Consider the following projects:

Year:	0	1	2	3	4	5	6	7
£ project A	−100	40	30	20	20	10	10	0
£ project B	−100	30	20	20	20	20	20	20

Over a period of 7 years project A pays back £130, whereas project B pays back £150. Thus a less conservative criterion for pay-back would result in a reversal of the firm's original decision to select project A, especially since project B may continue to earn profits beyond the seventh year, whereas project A earns nil profits after the sixth year.

Secondly, returning once again to our original set of data, we may note that for a project to satisfy a 4-year pay-back criterion, it must achieve a rate of return on capital employed of 25 per cent p.a. or better. This expectation of high returns contradicts somewhat the choice of this method on the grounds that it is essentially conservative in reducing risk. One would not, surely, expect many non-risk investments to yield such high rates of return. Consequently not only will very few projects satisfy the criterion where the pay-back period is comparatively short, but those which do so are surely likely to be much more uncertain of outcome than would be to the taste of a conservative firm.

Thirdly the likelihood of under-investment implicit above will be an even more serious disadvantage where borrowing costs (the opportunity cost of invested capital) are low. Even given a borrowing cost of 10 per cent per annum it would still be profitable to invest in any project having a pay-back period of 10 years or less (or of 12½ years or less where the borrowing cost is 8 per cent).

Lastly the method fails to allow for differing time patterns of cash flows. Consider the example below:

Year:	0	1	2	3	4	5
£ project A	−100	80	20	20	20	20
£ project B	−100	40	40	40	20	20

Both projects pay back the same amount over a 5-year period (£160). Hence, judged against a criterion of a 5-year pay-back period both projects appear equi-desirable. Common sense, however, tells us that project A is in fact superior to project B, firstly because the capital outlay is recovered over a shorter time period (2 years for project A as against $2\frac{1}{2}$ years for project B) and secondly because the firm is able to re-invest the early profits as soon as they are received, which renders the high initial return of project A highly advantageous.

The disadvantages of this method are therefore serious, but can its use be justified in certain circumstances?[1] In a specific sense it would be the best criterion to adopt where a firm is operating in a completely uncertain environment, such that speedy recouping of capital outlays is of the essence.[2] This might, for example, apply to a British firm's operations in a politically unstable country abroad.

In a more general sense Adelson[3] has commented that the difficulties inherent in trying to forecast very far into the future mitigate in favour of the pay-back criterion, and further, that most projects which satisfy the pay-back criterion also satisfy the D.C.F. criteria, whereas the converse does not hold true.

Return on Capital Employed

The principle of this method is to express profits as a per cent return on capital employed, where the calculation is done post

---

[1] A résumé of justifications for pay-back is to be found in J. Hellings, 'Technical Note. The Case for Pay-Back Re-examined', *Journal of Business Finance* (Spring 1972) pp. 99–102.

[2] A. J. Merrett and A. Sykes, *The Finance and Analysis of Capital Projects* (Longman, 1963) pp. 200–9.

[3] R. M. Adelson, 'D.C.F. The Other Point of View', *Moorgate and Wall St Review* (Spring 1971) p. 57.

tax and incorporating investment allowances. The calculation is very simple once the firm has decided *the precise nature of the variables to be used for the computation.* Consider the data below:

Year:	0	1	2	3	4	5
£ project A	−100	40	40	40	20	10
£ project B	−100	30	60	60	30	20

Total profit for project A is £150, and for project B is £200· Hence profit per annum will be respectively £30 and £40, which in relation to an original capital outlay of £100 suggests a rate of return for project A of 30 per cent and for project B of 40 per cent.

However, several disadvantages of this method spring readily to mind. Firstly, as for pay-back above, it ignores the question of re-investing profits. Where two projects yield the same average return but one yields a much greater return over the early years, this should be taken into account where a decision requires a choice between the projects.

Secondly the computation of an average rate of return ignores differences in the number of years over which the project exists. Two projects yielding the same average return over different periods are not equally worthwhile where the firm has no reason to suppose that the projects will not earn profits for their full expected lifetime. If this is so the project having the longer lifetime will in fact be the preferable alternative.

A further point leading on from the above relates to the fact that even where one project yields a higher annual return than another, this cannot be taken as evidence of the greater appeal of that project until the lifetime of the two projects is also considered. The method cannot differentiate satisfactorily between a project yielding a 10 per cent return for 10 years and another project yielding 9 per cent for 15 years.

Fourthly this method is unable to differentiate between £1 today and £1 next year (an objection which also applies to the pay-back method). This is a serious deficiency because money held today can be invested, and hence becomes a larger sum in the future. It is thus apparent that £1 today is worth more than £1 in the future and that it is worth increasingly more *pro rata* the further into the future we go.

All the above objections apply to the average annual rate of return on the full capital employed method. Yet it is not even satisfactory to assume that this is the ideal formulation for computing rate of return. There are several possible alternatives. We could for instance keep the original capital outlay as the lower half of the equation, but alter the numerator to read either 'profit over the first year of the project', or 'the highest annual profit irrespective of the year in which it was earned', or 'the average profit taking the first and last year's profits together'. Using the above data this will yield the results shown in Table 5.1. The confusion over which project

TABLE 5.1

	Capital employed	Average annual return	Return in first year	Return in best year	Average return, first and final year
£ project *A*	100	30%	40%	40%	25%
£ project *B*	100	40%	30%	60%	25%

to choose often becomes even worse if we base calculations upon average capital employed per annum, or upon any other measure of capital employed.

For all the above reasons return on capital employed must be considered the least acceptable of the methods considered in this chapter.

MODERN APPRAISAL METHODS (DISCOUNTED CASH FLOW)

Modern methods of investment appraisal all involve the principle of *discounting*. Discounting is nothing more than the inverse of compounding, where both methods seek to demonstrate the fact that a given sum of money in the future differs in terms of purchasing power from an identical sum today. Compounding implies that interest accruing in any one year is added to capital outstanding at the beginning of that year and interest is then charged on the total sum (interest plus capital) during the ensuing year. Thus, taking a sum £X invested at an interest rate of r per cent per annum, the capital will have accrued by year end to £$X(1+r)$. Interest on this amount is then charged during the second year at a rate of r per cent per annum, so that at year end the capital has grown to £$X(1+r)(1+r)$ or £$X(1+r)^2$. For years beyond year 2 we simply change the bracket to read $(1+r)^3$ for year 3 and so forth.

Now underlying what is known as the *time value of money* is the fact that where a person has available to him a certain sum of money in the present, he will, by investing it at a fixed interest rate, have available to him a larger sum measured in money terms in future years. (Notice, however, that we are talking here of a larger money amount, rather than a larger real amount, for reasons discussed further on.) He will not consider an offer to be repaid the *same* money amount say next year as being acceptable, even where he expects to be able to buy the same basket of goods next year as this year with the money, because he has given up the opportunity to spend the money at his discretion. His refusal to accept as equivalent a given sum this year and the same sum next year will also reflect the effects of inflation upon the real value of money (otherwise known as purchasing power). Where prices are rising by 10 per cent per annum a £1 note today will purchase 10 per cent fewer goods one year hence. Therefore if a person has £1 to invest, and is offered 10 per cent interest during a period when prices are rising at 10 per cent, he will in *real* terms be no better off than he was when he started. This tends to imply that a person will require from a would-be borrower an interest rate significantly above the going rate of inflation, and if he is unable to obtain such a rate, logic suggests that his best course of action would be to spend the money immediately, preferably on an earning asset.

Compounding therefore tells us the value in the future of a given sum today, invested at various interest rates for varying periods of years. Discounting on the other hand tells us how much *in present-day terms* any given sum accruing in the future

will be worth. It is a measure of indifference between two or
more sums accruing in different time periods.

To see how this works we can readily link the principles of
compounding and discounting. A given sum £X today will be
worth £X(1+r) next year as we have seen above. But it is
just as true to say that if we discount the year end sum by a
factor (1+r) we will once again arrive at our original investment, as follows:

$$£X \times (1+r) \times \frac{1}{(1+r)} = £X$$

Hence we can always discover what a given sum at year end
is worth in present-day terms by discounting by a factor (1+r).
Likewise we can equate a given sum at the end of two years
with its present value by discounting by a factor $(1+r)^2$. All
future cash flows can be discounted to their present value
equivalents in this way, such that we can derive a discounting
formula as follows (where E = expected net returns).

$$\text{Gross Present Value} = \frac{E_1}{(1+r)} + \frac{E_2}{(1+r)^2} + \frac{E_3}{(1+r)^3} + \cdots \frac{E_n}{(1+r)^n}$$

This formula can be summed into

$$\sum_{m=0}^{m=n} \frac{E_m}{(1+r)^m}$$

where m is the number of years of the project's life.

Once all expected net returns have been discounted to their
gross present values and summed, the capital outlay must be
subtracted to define Net Present Value (N.P.V.), namely

$$\text{G.P.V.} - \text{Capital cost} = \text{N.P.V.}$$

Where the Net Present Value is positive in sign this can be
taken to imply that the project is earning more than the rate of
return by which the expected net returns were discounted,
whereas if N.P.V. is negative in sign this implies that the
project is not earning as high a rate of return as that used for
discounting purposes.

All the above very much begs the question as to what the

discount rate means in economic terms. A discussion of this point will, however, be put aside for the moment while we consider what is meant by the *Internal Rate of Return* (I.R.R.).

The Internal Rate of Return may be defined as that rate of interest which will discount the stream of expected net returns (expected returns less expected costs) into equivalence with the capital cost of the project. This is the same thing as a discount rate which produces an N.P.V. of zero. Unlike N.P.V., however, I.R.R. can only be calculated by some form of trial-and-error process, although short-cut techniques do exist in the form of various tables.[1] These tell us, for example, for given discount rates, with what numbers to multiply expected net returns in order to transform them into their present value. For example, the present value of 1 discounted at 10 per cent for one year is 0·9091. Likewise the present value of 1 after two years at a 10 per cent discount is 0·8264.

Thus to take an example of a calculation where the discount rate is 10 per cent:

Year:	0	1	2	3
Cash flows	− 500	+ 200	+ 200	+ 200
Discount factor		0·9091	0·8264	0·7513
Discounted values	− 500	+ 181·8	+ 165·3	+ 150·3

Gross Present Value = 497·4.
Net Present Value = 497·4 − 500 = − 2·6.

Thus the above project would just fail to be acceptable at the 10 per cent discount rate. One can see by further inspection that the Internal Rate of Return will be very marginally below 10 per cent.

A fuller calculation to suggest very broadly the approach to discovering I.R.R. is as follows, using a discount rate initially of 14 per cent.

[1] See for example D. C. Hague, *Managerial Economics* (Longman, 1969) p. 124.

F

Year:	0	1	2
Cash flows	−400	+240	+253
Discount factor	1	0·8771	0·7694
Present value	−400	+210·5	+194·5

Therefore Net Present Value = 5·0.

We are, however, seeking an N.P.V. of 0 as indicated above. Let us therefore try discounting at 15 per cent.

Year:	0	1	2
Cash flows	−400	+240	+253
Discount factor	1	0·8695	0·7561
Present value	−400	+208·7	+191·3

Therefore Net Present Value = 0.

We note that where the I.R.R. is greater than the borrowing cost of funds used in the project, the project is acceptable, but where the I.R.R. is less than the cost of borrowing the project is rejected.

The accuracy of the discount factors quoted above (to four figures of decimals) may tend to camouflage the importance of the rate at which they decline. Once the discount factor becomes fairly small the application of such a discount factor to a cash flow produces only a marginal change in N.P.V., and is therefore unlikely to affect the viability of the project. Hence the precision of the discount factor is not of great importance. Note also that given sufficiently high discount rates, the net present value will be so heavily weighted by the returns from the first few years, that there will be no significant difference between N.P.V. and pay-back criteria.

THE COST OF CAPITAL

It is now time to consider the ubiquitous letter r above. This letter appears both in the compounding and discounting formulae as a suitable rate of interest. But saying that r is a suitable rate of interest for the problem in hand very much begs the question given that the N.P.V. will vary significantly for only small changes in r. Furthermore, although the I.R.R. can be calculated without reference to the value of r, we can only decide whether or not the project is acceptable by comparing the I.R.R. with the firm's borrowing cost, and this is not at all an easy thing to pin down.

The cost of capital to a firm first of all depends upon the nature of the capital in question. Firms finance themselves broadly via the issue of what are known as shares or equities which are linked to the firm's profits; and bonds or debentures, which are redeemed by the company after a stated number of years have passed, with interest being payable on the capital on an annual basis.

In principle it should therefore be extremely simple to calculate the cost to the firm of raising capital by bond issue. Unfortunately a firm is under no obligation to issue all bonds at a constant interest rate. Indeed we would expect the rate offered on bonds to take into account rates being offered on competing investments, and hence to vary as competitive circumstances vary. Thus we cannot be entirely certain of the appropriate interest rate to use, at least not without the most painstaking calculations.

When we talk of the firm's cost of capital, we generally refer, however, to its equity cost of capital. It could be said that in theory firms are trying to maximise the present value of potentially available profits on behalf of the shareholder, but it cannot very well do this unless it knows the equity cost of capital, which appears unlikely in an uncertain world.

Let us consider the case of a company wishing to raise capital from existing shareholders. When an individual is considering which shares to buy, he is in principle asking himself what he expects the value of the expected stream of future dividends to be worth, taking each share individually. He then discounts them to their present value and puts his money into the share with the greatest residual figure net of tax. Share purchasers are, however, not often such pristine examples of 'economic man', and it is more likely that they will compare just a few shares on a much more rough and ready basis, often using past dividend records as a guide. Thus a firm must broadly bear in mind the need to have a comparable dividend record to those companies most likely to be treated as alternative investments in the shareholder's mind. It is possible for a company to estimate the equity cost of capital in this sort of way, although it is hardly likely to be precise because, for example, the degree of risk involved in the operations of the different firms may differ, and a firm may anyway find that the result might change significantly through one or two firms being added to or subtracted from the original list of firms considered by investors as comparable.

The most often quoted method is, however, to be found in Merrett and Sykes.[1] At any rate their method has become sufficiently accepted to merit some fierce attacks in the journals of late.[2] What they did was to average out the returns to investors in a company over a recent period of a varying number of years. Included in the average were principally ordinary and preference shares, bonds, and retained earnings, and the average so computed became the firm's cost of capital. In order to reflect the way in which firms customarily obtain the bulk of their finance the major emphasis was upon dividends and capital gains, all adjusted to allow for the appropriate rate of taxation. They examined the period 1919 to 1966, although the pre-war period is not of great interest to us here. Over the post-war period as a whole they reckoned that an average return of 12 or 13 per cent in money terms (i.e. not adjusted for inflation) was a reasonable figure. This would then yield about 11 per cent after deduction of tax.

There are, however, two broad objections to this procedure. Firstly Merrett and Sykes obtained their average figure using a particular portfolio of shares and summing all the results obtained. If, however, we look at *individual* shares, which presumably is what the ordinary investor does, we find an enormous spread around the average such that the results would not satisfy any statistical test of significance.

[1] A. J. Merrett and A. Sykes, *The Finance and Analysis of Capital Projects*.

[2] See e.g. R. M. Adelson, *Moorgate and Wall St Review* (Spring 1971) pp. 43–58 and F. B. Pizzala, 'The Cost of Capital to the Private Sector. A Critique of Merrett and Sykes', *Moorgate and Wall St Review* (Spring 1972).

Secondly it is possible to pay out dividends not from gross profits but from retained earnings. The real value of shares, however, reflects both of these sources of dividends, so that an investor who is tempted to put his money in one company because its history of dividends is marginally better than that of another company, where the former company is paying dividends out of retained earnings and the latter company is paying them out of gross profits, will, at such time as the former company begins to run out of retained earnings, find the value of his share dropping rapidly.

This has drawn the following conclusion from Pizzala.[1]

The approach developed by Merrett and Sykes for estimating the cost of capital is invalid as a guide to the future, since it rests on the ability of companies to change their gross profit margins as tax and economic circumstances change in order to provide shareholders with an historically observed rate of return. The evidence presented here shows that companies cannot hope to do this.

If gross earnings do not show a significant improvement the long run real return to shareholders might not be much better than half of the amount they earned over the last fifteen to twenty years, unless proposed tax changes prove to be very advantageous to shareholders. Even if the profit situation improves shareholders must expect a lower real return for a number of years, because of the very small level of company retentions over the last ten years.

Other commentators have simply opted for the long-term interest rate on debentures as a reflection of the company's cost of capital on the grounds that higher returns on equities simply reflect the extra risk involved in their purchase. This does, however, require that firms are able to calculate risk premiums accurately.

According to Hawkins and Pearce,[2] however, a more complicated formulation of the cost of capital is required. If we ignore overspill effects (effects which different sources of capital will have on each other's prices) then the cost of capital

[1] Pizzala, *Moorgate and Wall St Review* (Spring 1972) p. 62.
[2] Hawkins and Pearce, *Capital Investment Appraisal*.

becomes a combination of (*a*) the after tax interest rate on all forms of fixed interest loans (*b*) the best rate of return available were the shareholder to invest his funds in the equity capital of another company. This is known as the shareholder's opportunity cost of capital, and is defined as being equal to Dividends plus Capital Gains minus all taxes. (*c*) the value of retained earnings and depreciation provisions. Since the cost of a fixed amount of funds varies in practice, depending upon the mix of debt and equity that is used, the cost of capital is that which obtains for an optimal mix of funds.

In conclusion then it is difficult to make any concrete statement about the meaning of the firm's cost of capital. Obviously we have kept here to a relatively simple exposition of the question at issue, and there is a great deal left unsaid. Unfortunately the complications introduced in more refined models serve only to create even more disagreement among commentators about the meaning of the concept. And yet, to repeat the opening comment of this section in a slightly different form, the use of discounting techniques is preferred to more traditional methods in large part because they are supposed to produce much better informed investment decisions. With so much doubt surrounding the definition of the discounting factor to be employed in the D.C.F. calculation, one cannot but have one's doubts.

Turning aside now from this thorny issue, we must ask ourselves what, in other respects, are the advantages or disadvantages of D.C.F. techniques over traditional methods of investment appraisal?

ADVANTAGES OF D.C.F. TECHNIQUES

What then are the respects in which D.C.F. techniques overcome the drawbacks of traditional methods?

(*a*) Discounting explicitly allows for the fact that a £1 today is worth more than a £1 in the future through the use of increasing discount rates the further into the future we look. This becomes clear when we look at the table of discount factors with which to multiply the expected returns each year, as they can be seen to decline steadily over a period of years, depending upon the firm's cost of capital. Hence expected future returns will be reduced in value in the process of converting them into present-day terms.

(*b*) Discounting also helps surmount the problem of choosing between projects which yield in total the same expected profit over a period of years, but where the bulk of the profits accrue in different years for competing projects. Since the rate at which expected profits are discounted rises the further into the future we look, a project which earns the bulk of its profits very quickly will have a greater N.P.V. and I.R.R. than a project which earns the bulk of its profits only after an initial lean spell.[1]

(*c*) D.C.F. methods automatically take account of depreciation. Where a project has a positive N.P.V. this implies that the discounted returns exceed the capital cost of the project. At the same time the firm is earning a higher return than the rate at which it borrows. Hence the project both earns a profit and recovers all the original capital outlay. The I.R.R. will tell us that rate of return on a project which exactly recovers the capital outlay, no more and no less. Thus, irrespective of the technique used there is no need to allow explicitly for depreciation which is simply the traditional way of ensuring that the capital outlay is recovered.

(*d*) It is possible to incorporate an allowance into the D.C.F. calculation for the effects of inflation. The annual figures for expected net returns can be adjusted to allow for the expected trend in costs and prices. Where these are predicted to move together the D.C.F. calculation will be unaffected. Where, however, either costs are expected to inflate more rapidly than prices or vice versa, this should then be incorporated into the expected net returns for future years. The difficulties inherent in such predictions are obvious, but become less and less important the further ahead we look, because the expected net returns will be heavily discounted after a few years because of the fall in value of the discount factor.

(*e*) D.C.F. techniques permit us to make allowances for taxation regulations. Traditionally accountants simply deduct tax from total expected returns as a lump sum. In practice, however, the taxation system does not operate uniformly over

[1] For a detailed calculation to demonstrate this point see Hague, *Managerial Economics*, pp. 316–17.

the lifetime of an investment. Various reliefs such as investment grants are often available over the early years of an investment, whereas taxes only become significant in later years. The D.C.F. calculations, however, give most weight to the returns in the first few years of an asset's life, whereas returns in later years are heavily discounted. Hence the application of the correct grant or rate of taxation to the correct expected return will boost the N.P.V. and I.R.R. to a greater value than where the average rate of taxation is levied on an annual basis in the calculation.

DISADVANTAGES OF D.C.F. TECHNIQUES[1]

The disadvantages of D.C.F. may be general to both N.P.V. and I.R.R. methods, or may be specific to one rather than the other.

So far we have simply been concerned with a decision as to whether or not to undertake a given project in isolation. We concluded that if the D.C.F. calculation yielded a positive N.P.V. or an I.R.R. in excess of the cost of capital, then the project was worthwhile. Furthermore both criteria must end up at the same conclusion given that a positive N.P.V. is the same thing as an I.R.R. greater than the borrowing cost.

To treat prospective investments in isolation is not, however, a true reflection of the situation facing most firms. Normally they will have available to them a range of investment opportunities from which to choose. This creates no difficulties in circumstances of unlimited capital availability since the firm will be enabled to undertake all projects which satisfy the D.C.F. criteria. Few firms are, however, in the happy position of having no limitations on capital. Indeed limitations on any inputs will have the same effect so far as the firm is concerned, preventing it from undertaking all worthwhile projects.

Limitations on inputs imply the need for ranking projects in declining order of desirability. It is, however, most unlikely that where the limitation is on available capital, the best set of projects can be selected by simply choosing those with the highest N.P.V. or I.R.R. until no further funds are available.

[1] A more analytical critique of D.C.F. techniques is to be found in J. Hirschleifer, 'On the theory of Optimal Investment Decision', *Journal of Political Economy*, vol. 66 (1958) pp. 329–72.

The reasons for this are largely beyond our scope here,[1] because the existence of large numbers of projects which all satisfy the D.C.F. criteria, but very few of which can be undertaken because of input constraints, presents difficulties which can only be resolved by the use of mathematical programming techniques. We can, however, make an attempt to analyse the situation in which the firm must choose only one from two possible investments where they must be treated as mutually exclusive. In such circumstances the N.P.V. and I.R.R. criteria may produce conflicting recommendations as to which investment to undertake.

Consider the example below:

	Year					I.R.R.	N.P.V. at 10%
	0	1	2	3	4		
£ project A	−286	100	100	100	100	15%	+31
£ project B	−130	50	50	50	50	20%	+29

The N.P.V. criterion would come down in favour of project A, but the I.R.R. criterion would favour project B. The I.R.R. tells us how much on average the project will yield per annum, but does not tell us how much it will yield in different years of its life. N.P.V. of course will be highest in the first few years of a project's life, and lowest at the end of its life, because the rate of discount steadily increases. The relationship between the two criteria hence fluctuates either with changes in the amount of capital invested or with changes in the discount rate (i.e. the number of years over which the investment produces profits).

One drawback of the I.R.R. criterion is that in a situation where the firm must choose between two projects both costing the same, it might discover the I.R.R. to be identical even though the returns in individual years are not identical, in

---

[1] But see for example Hague, *Managerial Economics*, pp. 328–9; Hawkins and Pearce, *Capital Investment Appraisal*, pp. 65–8; Adelson, *Moorgate and Wall St Review* (Spring 1971) pp. 54–5.

which case N.P.V. would not be the same for both projects. This is because it is possible to produce an N.P.V. of zero for a given capital outlay by multiplying two or more different sequences of profits by the same sequence of discount factors.

Furthermore in the above example, the I.R.R. criterion tells us that a 20 per cent yield on £130 outlay is preferable to a 15 per cent yield on £286 outlay. This is, however, not a logical conclusion to draw where the firm has available the funds to invest in either project, since it will then have to decide what to do with the £156 left unused as a result of choosing project B. Assuming reasonably that this money is not to be left idle, the investment of the £156 will itself yield an I.R.R. in addition to that yielded by the original £130. Let us, for example, suppose that the firm can invest £156 in another project yielding an I.R.R. of 10 per cent. The question it must then ask itself is whether or not it prefers one investment of £286 yielding 15 per cent, or a combination of two investments, one of £130 yielding 20 per cent, and one of £156 yielding 10 per cent. The preferable alternative is by no means immediately obvious.

We can, however, solve this problem by using something known as the incremental yield, which is the rate of return on the incremental capital invested in project A not invested in project B. This gives us an answer as follows:

	Year					N.P.V. at 10%	I.R.R.
	0	1	2	3	4		
£ project A	−156	50	50	50	50	+2	11%

Thus we find that the incremental yield is approximately 11 per cent. Had the firm chosen project B and invested the incremental capital it would have produced an incremental yield of only 10 per cent. Hence the firm is better off with a choice of project A.

The incremental I.R.R. technique will in fact bring I.R.R. into line with N.P.V. such that they both produce the same choice of project. The difference between the incremental

I.R.R. of the larger project and the incremental yield resulting from choosing the smaller project and investing the difference elsewhere gives the firm an indication of how much better one alternative is than the other. The usefulness of the incremental calculation from the firm's point of view is therefore that it obtains some idea as to whether or not to put the extra capital outlay at risk in the bigger project.

MULTIPLE DISCOUNT RATES

So far we have treated all cash flows as being identical in nature, with an initial outlay on an investment being followed by positive inflows of profits beginning in year one. It may, however, be possible to discount such a stream of profits into equality with the capital outlay using several discount rates. In all the cases so far examined only one of these discount factors would be positive in sign; this is because there are in practice as many positive discount rates as there are sign changes in the cash flow table, and hence there is only one where the initial flow is negative, and all subsequent cash flows are positive.

Where, however, the cash flows vary in sign from year to year, it is possible for there to be more than one positive value for the discount rate, in addition to several negative values. We can, however, disregard such negative discount rates and consider only the problem which arises where there is more than one positive discount rate.

To determine all positive values for r one needs to discount the stream of cash flows at every rate of discount in order to discover the N.P.V. at each value for r. We can then plot the two things against each other on a graph, with N.P.V. on one axis and the discount rate on the other. Whenever N.P.V. is zero then the discount rate in question must obviously be a potential value for I.R.R. We might get a series of points plotted as shown in Fig. 5.1 (see p. 162).

We thus have three potential values for I.R.R. of 5, 12 and 20 per cent.

Now given a cost of capital of 9 per cent, the project will not be acceptable, because at that rate of discount N.P.V. is negative. In fact the project will only be profitable where the cost of capital is between zero and 5 per cent, or between 12 and 20 per cent.

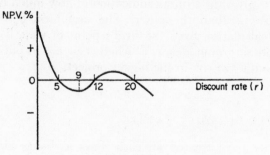

FIG. 5.1

Hawkins and Pearce[1] suggest a simple test to identify multiple discount rates as follows:

First find a solution rate for r. Then add up the discounted value of cash flows, year by year. If at any point this value is greater than the initial investment, then negative capital exists at that solution rate of return. Once negative capital has been found we know that the simple I.R.R. method is invalid, since one of two things must be true:

(a) either there will be multiple discount rates

(b) there will be a unique but 'economically meaningless' value of r

It is possible for two other situations apart from a multiple I.R.R. to occur. Firstly I.R.R. may have no value at all; that is to say N.P.V. is never zero, meaning that the curve of N.P.V. plotted against r would never cut the horizontal axis. Secondly there may be a unique solution where N.P.V. appears as a curve which lies below the horizontal axis at all points except one, where it is at a tangent to the horizontal axis. This would yield a unique value for I.R.R. at the point of tangency, but this would only imply that the firm was exactly covering its costs. At all other discount rates the firm would be making losses because the N.P.V. is negative. Hence the project is not acceptable.

[1] Hawkins and Pearce, *Capital Investment Appraisal*, p. 32.

PROJECT INTERDEPENDENCE

So far we have assumed that each feasible project under consideration has an existence completely independent of that of other actual or potential projects. This view is unsatisfactory because a firm normally only considers potential investments whose value largely stems from the fact that they harmonise with and improve upon the firm's existing business. Consider the following example. A firm has a possible investment which requires for its fulfilment a larger quantity of space than is currently available. The firm calculates that to build an extension to the factory in order to house the project will be so expensive that the project cannot prove viable at existing borrowing costs. Therefore the project is rejected. A month later a second project is proposed which also requires more space than is currently spare, and once again it is rejected since the allocation to the project of the entire cost of building a factory extension prevents it from earning an acceptable rate of return. Now clearly, if the firm were to appraise the need to build additional factory space for the first project in the light of a reasonable expectation of additional space requirements for further projects, it would not be necessary to allocate more than a small proportion of the cost of constructing the extension to this project, nor to later projects utilising the same general area. This being so, both the former and latter projects might earn an acceptable rate of return. It must be admitted that a firm can face extensive difficulties in trying to estimate how a project may interact with others that have not yet come up for consideration, or even how it may interact with itself where there is a probability that the project will need to be extended in future years if undertaken at all. Nevertheless it is not in principle valid to treat each project purely on its own merits – in isolation from its likely interactions with other activities of the firm.

RISK AND UNCERTAINTY

We have already noted that the rapid decline in the value of the discount factor tends to reduce to relative insignificance the net cash flows earned beyond, say, the fifth year of a project's life, except of course in circumstances where by far the greatest returns are earned several years after the project's inception. But even in the latter case we must allow for the considerable margin of error which is associated with forecasting cash flows well into the future. In all our above examples of discounting we have been cheerfully inserting numbers into the stream of cash flows as if they were known with certainty. In practice this is most unlikely to hold, so that we must turn now to consider the implications for discounting methods of the prevalence of risk and uncertainty surrounding an investment decision.

We can define the different possible states of knowledge as follows:

Certainty accompanies a decision where each alternative course of action is known to result in a specific pay-off.

Risk accompanies a decision where each alternative course of action produces one of a limited number of pay-offs, and where the probability of occurrence of each possible pay-off is known.

Uncertainty accompanies a decision where each alternative course of action produces one of a limited number of pay-offs, but where the probability of occurrence of each possible pay-off cannot be meaningfully assessed.

There are a number of possible ways of allowing for risk.[1] The simplest is to impose a risk premium, which either takes the form of increasing the discount factor used in N.P.V. calculations, or of raising the acceptable I.R.R. to a higher cut-off point. In both cases the firm allows itself a margin of error in excess of the return required under conditions of certainty. It is, however, difficult to objectively calculate the appropriate rate of premium, and the impact of increasing the discount rate

[1] For a detailed analysis of risk and uncertainty see for example M. Stamp and I. Peacock, ' "The Dusty Answer". Risk Analysis and Corporate Investment Decisions', *Moorgate and Wall St Review* (Spring 1972) p. 72 onwards; Hawkins and Pearce, *Capital Investment Appraisal*, sections 6 and 7; J. F. Helliwell and J. C. T. Mao, 'Investment Decision under Uncertainty, Theory and Practice', *Journal of Finance* (May 1969); Adelson, *Moorgate and Wall St Review* (Spring 1971) pp. 43–58.

will vary from year to year as a result of squaring, trebling, etc., the discount factor $(1+r)$, since this must necessarily imply a specific rate of increase in the risk premium over time.

On a more sophisticated level statistical techniques need to be employed which utilise the known probabilities of occurrence of each possible pay-off. Thus we can, for example, derive the Expected Value of an investment by multiplying each possible pay-off by its probability of occurrence, and summing the results. The investment with the greatest Expected Value is then selected. The drawback to this procedure, however, is that it only produces an *average* figure for Expected Value, and ignores the *range* of possible pay-offs. Thus we can obtain an identical Expected Value by assigning probabilities of 0·2; 0·4; 0·2 respectively to the pay-offs £10; £2; − £4; and £5; £2; £1. Yet the two projects will clearly only be equivalent to an investor who has no strong positive or negative attitudes to risk in the light of the much wider distribution of pay-offs of the first project.

To overcome this difficulty account has to be taken of the way in which the pay-offs vary around the average. Essentially what this means is that if two projects yield the same E.V., but one project has a narrower range of possible pay-offs, then this project will be preferred. Where, however, one project has a higher E.V. but also a wider range of pay-offs, each firm will have to assess its own rate of trade-off between increased return and increased risk, and the choice of project will ultimately depend upon whether the firm is a risk-taker or risk-avoider.

Uncertainty

As mentioned above, it is impossible to assign objective probabilities of occurrence to pay-offs in all circumstances. One possible approach to this problem is to substitute subjective probabilities of occurrence for each possible pay-off into the solution techniques outlined above. This Bayesian approach thus produces a set of subjective Expected Values, and the firm chooses from amongst them in accordance with the principles developed for conditions of risk. There is considerable debate as to whether or not subjective probabilities, which are not based upon objective data related to past experience, can be treated as meaningful. The approach is defended on the grounds that it is better than failing to assign probabilities at all. There are, however, alternative approaches to problems involving uncertainty, such as are set out below.

The general approach is essentially the same as that developed for the analysis of the Theory of Games as set out in Chapter 2. Instead, however, of treating the game as existing between two individuals or two firms, the firm is taken to be struggling against forces of Nature over which it has limited control. The term 'Nature' refers here to the general environment surrounding an investment decision which determines its profitability or otherwise, and will hence include, for example, the general level of demand within the economy, competitors' reactions, and changes in the cost of capital.

The first stage is for the firm to set out the list of possible investments, and to then compile a limited number of hypotheses about the likely states of Nature. One such hypothesis might, for example, incorporate the assumption of zero growth in National Income, whereas another might assume that National Income will grow at 5 per cent per annum. Each investment opportunity is then examined in the light of these various possible states of Nature, and a pay-off is computed in each case. This produces a pay-off matrix such as is set out in Table 5.2, where the entries in the table are the relevant pay-offs.

TABLE 5.2

Investment project	State of Nature		
	I	II	III
A	100	20	−10
B	50	0	70
C	20	15	35

(I) *Maximax*: to use this criterion the firm extracts the best pay-off associated with each investment, and chooses which-

ever of these pay-offs is the greatest. The best pay-off for
A is 100, for *B* is 70, and for *C* is 35. Project *A* is therefore
selected.

This criterion is basically for inveterate gamblers and is
generally ill-advised. It also ignores intermediate pay-offs,
which, if taken into account, suggest that *B* is the better
alternative should things not go as well as is expected.

(II) *Maximin:* to use the maximin criterion the firm extracts
the worst pay-off associated with each investment, and chooses
whichever of these pay-offs is the greatest. The firm is thus
maximising its minimum gain, which implies a pessimistic
view of the future. In effect the firm assumes that the worst will
happen, but tries to minimise the extent of the likely disaster.

The minimum gain for *A* above is -10; for *B* is 0; and
for *C* is 15. Investment *C* is therefore selected. The drawback
to this choice however is that Nature is assumed to be actively
seeking to do its worst, whereas it must in practice act in a
random fashion. Yet if Nature acts benevolently project *C*
offers little reward in addition to that available where Nature
acts malevolently. Project *B* on the other hand offers much
better prospects were Nature to do other than its worst. This
criterion therefore shares with the maximax criterion the
drawback of over-concentration upon one state of Nature to
the exclusion of all others.

(III) To overcome this drawback the firm can, for example,
adopt the *Hurwicz* criterion which explicitly allows for the
possibility of both good and bad outcomes for an investment.
The firm decides initially upon its general level of optimism
about the future, and assigns to the coefficient of optimism λ
a value between 0 and 1, where 0 represents absolute pessimism
and 1 represents complete optimism. The best possible pay-off
for each project is then selected and multiplied by the coefficient
λ whereas the worst possible pay-off is multiplied by the
coefficient $(1 - \lambda)$. The two values obtained in this way are
then added together to form a weighted average for each
project, and the project producing the greatest such value is
chosen.

Let us assume that the firm is optimistic in outlook, and
gives a value of 0·8 to λ and hence of 0·2 to $(1 - \lambda)$.

The best outcome for *A* is 100, and the worst outcome is -10.

This gives a weighted average of $(0.8 \times 100) + (0.2 \times -10) = 80 + (-2) = 78$. The same process for project B yields $(0.8 \times 70) + (0.2 \times 0) = 56$. The same process for project C yields $(0.8 \times 35) + (0.2 \times 15) = 31$.

Project A is therefore chosen. This reflects the firm's optimistic viewpoint which greatly favours A's best possible pay-off. Were λ equal to 0.3, however, project C would be chosen. Once again the drawback to this criterion is that it neglects intermediate pay-offs, which is to be expected since the criterion is basically a weighted average of the Maximax and Maximin criteria.

(IV) Account is, however, taken of intermediate pay-offs with the *Laplace* of *Equiprobability* criterion. This criterion assumes that Nature acts randomly, such that every possible state of Nature is equally likely to occur in practice. Since no firm can possess sufficient objective data to demonstrate the truth or otherwise of this proposition, the Laplace criterion is based upon subjective estimates of likely future states of Nature, and this is its major drawback.

In the matrix above each possible state of Nature is assigned a probability value of $\frac{1}{3}$, and weighted values for each project are calculated as follows:

Project A's weighted average
$$= (\tfrac{1}{3} \times 100) + (\tfrac{1}{3} \times 20) + (\tfrac{1}{3} \times -10) = 33\tfrac{1}{3} + 6\tfrac{2}{3} - 3\tfrac{1}{3} = 36\tfrac{2}{3}$$
Project B's weighted average
$$= (\tfrac{1}{3} \times 50) + (\tfrac{1}{3} \times 0) + (\tfrac{1}{3} \times 70) = 16\tfrac{2}{3} + 0 + 23\tfrac{1}{3} = 40$$
Project C's weighted average
$$= (\tfrac{1}{3} \times 20) + (\tfrac{1}{3} \times 15) + (\tfrac{1}{3} \times 35) = 6\tfrac{2}{3} + 5 + 11\tfrac{2}{3} = 23\tfrac{1}{3}$$

Therefore project B is chosen because it has the highest weighted average.

(V) So far we have been wholly concerned with comparisons between various pay-offs on the basis of an implied presumption that what is expected to happen will so happen. An alternative approach, however, concerns itself with the consequences of incorrect guesses about the future, and reintroduces the now familiar idea of opportunity costs. If a firm invests in one project rather than another, and it transpires that the choice of project was incorrect, the firm will feel regret at having made the wrong decision. This regret, or opportunity cost, is equivalent to the pay-off associated with the correct decision less the pay-off actually obtained as a result of undertaking the wrong investment.

Now for each possible state of Nature there can only be one optimal investment. The regret associated with the choice of any other project can thus be calculated by subtracting its pay-off from the pay-off of the optimal project. In this way we can build up a Regret matrix in which the optimal project under each state of Nature has a value of zero. The Regret matrix derived from our original matrix above appears as shown in Table 5.3. The regret for BI is obtained, for example, by subtracting B's pay-off (50) from A's pay-off (100) assuming state of Nature I prevails.

TABLE 5.3

Investment projects	States of Nature		
	I	II	III
A	0	0	80
B	50	20	0
C	80	5	35

Once the Regret matrix has been formed the objective is to minimise the greatest possible regret. The greatest regret for A is 80; for B is 50; and for C is 80; therefore project B is chosen.

The drawbacks to the criterion are firstly that it is pessimistic, concentrating as it does on the worst possible outcomes under each state of Nature, and secondly, that it once again ignores all intermediate pay-offs.

It can be seen in conclusion that different criteria produce radically different recommendations. It can thus be said that the use of the above criteria is rather limited. The choice of criterion is heavily dependent upon the psychological make-up of the decision maker, which is itself subject to variation over time. No criterion is therefore likely to prove acceptable in the longer term for use as a general yardstick by any firm. This is not however considered by some commentators to be much of a drawback, perhaps because, when all is said and done, anything is better than ignoring the problem of uncertainty altogether.

ARE DISCOUNTING TECHNIQUES WORTHWHILE?

It is perhaps appropriate at this point to try to sum up the gist of the argument so far. We have discarded the rate of return criterion as unsuitable for investment appraisal, and accepted the pay-back criterion as worthwhile only in a limited set of circumstances. With respect to discounting techniques we have for the most part been ambivalent. We have seen how they surmount most of the difficulties inherent in the traditional methods, but at the same time we have discovered a new set of difficulties peculiar to discounting techniques including difficulties which originate because of a failure of the I.R.R. and N.P.V. approaches to agree as to which of two mutually exclusive projects to select. It is fair to say, however, that some of these difficulties can be surmounted by the application of certain additional techniques such as incremental analysis or risk analysis, and it is hardly surprising that D.C.F. techniques are extremely popular today. The fact is of course that at present no better techniques exist. This may not in practice be a lasting situation as there is a continuing search for methods which improve upon discounting techniques. It has been pointed out, for example, that a decision to invest today should only be taken in the light of the expected stream of future investment proposals, since a firm, limited by a constraint on capital availability, must necessarily be foregoing the opportunity to invest in the future when it decides to invest today. If, for example, using past data to obtain a trend line which can satisfactorily be projected into the future, it is possible to obtain a probability distribution of projects having given I.R.R.s, then the firm will be enabled to decide reasonably scientifically whether to invest today or to hold back the money in the expectation of a better investment coming along in the near future.

Finally we note a suggestion by Adelson[1] that it is possible to do away with discounting and cost of capital concepts altogether. He suggests

[1] R. M. Adelson, *Moorgate and Wall St Review* (Spring 1971) p. 58.

Building a model of the firm and its environment (which contains probabilistic information about future investment opportunities) and looking to a horizon some years ahead. Projects for appraisal are inserted into the model as they become available, and the effect of particular projects or particular groups of projects on various measures of the company's well-being at this horizon can be investigated.

Such an approach would doubtless be regarded as extremely complex by most firms and therefore disregarded. After all many firms regard existing discounting techniques as too complicated for their purposes.[1] If so it is to be hoped that they will keep their eyes open to the drawbacks of the methods which they employ, although this proviso can also reasonably be extended to firms which employ discounting methods.

BIBLIOGRAPHY

R. M. ADELSON, 'D.C.F. The Other Point of View', *Moorgate and Wall St Review* (Spring 1971) pp. 43–58.
——, 'D.C.F. Can We Discount It? A Critical Examination', *Journal of Finance* (Summer 1970).
A. M. ALFRED, 'Discounted Cash Flow and Corporate Planning', *Woolwich Economic Papers,* no. 3 (Woolwich Polytechnic, 1964).
A. M. ALFRED and J. B. EVANS, *Discounted Cash Flow Principles and Some Short Cut Techniques* (Chapman & Hall, 1965).
S. H. ARCHER and C. A. D'AMBROSIO, *The Theory of Business Finance. A Book of Readings* (New York: The Macmillan Co., 1967).
M. J. GORDON, 'The Pay-off Period and the Rate of Profit', *Journal of Business* (Oct 1955).
J. R. GOULD, 'On Investment Criteria for Mutually Exclusive Projects', *Economica* (Feb 1972) pp. 70–7.
J. GRINYER, 'The Cost of Equity Capital', *Journal of Business Finance* (Winter 1972) pp. 44–53.

[1] See for example T. Klammer, 'Empirical Evidence of the Adoption of Sophisticated Capital Budgeting Techniques', *Journal of Business* (July 1972) pp. 387–98 for some evidence on this point.

D. C. HAGUE, *Managerial Economics* (Longman, 1969), chaps 6 and 15.

T. M. HAMMONDS, 'Discounting for Risk', *Quarterly Journal of Economics and Business* (Autumn 1971) pp. 77–83.

C. J. HAWKINS and D. W. PEARCE, *Capital Investment Appraisal* (Macmillan, 1971).

J. HELLINGS, 'Technical Note. The Case for Pay Back Re-examined', *Journal of Business Finance* (Spring 1972) pp. 99–102.

J. F. HELLIWELL and J. C. T. MAO, 'Investment Decision under Uncertainty, Theory and Practice', *Journal of Finance* (May 1969).

J. HIRSCHLEIFER, 'On the Theory of Optimal Investment Decision', *Journal of Political Economy,* vol. 66 (1958) pp. 329–72.

T. KLAMMER, 'Empirical Evidence of the Adoption of Sophisticated Capital Budgeting Techniques', *Journal of Business* (July 1972) pp. 387–98.

G. H. LAWSON and D. W. WINDLE, *Capital Budgeting and the Use of D.C.F. Criteria in a Corporation Tax Regime* (Edinburgh: Oliver & Boyd, 1967).

A. J. MERRETT and A. SYKES, *The Finance and Analysis of Capital Projects* (Longman, 1963).

F. B. PIZZALA, 'The Cost of Capital to the Private Sector. A Critique of Merrett and Sykes', *Moorgate and Wall St Review* (Spring 1972).

C. I. SAVAGE and J. R. SMALL, *Introduction to Managerial Economics* (Hutchinson, 1967) chap. 4.

E. SOLOMON, 'Measuring a Company's Cost of Capital', *Journal of Business* (Oct 1955).

C. S. SOPER, 'The Marginal Efficiency of Capital. A Further Note', *Economic Journal* (Mar 1959).

M. STAMP and I. PEACOCK, ' "The Dusty Answer". Risk Analysis and Corporate Investment Decisions', *Moorgate and Wall St Review* (Spring 1972).

6

Forecasting

Forecasting and planning are to a great extent interdependent. A plan must involve an objective or set of objectives towards the attainment of which the firm directs its efforts. There is in theory nothing to prevent the firm choosing its objectives without paying the least regard either to what has happened in the past or to what can reasonably be expected to happen in the future. In other words it can choose its objectives because they are desirable *per se*, without worrying about the problem of constraints which, in a large variety of forms, impose external or internal controls upon the firm's operations. It is, however, at best illogical for a firm to set objectives which can be seen to be wholly impossible of realisation in practice. A firm obviously needs to set its objectives at an attainable level, taking into consideration all those factors, such as limitations on the availability of skilled manpower, or historic levels of capacity utilisation, which materially affect its operations. But above all the firm cannot produce profitably without careful consideration of market circumstances such as the number and type of customers it expects to serve. Moreover in a mixed economy such as that of the United Kingdom, market circumstances will themselves vary according to the attitude of the government of the day towards the private sector.

It is thus obvious that a firm needs to know a good deal of information about both internal and external constraints upon its behaviour before it makes any operating decisions. The firm cannot hope to accurately quantify all such constraints (a factor which, as we have seen in an earlier chapter, may prevent the firm from maximising profits), but this is not of itself a satisfactory argument for neglecting to quantify the constraints at all. The first task of the firm is thus to assess which are the constraints most likely to affect its chosen objectives in the future. The best indicator in this respect, assuming that we are not taking into consideration the introduction of a completely new set of objectives, which will happen only rarely, is any available statistical data about the firm's past operations. To the list of constraints which have operated in the past should then be added such constraints as are predicted to apply in the future due to changing circumstances. This may be a difficult process because the future is always to some extent uncertain, but there are often helpful guide-lines already in existence. For example, the government lays many plans considerably in advance of their execution. The projected changeover to a value added tax was known well in advance of its being put into effect. Likewise the decision to join the Common Market was not made overnight. The government now publishes large quantities of statistics, as do many organisations in the private sector. Predicting the future is therefore not entirely a hit and miss affair for the firm which takes the trouble to search out the information relevant to its future activities.

Unfortunately to simply draw up a list of constraints likely to operate upon the firm's future activities is only the first stage of the operation. The much more difficult second stage is to attempt to quantify the constraints as accurately as possible. With respect to the value added tax mentioned above this is a relatively simple operation once the government publishes the rates at which it will be levied. But quantification of expected future levels of consumer demand may prove rather more problematical. Obviously a firm cannot predict exactly how much of a good it will be able to sell at any given price next year, let alone in five years' time. But this does not imply that the firm is unable to considerably narrow-down the range of possible levels of demand through recourse to intelligent forecasting methods, and this therefore is what we must now turn to consider.

FORECASTS AND BUDGETS

As we have suggested above the future is uncertain. A forecast is intended to reduce uncertainty by attempting to predict, within acceptable limits, the value of the major constraints affecting the firm, in particular the value of market demand. The forecast of market demand, known as the sales forecast, is integral to the whole operation of forecasting. Without a forecast for expected sales it will be impossible to forecast how many factor inputs in the form of raw materials, labour or capital will be required, the requisite amounts of working capital, or the requisite level of inventories and so forth.

The forecast will obviously precede the setting of objectives, which, as we have mentioned above, should be set at an attainable level. The objectives will themselves then be transformed into a series of budgets. The budgetary procedure describes how the firm, in the light of its objectives, makes the necessary plans for the attainment of these objectives. Each department within the firm will be given its own individual set of objectives, and will be allocated sufficient resources to enable it to attain them. Each department's objectives will be set at such a level as to make it possible for other departments to simultaneously attain their own objectives. The key to the whole procedure will be the sales budget, since the desired end product of the whole budgeting process is to make available a certain amount of goods for sale at a certain price. One stage set back from the sales budget will be the production department's budget, the latter itself being translated into budgeted levels of inventory, machinery, and labour of varying skills. Since each budget is dependent upon some or all of the others, the failure of one department to keep to its budget (e.g. through an inability to hire enough skilled labour) will normally imply that other departments are themselves unable to proceed as planned. The great advantage of the budgetary process, however, is that it can be used for control purposes in the sense that the firm can compare what has transpired in practice with what it desired to achieve. It may then be possible for the firm to determine what has gone wrong, and to remedy the fault the next time it occurs. Alternatively the firm can calculate its next set of budgets in the light of what has happened.

CONSIDERATIONS PRIOR TO THE FORECAST

The firm needs to consider several things before it undertakes the process of forecasting. Savage and Small[1] have isolated six major areas for consideration:

The Relevant Time-Period over which the Forecast is to be Applied

Short-term forecasts are generally made for a period of a year or less, depending upon the particular problems faced by the individual firm. The object of such forecasts is to determine whether or not the firm should undertake a change of tactics in order to secure a temporary advantage. Long-term forecasts are concerned more with the question as to whether or not any changes in the firm's objectives themselves are desirable as a result of predicted changes in the constraints acting upon the firm. In the short term 'intuitive' forecasts (i.e. those dependent upon the judgement and experience of the forecaster) may be more suitable than statistical forecasting techniques, although the latter will predominate in the longer term.

The Level of the Forecast

We are largely concerned in this chapter with forecasting at the level of the individual firm. As indicated above, however, a good deal of information is produced by the government, and firms are well advised to have such information to hand. Where many firms belong to some form of trade association covering their industry, the association will probably provide them communally with information gleaned from surveys of consumer intentions or analysis of statistical trends. It is obviously more economical for a firm to obtain information in this way than to seek it out by itself.

General or Specific Forecasts

A firm must decide how specifically to forecast, e.g. a car manufacturer must decide whether to forecast sales of a given

[1] C. I. Savage and J. R. Small, *Introduction to Managerial Economics* (Hutchinson, 1967) pp. 164–5.

model irrespective of engine size or to forecast for each model and for each different engine size; to forecast sales of a model taking all markets together or taking home and export markets separately, etc.

New Products vs Well-Established Products

It is more difficult to forecast sales of new products as compared to established products because many of the statistical techniques explored later depend upon the existence of past data, which is obviously unavailable for new products. Hence new-product forecasting will have to rely disproportionately upon non-statistical techniques.

Producers Goods; Capital Goods; Consumer Durables; Consumer Goods

The major reason for distinguishing between the above categories relates to the variability of demand for each category. For this reason certain techniques are more suited to each category than to the others.

Special Factors

Such as, for example, the greater uncertainty in estimating demand for fashion goods as against consumer durables.

Bearing all the above in mind, we must conclude that forecasting is not an easy business, and that it is best done by people qualified in such techniques as exist, rather than by placing undue reliance upon intuition. However, it is difficult to determine the optimal combination of intuition and statistical techniques. Statistical analysis is obviously extremely useful, but its utility is very much dependent upon the quality of the data fed into the equations. Overmuch reliance upon past data can prove unwise in a constantly changing environment. On the other hand judgement or intuition may, if taken by itself, suggest policies which elementary statistical analysis would prove to be misguided.

CRITERIA FOR CHOICE OF FORECASTING METHODS

Before going on to discuss the actual techniques of forecasting, it is desirable to consider some criteria against which to judge the choice of method. The problem of choosing a suitable forecasting method is in itself an economic problem, i.e. the result achievable through the use of any particular method must be weighed against the cost of that method. The first useful criterion is therefore the comparison of costs and benefits of different methods. It is perhaps true to say, however, that it is difficult to predict how good the results of using any particular method will turn out to be until the greater part of the cost of that method has been incurred. Hence the choice among available methods must be made on *a priori* grounds as to which method is likely to yield the best results. The balancing of costs and benefits is analagous to the balancing of speed and accuracy. The speedier the results obtained the less accurate on the whole they may turn out to be. It may consequently be better to delay the forecasting procedure where this may be expected to lead to more accurate results.

But no matter what techniques are used, how much they cost or when they are undertaken, the forecasting exercise will prove redundant unless the results are utilised. This will not happen, however, unless operating management have faith in the forecasts. If they feel that forecasts made in the past did not turn out to be very reliable, they are unlikely to accept the results of later forecasts even if the latter are technically much more sophisticated. In part this suggests that a major effort must be made to educate managers who are expected to act upon the forecasts. In this respect undue methodological sophistication has its drawbacks, because the manager may be unable to comprehend at all the principles underlying the forecasting techniques. Partly for this reason changes in forecasting techniques will not be worthwhile unless they significantly improve the accuracy of the results obtained.

APPROACHES TO FORECASTING

One can distinguish four basic approaches to forecasting.

(1) *Opinion Polling,* which broadly encompasses surveys of

intended purchasing behaviour by individuals or by firms, and is one form of market research.

(2) *Barometric Techniques,* which involve the use of indicators.

(3) *Extrapolation,* which involves the projection of past trends into the future.

(4) *Econometric Models.*

Opinion Polling

The easiest way to obtain information about purchasing behaviour in the future is to go out and ask people whether or not they intend to buy the product in question. Unlike statistical techniques which are essentially impersonal, this method requires personal contact of some sort between the body seeking the information and the respondent. The whole exercise depends very much upon the expectation that people will behave approximately in line with their answers to the opinion poll. Although this will not be true for all respondents, the results will be accurate so long as some who replied negatively decide later to buy, to make up for those who later decide not to buy after stating that they intend to do so. Whether this expectation is a reasonable one is thus a matter for further discussion. Opinion polling is not, as we shall see, purely restricted to questioning potential purchasers about their intended behaviour, although there are certain circumstances in which this will prove most effective. Consumer surveys are easiest to conduct where the number of potential respondents is small, because it may then be possible to question all of them. Once the number of respondents becomes too large to allow for questioning each one individually, some form of sampling technique will have to be employed. The purpose of samples is to make it possible to validly consider the views of a few respondents to be representative of the views of all potential purchasers. Many sampling techniques now exist which enable a firm to place a good deal of faith in sample surveys, as the techniques are based upon a fairly sophisticated branch of mathematics known as probability theory. The need for technical sophistication in undertaking surveys has been one factor contributing to the appearance of specialist market research organisations.

Obtaining good results from sampling techniques depends firstly upon the collection of accurate information, which very much depends itself upon the quality of techniques used, and also upon the elimination of sampling errors. Samples must above all be unbiased or random, for a sample must obviously be representative of the whole market under study if it is to be of any use. Various ways of ensuring this are available, such as random number tables, but it is idle to suppose that errors will not occur. The smaller the sample the more likely are errors to occur, but, on the other hand, the larger the sample the more expensive it will be. Thus each firm will have to decide individually how much accuracy to trade off against how much expenditure.

As mentioned above it is possible to conduct opinion polls within the firm itself in addition to, or instead of, polling potential purchasers. In certain circumstances it may prove expedient to ask the firm's managers to pool their knowledge with the intention of constructing a demand schedule for the firm's products. At other times it may prove expedient to obtain information from the sales force, who have the advantage of being in close contact with the firm's customers. In both cases the information is virtually costless. Unfortunately it is also rather subjective, perhaps even more so than is true for consumer intention surveys, where there is a noted tendency for respondents to give the answer they think the questioner wants to hear. The members of the sales force may be either tempted to predict too high a level of sales because by nature they are more than usually optimistic, or too low a level of sales in order to make it easier to meet their sales targets.

Barometric Techniques

A barometer is an instrument for measuring change. Barometric techniques are methods involving indicators which can be used as proxies for changes whether in the condition of the economy or in the condition of the firm. The condition of the economy is reflected in various measures, of which one commonly used is Gross Domestic Product (G.D.P.). The condition of the firm is reflected in changes in whatever happens to be its main objective, such as profits or sales revenue. The firm obviously wants to be able to predict future profits or sales. The objective of the above technique is to try to discover other variables which will give advance warning of upwards or downwards movements in profits or sales. If such variables can be isolated, the firm will be able, by observing how they fluctuate, to predict at what time, to what extent, and in which direction, profits or sales will fluctuate.

The principle involved can best be illustrated by reference to the use of indicators in forecasting on a national scale, although it is relatively simple to draw an analogy with the use of indicators at individual firm level. On a national scale this method has been extensively developed[1] over many years, with some success, by the National Bureau of Economic Research in the United States. Such a method, however, can aim at little more than forecasting, a few months ahead, turning points in economic activity; it cannot clearly indicate the strength of a movement up or down. But to detect turning points in advance would itself be a considerable achievement. There are basically three types of indicator.

Leading indicators (Fig. 6.1)

Such indicators will attain their highest and lowest values before these are reached by the variable which the firm is trying to predict.

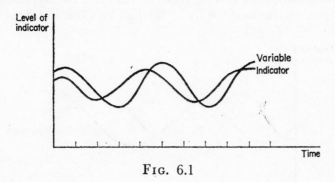

FIG. 6.1

---

[1] American experience is reported at length in *Business Cycle Indicators* ed. G. H. Moore (Princeton University Press, 2 volumes, 1961).

Coincident indicators (Fig. 6.2)

Such indicators will attain their highest and lowest values at the same time as these are reached by the variable which the firm is trying to predict.

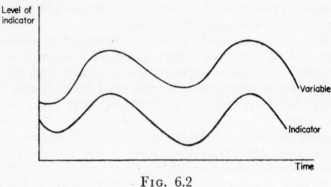

Fig. 6.2

Lagging indicators (Fig. 6.3)

Such indicators will attain their highest and lowest values after these are reached by the variable which the firm is trying to predict.

For predictive purposes the most useful indicators are those which can be classed as 'leading'. Hence the firm sets out to try to identify such leading indicators as exist, and to establish the precise temporal nature of the link between such leading

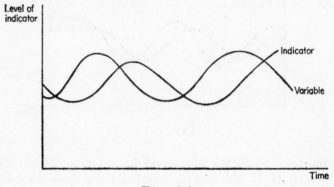

Fig. 6.3

indicators and the variable in which the firm is most interested. Once such a link has been established, the firm will be enabled, by observing changes in the leading indicators, to estimate in advance changes in the value of its objective.

The major study in the United Kingdom in which an attempt has been made to identify leading indicators for the economy as a whole, is by Dr Drakatos.[1] In his study Dr Drakatos took the period 1947–59 which covered three, full business cycles, with peaks in 1951, 1955 and 1957, and troughs in 1952, 1956 and 1958. This makes a total of six turning points. Dr Drakatos managed to isolate seven leading indicators, all of which gave good advance warning of four or more of the six turning points in economic activity. The data is set out in Table 6.1.

TABLE 6.1

Indicators	Frequency of series	Approximate time lag
1. Retail Sales – clothing and footwear	Monthly	6–7 weeks
2. Producer's stocks of crude steel	,,	1 month
3. Production of building bricks	,,	1 month
4. Index of security prices – total	,,	1 week
5. Consumption of pig iron	,,	1 month
6. Industrial production – construction	Quarterly	4 months
7. Industrial profits earned	,,	3–4 quarters

The usefulness of leading indicators is obviously related to the length of the lead period. The longer the lead the easier it will be for a firm to make the necessary adjustments in its operations to allow for the expected change in its objective. Time for remedial action to take effect is of the essence. Nevertheless it also takes time to collect data on changes in any indicator, and further time before the information finds its way into the hands of operating managers. It is quite possible for this process to nullify the advantage of certain leading indicators. In the above

[1] C. Drakatos, 'Leading Indicators for the British Economy', *National Institute Economic Review* (May 1963) pp. 42–9.

G

example the time lag involved in the collection of data for industrial profits rendered the series valueless for predictive purposes. The other six indicators were, however, rather more satisfactory in this respect. A firm is not, however, advised to rely upon one indicator alone, because its lead time may not be constant. In fact it is preferable to use all available leading indicators where possible. To do this it is necessary to calculate a *Diffusion Index*. This can be calculated in a variety of ways, but might typically show the percentage of the series increasing over the time interval being measured. Often the 50 per cent mark is used as a guide, so that where more than 50 per cent of the leading indicators are rising it might be plausible to predict an upturn in aggregate business activity. In a more general sense, however, diffusion indices can be employed to help measure and interpret the breadth and intensity of cyclical recessions and recoveries, the state of business in general, and the degree of optimism or pessimism on the part of businessmen. The diffusion index will indicate the direction of change of the firm's objective, but will only in a broad sense suggest how rapidly profits or sales can be expected to rise or fall, which to some extent offsets its advantages. It is furthermore important that the lead time of the indicators used is fairly reliable. The whole purpose of using indicators is to allow the firm to take remedial action well in advance of the expected change in its objective. It will only be willing to undertake such remedial action when it feels sure that the objective will alter in a specific way if left to vary freely, otherwise the remedial action might worsen rather than improve the situation. A diffusion index, preferably weighted in accordance with the relative importance of different indicators, will be helpful here.

Extrapolation

This is an essentially mechanical process, and involves the projection of past behaviour or past trends into the future, without any attempt to integrate the techniques with relevant economic theory or statistical data. The basic premise here is that the future will be a replica of the past in the sense that the same variables which in the past have affected the objective will continue to affect it in the future; and further, that each determining variable will continue to have a roughly similar quantitative effect to that in the past. Certain variants of this method have the advantage of simplicity and convenience while at the same time rendering fairly reliable long-term forecasts.

The simplest trends to project are those which can be identified at first sight, although they will tend to be fairly rare in practice. It is possible for there to be no progression at all, with the data remaining constant year after year. In the latter case the firm can hardly go wrong in forecasting no change over the ensuing year. Some trend lines will be linear, i.e. it will be possible to draw a straight line through the data once it has been graphically plotted. Such a trend might be the sequence 9, 10, 11, 12, 13, in which case the firm could safely predict a value of 14 for the following year. Likewise the series 20, 40, 80, 160, 320 indicates that the numbers double annually, and the firm can easily predict that the next item in the series will be 640. This process works also in reverse, so that where, for example, the series reads 64, 32, 16, 8, 4 the obvious prediction for the next year is 2. On the other hand the firm cannot for obvious reasons expect its sales or profits to increase or diminish in this way without limit. Although, for example, what starts out as a group of very small firms can grow very rapidly for a number of years in this way, they will have to take care not to expect the process to be indefinite, and should allow for the rate of growth to trail-off over the years.

Often data is cyclical in nature. Where the cycle is completely regular, as applies to the series 12, 15, 20, 12, 15, 20, 12, projecting the trend is very simple. This becomes more difficult however where typically the data exhibits both cyclical characteristics and evidence of growth. For example, the series 58, 54, 60, 66, 62, 58, 64, 70 exhibits both cyclical and growth patterns, with a cycle of 4 years' duration.

In the above examples the sequence of the figures is clear. But where such sequences cannot be readily identified more complex methods must be used.

Moving Averages

In order to isolate the trend of a series which does not exhibit any obvious regularity it is possible to construct a new sequence from the old by means of a moving average. Each number in the original sequence is replaced by an average containing both itself and an equal number of those values which immediately precede or follow it. An illustration of this technique is set out in Table 6.2. Ideally the time span of the moving average

TABLE 6.2

| Month | Sales | Moving average | | |
		3-month	5-month	7-month
January	100	–	–	–
February	120	108	–	–
March	105	113	114	–
April	115	118	124	123
May	130	132	128	126
June	150	140	132	125
July	140	138	131	126
August	125	125	127	123
September	110	115	117	119
October	110	107	109	–
November	100	103	–	–
December	100	–	–	–

should be equal to the average period of the cycle in the series; that is, the average time span from peak to peak and trough to trough. The extent to which this can be done will determine how well the moving average has succeeded in smoothing out the fluctuations in the original series. The ultimate objective is to produce a series which changes gradually over time.

The advantage of this method is its simplicity and long-run accuracy. On the other hand, as can be seen above, it inevitably leaves gaps in the data. Furthermore, taking, for example, the 7-month moving average, there will also be time lags in the data to the tune of 3 months. The time lag can always be assessed by using the formula

$$\text{Time lag} = \tfrac{1}{2} \quad (\text{Time span} - 1)$$

Clearly the greater the number of periods over which a moving average is taken, the greater is its time lag, which is a disadvantage. A further disadvantage is that where the figures exhibit a constant upward or downward trend, the moving average will yield either consistently low or consistently high estimates.

The use of a moving average can thus pose some difficulties unless the average is reasonably stable and easy to predict (although improvements are possible through the introduction of trend corrections and weighting).[1] Since this is not often the case, moving averages have perhaps been more frequently employed in order to study deviations from the trend rather than the trend itself.

Naive Models

These are simple models which assume that the future value of the variable being forecast is in some way a function of its present or recent value.

Let x = the realised value of the variable
$\quad x'$ = the forecast value of the variable
$\quad t$ = the time period (t = present period; ($t+1$) = next period)

(a) *No change model.* If we predict that the value of the variable in the next period will be the same as its value in the present period, this can be formulated as follows

$$x'_{(t+1)} = x_t$$

(b) *Models incorporating change.* The above principle can be extended to allow for changed expectations in the future as compared to the present. If, for example, we expect the value of the variable to double within the next time period we get $x'_{(t+1)} = 2x_t$ and so forth. This process can of course be applied

[1] See for example A. Battersby, *Sales Forecasting* (Cassell, 1968/ Pelican Books, 1970) chaps 2 and 3.

for any number of future time periods. The relatively straight-forward nature of such models makes them popular, and they fulfil the requisites of a short-term forecasting method, which are speed of computation, cheapness, and ease of applicability. Relatively little data is needed for naive models as can be seen above, and most firms will have the necessary information available. An alternative model is known as 'exponential smoothing and forecasting'. For this model it is often only necessary to take a weighted average of actual sales in the current period and the forecast of sales for the current period made in the previous period.[1] This method can, however, only be projected forward one period at a time.

It is possible for such simple models to forecast more accurately than methods of greater sophistication, particularly where the data is stable or where it is changing in a fairly uniform or gradual way. However, for a complex dynamic system in which fundamental changes occur frequently, it is likely that something more elaborate than a naive model will be required for making reliable predictions.

Time Series Analysis

A time series is a sequence of values corresponding to particular points or periods of time. Thus one might, for example, arrange observed figures for profits on an annual basis. The line chart is a typical time series plotted on a graph having the variable under examination on its vertical axis, and 'time' on its horizontal axis measured in suitable units.

It is unlikely that data with respect to an economic variable when plotted on a graph will exhibit straight-line (i.e. linear) characteristics.[2] This is because there are four widely recognised sources of variability in such time series, these being known as trend; seasonal; cyclical; and irregular variations.

Trend represents the long-term expansion or contraction of a series.

---

[1] For a full exposition see for example I.C.I. Monograph No. 2: *Short-term Forecasting* (1964).

[2] See for example I.C.I. Monograph No. 1: *Mathematical Trend Curves – An Aid to Forecasting* (1964).

Seasonal fluctuations occur regularly at different times of the year.

Cyclical fluctuations occur where the data periodically rises and falls.

Irregular fluctuations are random and hence unpredictable changes in the variable values.

Seasonal fluctuations are readily identifiable provided data is given covering a period of years. Irregular fluctuations cannot be predicted and are best ignored. It is thus trend and cyclical forces which attract most attention. We have already referred to trend projection in some detail, and cyclical forces can also often be readily identified from available past data. Unfortunately none of the above factors is any great help in determining when the cycle will reach its turning points. Thus they cannot be used in isolation with complete confidence (but can be improved through combination with barometric techniques as previously described).

Econometrics

Econometrics explains past economic activity and predicts future economic activity by deriving mathematical equations that will express the most probable interrelationship between a set of economic variables. The object is to construct a model which takes the form of an equation or system of equations that seems the best to describe the past set of relationships according to economic theory and statistical analysis. The model, in other words, is a simplified abstraction of a real situation, expressed in equation form, and employed as a prediction system that will yield numerical results. Some relatively simple yet useful econometric techniques are known as *correlation* and *regression* analysis. These consist of plotting relationships between dependent and independent variables (for example, the relationship between a firm's price level and its sales). In *simple* correlation one independent variable (e.g. price) is correlated with one dependent variable (e.g. sales).

In multiple correlation more than one independent variable is correlated with one dependent variable. A regression equa-

tion may be drawn up to show the relationship between one
dependent and several independent variables.

In practice the firm begins by plotting a graph, such as
appears below, with the dependent variable on one axis and
the independent variable on the other axis. The firm then
turns to its past records and reads for each time period the level
of the two variables corresponding to it. This defines a single
point on the graph for each time period. The firm repeats the
process for every time period, and the net result is a scatter
diagram shown in Fig. 6.4. The grouping of the points plotted
gives us a visual measure of the relationship between the
variables. It is apparent in the example given that both
variables increase in size together, so that they are possibly
closely correlated. If, on the other hand, the plotted points
appeared haphazardly in the diagram, a close relationship
between the variables would seem prima facie unlikely. One
must always remember, however, that the existence of a high
degree of correlation between variables does not prove causa-
tion. If we plot rhubarb sales against pig iron output we might
find the two variables to be closely correlated. This would,
however, be coincidental. The value of neither variable can
conceivably be thought to depend upon the value of the other.
When, however, we discover a close correlation between
average income and sales we can reasonably assume that the
level of sales is in part dependent upon the level of average
incomes, because common sense and past experience lead us
to conclude that this is so. In other words the level of correlation
between any number of variables can only be accepted as
important if we have good reason for supposing that the
variables are in some way interdependent.

Once the firm has plotted the sort of graph illustrated in
Fig. 6.4 it can read from it the expected level of the dependent
variable associated with any given level of the independent
variable. To simplify this we want first of all to establish a
typical or average relationship between the variables. We thus
need to plot a curved (curvilinear) or straight-line (linear)
relationship which will enable us to read off a set of best
estimates of combinations of the variables. This is often called
the 'regression' equation. In Fig. 6.4 the points plotted appear
to fall approximately on a straight line. Hence the relationship

will probably be linear in nature. We can establish the average relationship by statistical techniques such as the 'method of least squares' or 'maximum likelihood'.[1]

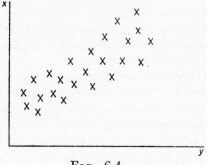

FIG. 6.4

Let us suppose that such techniques have been applied to the above data in order to produce a relationship such as is shown in Fig. 6.5. The relationship between variables can always be described in mathematical terms irrespective of whether it is linear or curvilinear. It is, however, considerably easier to do so for linear relationships, which will generally be of the form

$y = a + bx$ where the regression line is upward sloping
or $y = a - bx$ where the regression line is downward sloping

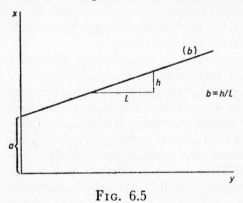

FIG. 6.5

[1] See for example Savage and Small, *Introduction to Managerial Economics*, pp. 171–81.

Where y is the dependent variable;

  x is the independent variable;

  a is the value of the dependent variable when the independent variable is zero; and

  b is the slope of the regression line (or, in other words, the change in the dependent variable per unit change in the independent variable). This is often known as the regression coefficient.

Once the regression line has been drawn the firm will want to know how well it describes the relationship. This can be done by measuring the dispersion of the plotted points around the regression line by computing what is known as 'the standard error of the estimate' and by calculating the actual degree of association between the variables by the 'coefficient of correlation'. Coefficients of correlation may have values between zero and one. Perfect correlation between two variables would yield a value of 1, whereas weak correlation would yield values only slightly in excess of zero.

Unfortunately there are a large number of drawbacks to the use of correlation and regression analysis.[1] There is firstly the problem of multi-collinearity. Where a dependent variable is influenced by several independent variables, analysis is greatly expedited if the dependent variable can be correlated with each independent variable taken in isolation. This, however, is not possible where the independent variables are themselves interdependent. If an attempt is then made to include all the variables in the relationship the regression coefficients may be meaningless for practical purposes.

Secondly there is an identification problem where several variables are simultaneously determined. In fact it is extremely difficult in economics to isolate any causal relationships, because a change in any variable will often set up forces which will eventually change the same variable on further occasions. The application of statistical techniques to relationships in which the dependent and independent variables are not clearly defined will serve only to compound the original error.

It is furthermore evident that forecasts of dependent variables

[1] For a full exposition of these drawbacks see B. Wagle, 'Some Recent Developments in Forecasting Techniques', *Journal of the Institute of Petroleum*, vol. 52, no. 509 (May 1966).

depend upon forecasts of independent variables. It is, as we
have seen above, necessary to plot all variable values together
for each time period in order to derive a series of points on a
graph. Before any attempt can be made to derive a value for
the dependent variable, the value of the independent variable
must be accurately forecast so that an appropriate point on the
regression line can be identified. It is perhaps fortunate for the
firm that the forecasting of most of the significant independent
variables for the economy is done for it by either the government or trade associations.

Finally we may note that the whole forecasting concept relies
in good measure upon the continuance of established relationships. Unfortunately the general lack of empirical data on
economic matters renders most relationships less than water-
tight over time, and it is a severe drawback that laboratory
experimentation to determine the nature of relationships in
the Social Sciences is not possible. Nevertheless one is driven to
fall back upon the often held assertion that suboptimal results
are better than no results at all. So long as the forecasting
process is undertaken with care and the firm utilises the
appropriate techniques, its future operations will undoubtedly
be seen in a clearer light.

BIBLIOGRAPHY

A. BATTERSBY, *Sales Forecasting* (Pelican Books, 1970).
C. DRAKATOS, 'Leading Indicators for the British Economy',
National Institute Economic Review (May 1963) pp. 42–9.
I.C.I., Monograph No. 1: *Mathematical Trend Curves – An Aid to
Forecasting* (1964).
——, Monograph No. 2: *Short-term Forecasting* (1964).
C. SAVAGE and J. SMALL, *Introduction to Managerial Economics*
(Hutchinson, 1967).
M. SHUPACK, 'The Predictive Accuracy of Empirical Demand
Analysis', *Economic Journal* (Sep 1962).
B. WAGLE, 'Some Recent Developments in Forecasting Tech-
niques', *Journal of the Institute of Petroleum*, vol. 52, no. 509
(May 1966).

7

Monopoly Policy

This section is concerned with a discussion as to whether in a general sense monopolies should be preferred to competitive industries or vice versa. As we shall go on to discover below, the evidence is somewhat ambivalent at the present time, implying that value judgements re monopoly policy cannot yet be superseded by decisions based upon hard facts. Nevertheless the basic issues can now be explored in detail in a way which was not possible only a short time ago.

The starting point for our analysis is the discussion of competition which we had in Chapter 2. Then you may remember we developed a monopoly model based upon the premise that a monopolist earns abnormal profits by equating marginal cost and marginal revenue in order to determine his most profitable output. We also developed a model of long-run equilibrium for a firm in perfect competition. This firm earns no abnormal profits, and produces an output corresponding to the lowest point on the firm's average cost curve, implying that the firm is operating at maximum efficiency (because it is minimising costs). The competitive firm in equilibrium also equates marginal cost and price, implying that it is maximising the welfare of purchasers.

If we turn now to consider the perfectly competitive *industry*, we obtain the appropriate curves for our model by aggregating the curves for all the individual firms constituting the industry. The industry supply curve is hence the aggregated *MC* curve, but notice that, although the aggregated average revenue curve is the industry demand curve, it now slopes downwards to the right rather than remains horizontal, as is true for individual firms. This is because, although variations in the output of individual firms cannot affect price, an appreciable alteration in supply by the entire industry will undoubtedly cause price to fall, since customers cannot be expected to absorb unlimited quantities of any given product at an unchanged price. Thus we derive a model of the competitive industry in equilibrium as shown in Fig. 7.1. In the model the competitive firms in aggregate sell Oq_1 at a price Op_1, equating supply with demand.

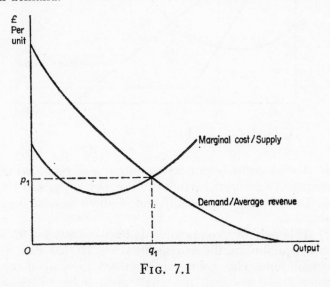

FIG. 7.1

The next step in our analysis is to superimpose the above diagram upon the monopoly model from Chapter 2 (see Fig. 7.2). The monopolist, equating MC and MR, produces Oq_2 at a price Op_2. The competitive industry produces in total Oq_1 at a price Op_1.

Now to construct Fig. 7.2 we have explicitly had to assume that *both revenue and cost curves are the same for both the monopolist and for the competitive industry*. There is broadly no reason to suppose in practice that demand varies much in aggregate however many suppliers serve the market. The assumption of identical cost curves will however need to be discussed in more detail further on.

The diagram shown in Fig. 7.2 was used by neo-classical economists as the foundation for their attack upon monopoly power. Several points are immediately clear from the diagram.

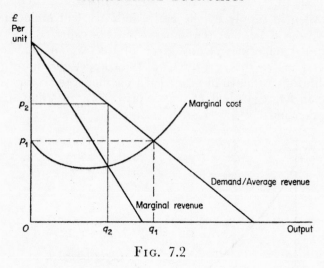

FIG. 7.2

(1) A monopolist both restricts output and raises prices as compared to a competitive industry (i.e. $Oq_2 < Oq_1$ and $Op_2 > Op_1$). This can be seen visually and requires no further comment.

(2) Although the competitive industry equates MC and price at equilibrium, the monopolist keeps MC less than price at equilibrium. This point was discussed in some detail in Chapter 2 and we shall not dwell upon it here because it takes us into the realm of what is known as Welfare Economics. The implications of monopoly for the welfare of the populace is of some importance in its own right, but analysis in this area is both complex and inconclusive. Hence we shall in this chapter only be concentrating upon whether monopoly or competitive conditions are the most economically efficient.

(3) The monopolist earns abnormal profits whereas only normal profits are earned by firms in a competitive industry. This provides us with the second justification in neo-classical theory for monopoly controls. The argument we shall adopt below will be to the effect that abnormal profits are not *per se* to be condemned, but that they must not be permitted to grow without limit.

Three other anti-monopoly arguments can be made which do not arise specifically from the above diagram:

(*a*) Because the monopolist has no fear of being driven out of business he will have no incentive to be efficient. On the other hand a firm in a competitive industry will be driven out of business if it is not operating on the lowest point of its *AC* curve – we shall have more to say on this point later.

(*b*) The monopolist does not need to maximise profits, but can seek to pursue other goals provided sufficient profits are being earned to satisfy shareholders. Alternative goals for firms were discussed in a previous chapter. In a general way this point is another aspect of point (*a*) above since a firm which does not maximise profits will not be operating at full efficiency. A competitive firm must maximise profits or go out of business, since maximum profits are only just sufficient for factors employed by that firm to earn a normal return for their services in the long run.

(*c*) The monopolist can discriminate with respect to price whereas the competitive firm cannot. Discrimination is supposedly unfair to consumers but may in fact be desirable (e.g. where a doctor is able to perform operations free for poor patients because he is imposing very high charges upon his richest clients). This again is an issue which we shall not pursue, because it does not affect the firm's cost efficiency.

Thus, to sum up, the neo-classical case for monopoly controls consisted of taking a model of a perfectly competitive industry, converting it into a monopoly model assuming no changes in market circumstances (costs and revenues), and drawing the conclusion that monopoly is prima facie undesirable.

The neo-classical case against monopoly provided the economic impetus for the introduction of the Sherman Act in America in 1890, although the Act was probably as much concerned with curbing the political powers of large corporations as with curbing their market powers.

The arguments given above did not however satisfy certain economists, who sought to provide an economic justification for monopoly power which would demonstrate that, in certain circumstances, monopolisation of a competitive industry would be in the public interest. This is often referred to as the Scale-Economies approach to monopoly since it sets out to demonstrate that, where large size goes hand in hand with economies

of scale (as could potentially occur where many small competitive firms are combined into one large monopoly) the
monopoly will be operating under the conditions of lower costs
as compared to the competitive industry it has superseded. The
net result might then be summarised in a diagram such as is
shown in Fig. 7.3, where the cost curves are assumed constant
over the normal operating range of the firm. In the diagram
the competitive industry produces quantity OA at a price
OY per unit. The monopolist produces a greater quantity OB

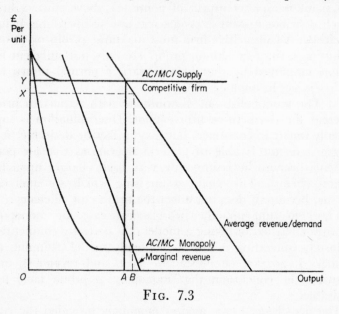

Fig. 7.3

at a lower price of OX per unit. Note however that the monopolist is still earning abnormal profits.

Acceptance of the scale economies argument completely
reverses the conclusion derived from neo-classical analysis,
and we must therefore consider the evidence carefully. Bear
in mind however that we shall be referring to 'monopolisation'
of a competitive industry not as requiring a transformation of
a many-firm into a one-firm industry, but rather more loosely
to describe a situation where the number of firms within the
industry is reduced to the point at which one or two firms are
able to fix their price–output relationship in such a way as

to satisfy their major objectives, without this decision being affected by the actions of any other firms within the same industry. It may be possible for a firm to dominate the industry without producing the greater part of total output. This is explicitly recognised in law where the Monopolies and Restrictive Practices (Inquiry and Control) Act 1948 was made applicable to any market where one firm produced more than $33\frac{1}{3}$ per cent of total production.

There is nevertheless a clear disposition in many minds to associate market power with size, as is evidenced, for example, by the terms of the 1965 Monopolies and Mergers Act. However, what is generally considered to be a large firm may have little market power in an industry characterised by many large firms, whereas what is generally considered to be a medium-sized firm may have considerable market power in an industry characterised by many small firms.

With the above provisos clearly in mind, we may note that it is not at all easy to produce a generalised hypothesis with respect to the circumstances in which increasing the average size of firms within an industry will lead to improved efficiency. An optimum size of plant or firm may be defined as 'that size of plant or firm that has minimum average costs of production in the light of its total economic environment',[1] where the environment consists of 'the demand conditions facing the firm, the supply conditions of the factors of production facing the firm, any taxes, subsidies or other type of government interference (both real or potential), and any other factor which may affect the economic operation of the firm'.[2] This tends to suggest immediately that optimum size may not be a given size but is likely to be a range of sizes.

In practice the determination of optimum size in an industry is an empirical matter subject to considerable computational difficulties.[3] Several approaches have appeared in the literature.

[1] T. R. Saving, 'Estimation of Optimum Plant Size by the Survivor Technique', *Quarterly Journal of Economics* (Nov 1961) p. 569.

[2] Ibid., pp. 569–70.

[3] These are set out for example in Saving, *Quarterly Journal of Economics* (Nov 1961) pp. 570–2 or A. Silberston, 'Economies of Scale in Theory and Practice', *Economic Journal* (Special issue; March 1972) pp. 369–91.

These include:

(a) Questionnaire methods which rely on data supplied by businessmen. This approach is, however, unlikely to lead to accurate results.

(b) Comparisons made either of production costs in plants of various sizes, or of rates of return for the various sizes of firm.

(c) Engineering estimates of costs of production by size of plant.

(d) The survivor technique.

A discussion of the merits or otherwise of various estimation methods appears in Pratten and Dean[1] and in Pratten.[2] The bulk of evidence for the United Kingdom which appears in these studies, and which is summarised by Silberston,[3] is based upon the 'engineering' approach.

The engineering approach involves estimating what the costs of producing various levels of output will be whether or not any firm is producing at these various levels. Past and present cost data serve as a basis for these estimates. The results of engineering studies tend to suggest that the average cost curve of a product tends initially to fall and subsequently to level out. The point at which the curve becomes horizontal is the *minimum efficient scale* of operation. Once this point has been determined the two most important factors are, firstly, the amount of capital required in order to construct a plant of efficient size and, secondly, the cost penalty incurred by a firm operating on a scale less than the minimum efficient scale. The point here is that cost savings due to scale effects are not a strong argument in favour of merging together two firms of half minimum efficient size where the cost disadvantage per unit of output of a firm of half the minimum efficient size is

[1] C. Pratten and R. Dean, *The Economies of Large Scale Production in British Industry*, Department of Applied Economics Occasional Papers, no. 3 (Cambridge University Press, 1965).

[2] C. Pratten, *Economies of Scale in Manufacturing Industries*, Department of Applied Economics Occasional Papers, no. 28 (Cambridge University Press, 1971).

[3] Silberston, *Economic Journal* (Special issue; Mar 1972) pp. 369–91.

only of the order of a few per cent as compared to the unit cost of a firm of efficient size.

The importance of scale effects thus depends both upon the need for capital as compared to its ready availability, and upon the cost differentials as between different scales of operation. Of great importance also is the relationship of the minimum efficient scale of operation to the total market size. If the number of efficient firms which a market can contain is small, then the price to be paid in return for high efficiency is a lesser or greater degree of monopoly power. It is quite possible, as is true, for example, of the British aircraft industry, that the market is insufficiently large for even one firm of efficient scale to operate within it. Bear in mind, however, that what holds true for one country may well not hold true for another because of differences in absolute market size. Thus, although the minimum efficient scale for aircraft production is much the same in the United Kingdom and the U.S.A., the American market, unlike the British, can absorb several firms of efficient size. This suggests that the implications of scale effects for monopoly policy will vary between countries for the same industry. In addition of course what may be a large amount of capital for one country may only be a small amount elsewhere. A final point to note is that a market may well not be defined by national boundaries. Imports will reduce the size of the available domestic market, whereas exports will expand the market size. Thus market size is affected by the competitive performance of the firms concerned.

No general conclusions on scale effects based upon engineering estimates can be made at the present time for the United Kingdom. The valuable study by Silberston which defines 'significant' scale effects to apply to markets where the cost disadvantages of operating below minimum efficient scale are considerable, and where capital and other entry costs are high, concludes that[1] 'it is probably fair to conclude that there are comparatively few industries which have "significant" economies of scale in this sense – in relation always to the size of the U.K. Market'.

Another way of estimating the optimum size for a plant or

---

[1] Silberston, *Economic Journal* (Special issue; March 1972) p. 386.

firm is by using the Survivor principle. This first appeared in the work of J. S. Mill[1] when he said: 'Wherever there are large and small establishments in the same business that one of the two which in existing circumstances carries on the production at the advantage will be able to undersell the other.'

The way in which the Survivor principle might work is by listing all firms within an industry according to their output, selecting suitable output ranges, and then adding up the percentage share of the industry output produced by each output range. Logic then suggests that a given output range which, over time, increases its share of total output, is doing so at the expense of firms within other output ranges. Hence firms falling within the expanding output range must be the most efficient.

The optimum firm size may turn out to be either very large or comparatively small. In the former case it may be closely related to the degree of monopoly power, in which event the breaking up of a monopoly within such an industry will be harmful to efficiency. Alternatively, where very few firms are anywhere near large enough to be efficient, this may suggest circumstances in which mergers or takeovers should be advocated.[2]

Obviously optimum size is a concept which might be expected to vary for any industry over time, so that the analysis would have to be conducted over a long time period to be acceptable, and there would have to be a sufficiently large number of firms within the industry to be statistically significant.

An early attempt to apply the Survivor principle was made by Stigler[3] using initially the American steel industry for investigation. He restricted his analysis to firms using open-hearth or Bessemer processes, and employed capacity as a

[1] J. S. Mill, *Principles of Political Economy* (Ashley Edition) p. 134.

[2] The view that the Survivor Technique is not applicable to an industry comprised only of small firms is put forward in N. Owen, 'Competition and Structural Change in Unconcentrated Industries', *Journal of Industrial Economics* (April 1971) p. 136. He contends however that there are economic costs associated with 'excessive competition' because advantage is not taken of available scale economies.

[3] G. J. Stigler, 'The Economies of Scale', *Journal of Law and Economics* (Oct 1958).

substitute for size. He found that firms with from $2\frac{1}{2}$ to 25 per cent of the industry capacity grew or held their share, and concluded that these constituted the range of optimum size. In effect he postulated that there were no net economies or diseconomies of scale available to firms with a capacity within the efficient range. Small firms did not have access to scale economies, and the biggest firms had run into scale diseconomies. Stigler also suggested that the most efficient plant size was one having between $\frac{3}{4}$ per cent and 10 per cent of the industry capacity.

Stigler than considered the American automobile industry, and concluded that there were diseconomies of large size, at least for the largest size of firm, in inflationary periods with private or public price control, but substantial economies at other times.

Notice Stigler's point about the optimum output range over which no scale economies exist, hence costs per unit are constant. If this were not so presumably an expansion of demand would be met not by existing firms, since they would incur scale diseconomies in so doing, but by new firms taking advantage of potential scale economies. In practice, however, the bulk of an expansion of output is met by existing firms.

Later empirical studies discovered, however, that a significant minor proportion of industry output – in one sample of industries from 10 to 30 per cent – is generally supplied by a fringe of small firms that suffer significantly from diseconomies of small scale. Yet these firms survive. Hence large size is not *per se* a condition for survival.

The Stigler data relates to the U.S. economy and does not therefore tell us anything about the minimum efficient scale for equivalent industries within the United Kingdom. The same objection can be levelled at Saving who concludes that[1]

An analysis of the survivorship estimates of optimum size of plant yielded the following conclusions: (1) Both the mean optimum size and the minimum optimum size are usually small when compared with their respective industry sizes. (2) The range of optimum size is usually large relative to its respective mean optimum size. (3) In those industries in

[1] Saving, *Quarterly Journal of Economics* (Nov 1961) pp. 596–7.

which the plants compete in national markets optimum size
is rarely so large as to necessitate non-competitive industry
behaviour. (4) The primary determinants of optimum size
are the industry size and capital intensiveness.

Nevertheless the above studies do tend to show that, where the
issue of scale effects is integral to an investigation of alleged
monopoly power, reasonably accurate estimates of the efficient
operating range for different industries can be calculated in
more than one way. (It should, however, be borne in mind
that, as Dewey has pointed out,[1] most mergers 'have virtually
nothing to do with either the creation of market power or the
realisation of scale economies'.)

Clearly the role and importance of scale effects can in
practice only be determined on an *ad hoc* basis for individual
firms under investigation.

It is, however, useful to try to weigh the possible benefits to
be obtained from increased scale against the welfare losses
apparent in the Neo-Classical case against monopoly, in order
to reach an opinion as to which is the more important. This
approach has been taken up by several economists[2] among
them Williamson[3] who stated that[4] 'a rational treatment of the
merger question requires that an effort be made to establish
the allocative implications of the scale economy and market
power effects associated with the merger'. Williamson's
approach can readily be generalised to the whole question of
the trade-off between the Neo-Classical and Scale Economy
arguments, and we therefore illustrate it with Fig. 7.4 in
which AC_1 is the pre-merger average cost curve. When, as a
result of the merger, price rises from Op_1 to Op_2, the 'dead-

[1] D. Dewey, 'Mergers and Cartels. Some Reservations about
Policy', *American Economic Review*, Papers and Proceedings (May
1961) p. 257.

[2] C. Kaysen and D. Turner, *Anti-Trust Policy. A Legal and Economic
Analysis* (Cambridge, Mass., 1959).

[3] O. E. Williamson, 'Allocative Efficiency and the Limits of
Anti-trust', *American Economic Review* (May 1969) and 'Economies
as an Anti-trust Defense', *American Economic Review* (March 1968)
pp. 18–36.

[4] Williamson, *American Economic Review* (Mar 1968) pp. 5, 18, 19.

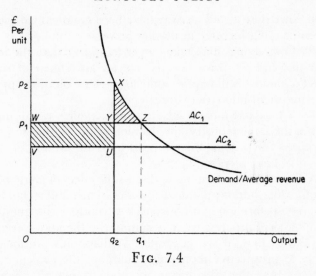

FIG. 7.4

weight' loss to the consumer[1] would be equivalent to area XYZ (resulting from higher price and lower output). On the other hand, where the merger produces scale economies, and hence a lower AC curve (e.g. AC_2 above), the producer simultaneously gains in profits the area $UVWY$. If we assume that £1 gained by a producer can be treated in the same way as a £1 gained by the consumer (an assumption with which the reader may not be inclined to agree)[2] then the general well-being of the economy will be improved wherever area $UVWY$ exceeds that of XYZ. Williamson provided data to show that in general this would be true, subject to a number of qualifications. These were:

(1) Where the companies concerned would have achieved scale economies without the need to merge as a result of market growth over time, the cost savings above are largely inadmis-

---

[1] The 'dead weight' loss to the consumer represents the total loss of consumer's surplus (see section on 'price discrimination' in Chap. 2) as a result of price per unit rising from Op_1 to Op_2 ($p_2 \times Zp_1$) less the gain of surplus by the producer on the lower output sold ($p_2 \times Yp_1$). This leaves a net loss of surplus equal to XYZ.

[2] A justification for this assumption appears in C. Rowley, *Anti-trust and Economic Efficiency* (Macmillan, 1973) chap. 2.

sible, since they would anyway have been obtained without any accompanying increase in market power.

(2) Cost-savings may take longer to appear than the impact of a post-merger price rise. Hence an assessment of the net effect of the two will require some form of discounting approach to bring them into strict equivalence.

(3) Where one merger sets in train a whole series of mergers within the same industry, the decision as to whether to support or repress the original merger must make allowance for the net effects of later mergers.

Williamson then went on to discuss the effect of mergers upon income distribution; political considerations; and technological progress. Before going on ourselves to consider the question of technological progress we may summarise the above argument by stating that, if we generalise Williamson's arguments to apply to prospective monopoly situations, the evidence so far suggests that the advantages accruing from scale economies more often than not will outweigh the possible disadvantages accruing from increased market power.

FIRM SIZE, INNOVATION AND TECHNOLOGICAL PROGRESS

Running in parallel with the Scale Economies issue, is a controversy as to whether or not increasing the average size of firms will be beneficial for the rate of invention, innovation and technological progress. If the evidence suggests that benefits in these areas would result from large manufacturing units, this would seem to strengthen the case for allowing monopolies to operate without hindrance, and if such benefits are not found to exist, then this strengthens the case for monopoly controls.

The argument goes broadly as follows. A monopoly always has the incentive to innovate and to be technically progressive because it will always be able to retain any abnormal profits which result from its ability to lower costs on existing products or to introduce new products. On the other hand there is no necessity for the monopoly to innovate where it can prevent the entry into its markets of competitors who would eat into its abnormal profits. Much depends upon the strength of the monopoly's protection from competition as to whether the drive to maximise profits by innovating or to accept existing profits will predominate. It is further possible that, where a monopoly succeeds in maximising profits by innovating, the extra profits will stimulate competition which would otherwise not have materialised.

The situation is, however, rather different for a competitive firm. Such a firm can only retain abnormal profits in the short term, however defined. In the long term other firms operating along identical cost curves will reduce all abnormal profits to zero. Thus the incentive to innovate does exist, but its strength will vary according to the size of the abnormal profits and according to the length of the short term.[1] Clearly a competitive firm cannot afford to not innovate at all where its competitors are introducing innovations which are hard to copy. But if innovations are easy to copy the competitive firm may prefer to sit back and to simply borrow the new technology as it is developed.

Research and Development

Much of the discussion revolves around the question as to whether a competitive firm can afford to undertake Research and Development if it is earning only normal profits. The monopoly will of course not be short of funds to invest in this area. An interesting though perhaps extreme view is put forward by Galbraith[2] who suggests that the costs of innovating are today beyond the pockets of all but the largest firms; that big profits accrue from risky projects which only a large firm

[1] See for example K. J. Arrow, 'Economic Welfare and the Allocation of Resources for Invention' in *The Rate and Direction of Inventive Activity* (Princeton, 1962.) Also B. Yamey, 'Monopoly, Competition, and the Incentive to Invest. Comment', *Journal of Law and Economics*, pp. 253–6; H. Demsetz, 'Information and Efficiency. Another Viewpoint', *Journal of Law and Economics* (Apr 1969) pp. 1–23; R. Jackson, 'Market Structure and the Rewards for Patented Inventions', *Anti-trust Bulletin* (Fall 1972) pp. 911–26.

[2] J. K. Galbraith, *The New Industrial State* (Hamish Hamilton, 1967).

can afford to undertake (in the sense of being able to absorb losses without failing overall to earn normal profits); and that there is often such a lengthy time-span between a decision to undertake a major project and the actual appearance of the finished good on the market (e.g. the gestation period for a new motor car is of the order of 4 or 5 years) that again only a very large firm can afford to fund the project in its developmental stages before any revenues have been earned.

The main contributor to the debate has been Mansfield.[1] In various studies he found that in the petroleum, drug and glass industries the largest firms spent less on R and D relative to sales than did somewhat smaller firms, though differences for the steel industry were not statistically significant. He also considered that the productivity of an R and D programme of given scale appeared to be lower in the largest firms than in somewhat smaller firms.

There is evidence[2,3] that in many industries today there is a threshold level of R and D expenditure below which a firm should not bother to invest at all. This suggests that mergers between smaller firms in an industry would be advantageous in this respect, but both Mansfield and Comanor[4] indicate that once this threshold is reached R and D diseconomies rapidly set in. Hence mergers between larger firms would bring no definite advantages, and perhaps quite the opposite.

The majority of large firms do not appear to produce many inventions in their laboratories. Mansfield,[5] drawing upon

[1] E. Mansfield, *Industrial Research and Technological Innovation* (Longman, 1969); 'Size of Firm, Market Structure, and Innovation', *Journal of Political Economy* (Dec 1963) pp. 556–77.

[2] B. R. Williams, *Technology, Investment and Growth* (1967).

[3] C. Freeman, 'Research and Development. A Comparison between British and American Industry', *National Institute Economic Review* (May 1962) pp. 21–39.

[4] W. S. Comanor, 'Research and Technical Change in the Pharmaceutical Industry', *Review of Economics and Statistics* (May 1965). Also *Economica* (1964).

[5] E. Mansfield, *The Economics of Technological Change* (Longman, 1968). Also 'Industrial Research and Development: Characteristics, Costs, and Diffusion of Results', *American Economic Review*, Papers and Proceedings (May 1969) p. 66.

a McGraw-Hill Survey[1] which suggested that 90 per cent or so of firms expected their R and D expenditures to be recouped within five years, pointed out that most major innovations take a good deal longer than this to appear in marketable form. Hence most of the laboratory work in large firms can only be classified as improvements to existing products. This is borne out by an F.B.I. investigation in the United Kingdom[2] and by Bright[3] and others. Hence we must look outside the major corporations for the origins of major technological break-throughs. Nevertheless the evidence is not sufficiently water-tight to allow either definite support for or condemnation of monopoly on the grounds of its effects upon research and development.

Invention and Size

Some commentators prefer to investigate not the ratio of R and D expenditures to firm size, but the rate at which inventions appear in firms of varying sizes. Again, however, the conclusion to be drawn is much the same as in the section above, parti-cularly as almost all the data has been gathered in the U.S.A. One approach to this question is to look at patent statistics, bearing in mind that it is often argued that many small firms have little faith in patents which they believe can be easily circumvented, whereas monopolies are thought to use patents to hold in cold storage, so to speak, inventions which they do not intend to make use of, but which they do not wish their competitors to develop. Such an assertion is difficult to prove either way, but its implications for monopoly policy are clear.

Scherer[4] sampled 448 firms drawn from the Fortune list of

[1] See D. Hamberg, 'Invention in the Industrial Research Labora-tory; *Journal of Political Economy* (Apr 1963) pp. 95–115, where he provides evidence in support of the hypothesis that the large industrial laboratories are likely to be minor sources of major inventions.

[2] F.B.I., *Industrial Research Survey* (1960).

[3] J. R. Bright, 'Evaluating Signals of Technological Change', *Harvard Business Review* (Jan 1970).

[4] F. M. Scherer, 'Firm Size Market Structure, Opportunity and the Output of Patented Inventions', *American Economic Review* (Dec 1965) pp. 1097–126.

the 500 largest industrial corporations in the U.S.A. in 1955. He concluded that 'the evidence does not support the hypothesis that corporate bigness is especially favourable to high inventive output'. Also that 'a heavy burden of proof must be sustained by firms emphasizing research and development potential as a justification (e.g. in merger cases) for bigness'.[1] This conclusion appears to be even more relevant to the United Kingdom in the light of Freeman's conclusions that[2]

> it seems that American Industry's research expenditure is over five times as large as British Industry's, as an absolute figure; it is nearly three times as large per employee, and twice as large as a percentage of net output. Taking the 350 largest firms in each country which do research, the average large American firm spends five times as much as the average large British one.

Other studies have traced major inventions to either inventors working by themselves, small firms, universities, and, particularly in the agricultural sector, to government financed research institutions.

In a study using data on patents for three large American industries Smyth, Samuels and Tzoannos[3] conclude that there is no direct relationship between the extent to which patenting occurs and firm size.

On the other hand the lack of inventiveness by large firms may be a conscious decision on their part to concentrate upon innovation rather than invention, since this is the area where the advantages of large size should become most apparent.

Innovation and Size

It follows from the foregoing analysis that many inventions originate from individuals or firms working on small budgets. Innovative activity, however, often requires very large budgets, and hence seems admirably suited to the resources available to

[1] Ibid., p. 1114.

[2] Freeman, *National Institute Economic Review* (May 1962) p. 21.

[3] D. J. Smyth, J. M. Samuels and J. Tzoannos, 'Patents, Profitability, Liquidity and Firm Size', *Applied Economics*, vol. 4 (1972) pp. 84–5.

the largest firms which can both afford to pump huge sums of money into capitalisation before any revenues are seen at all, and which can also afford to take risks, only provided that the innovative process does not stretch them too far in relation to their other capital requirements. The main advocate of the view that large size and innovation go together is Schumpeter[1] who considered that where one firm innovated, this would spur on other firms to do likewise. Thus a process of 'creative destruction' would gradually replace old capital by new. It appeared to him, however, that this process would only take place if the firms concerned felt secure in their ability to sell the goods resultant from the innovative process, or alternatively where they felt sufficiently sure of selling their existing range of products to make the risks worthwhile. This, however, required elements of monopoly power in such markets, and its existence would provide a 'powerful engine of progress'. The most commonly occurring refutation of this view is enshrined in the argument that large firms become so conservative and bureaucratised in their ways that ready adaption to market circumstances, which is a requisite of innovation, is no longer possible. There is considerable evidence that large firms are in general unwilling to take risks, perhaps because if the project is successful it is the shareholders who benefit most, whereas if it is unsuccessful the originator of the innovation is liable to be dismissed. On the other hand the owner-manager can see the benefits to himself of innovation much more clearly.

Mansfield[2] found that the ratio of innovations to firm size reached a maximum at about the sixth largest firm for the petroleum and coal industries, and at a much lower rank for steel. On the other hand the four largest coal and petroleum (but not steel) firms were responsible for a larger number of innovations than their market share. Adams and Dirlam, investigating the oxygen steelmaking process[3] conclude that

the small firms may be the innovators because, unlike their

---

[1] J. A. Schumpeter, *Capitalism, Socialism, and Democracy* (Allen & Unwin, 1950).

[2] E. Mansfield, *Journal of Political Economy* (Dec 1963) p. 566.

[3] W. Adams and J. Dirlam, 'Big Steel, Invention and Innovation', *Quarterly Journal of Economics* (May 1966) pp. 167–89.

giant rivals, what they do in the way of cost reductions is unlikely to cause so violent a disturbance of the status quo. Hence, based on the steel industry experience, it seems as reasonable to assume that innovation is sponsored by firms in inverse order of size as it is to assume the contrary.

Other studies indicate, for example, that a significant part of innovative activity originates in attempts by outsiders to break into a new market dominated by large established firms. If this is so it suggests that monopoly power based on entry barriers is undesirable.

Scherer considers[1] that

A little bit of monopoly power in the form of structural concentration is conducive to invention and innovation, particularly when advances in the relevant knowledge base occur slowly. But very high concentration has a favourable effect only in rare cases and more often it is apt to retard progress.... Likewise it is vital that barriers to entry be kept at modest levels and that established industry members be exposed continually to the threat of entry by technically audacious newcomers.

We may note in conclusion that given the available evidence the above analysis does not significantly affect the original trade-off argument between the classical case against monopoly and the advantages of access to scale economies. The evidence on technological progress does not allow us to do any more than to draw the general conclusion that in certain industries at certain periods monopolisation will be an agent of technological progress, whereas at most other times it will not, and further that we have at present no way of predicting when such periods will appear in any given industry.

This is reflected in the somewhat stronger viewpoint of the authors[2] of the most comprehensive survey of technical progress so far to appear in the literature that: 'As it stands, the evidence appears to be heavily weighted against the hypothesis

[1] F. M. Scherer, *Industrial Market Structure and Market Performance* (Rand McNally, 1970) pp. 377–8.

[2] A. P. Thirlwall, and C. Kennedy, 'Surveys in Applied Economics: Technical Progress', *Economic Journal* (Mar 1972) p. 61.

that a necessary condition for technological change and progressiveness is that firms should be large scale and dominate the market in which they operate.' Thus we cannot in general accept the argument where put forward by firms intent upon a merger, that the merger will bear fruits through a faster rate of technological advance.

THE IMPLICATIONS OF X-EFFICIENCY

At the very end of his article[1] Williamson introduced what he called the 'management discretion' argument which suggests 'that market power provides a firm with the opportunity to pursue a variety of other-than-profit objectives'. As he pointed out, this argument had been mooted around in the literature for well over half a century without, however, having much impact, largely because the evidence was rather sparse. He did however point out, in partial refutation of his own arguments concerning the benefits of scale economies, that 'if indeed a predictable relaxation in the least–cost posture of a firm which has acquired market power through merger can be made, the estimated cost savings...should be adjusted accordingly. Economies which are available in theory, but, by reason of market power, are not sustainable, are inadmissible.'

Williamson's decision not to discuss the matter further probably reflects the fact that there had been, in the years prior to his own publication, only one major article on this subject. This article by Leibenstein[2] has, however, touched off of late a considerable controversy as to whether or not the benefits yielded by monopolisation through access to scale economies are, or are not, outweighed by the monopolist's subsequent lapse into inefficient operating techniques when he finds himself relieved of competitive pressures. The concept of X-inefficiency thus refers to a situation where a firm is not in practice maximising profits (i.e. not minimising costs). We have had much to say about company objectives other than profit maximisation, but for the moment we are assuming that the goal of both competitive firms and monopolies is in principle to

[1] Williamson, *American Economic Review* (Mar 1968) p. 31–2.
[2] H. Leibenstein, 'Allocative Efficiency versus X-Efficiency', *American Economic Review* (June 1966).

maximise profits. A competitive firm must also maximise profits in practice because it will be unable to make normal profits in the long run where it does not so do, and will be driven out of business. But will a monopolist be cost-efficient in practice?

In Leibenstein's opinion a monopolist will not be cost efficient. He begins his analysis by pointing out that the misallocation of resources which results from monopolising a competitive industry is very small. This misallocation is represented by the area XYZ in Fig. 7.4 above. There are, however, more significant conclusions to be drawn about X-efficiency. He blames X-inefficiency upon several factors, among them the lack of knowledge possessed by a firm with respect to the optimum combinations of factor inputs, and the propensity of labour factors to work at less than full capacity (what Leibenstein calls 'intellectual slack' with respect to management). He concludes[1]

> that for a variety of reasons people and organisations normally work neither as hard nor as effectively as they could. In situations where competitive pressure is light many people will trade the disutility of greater effort, of search, and the control of other people's activities for the utility of feeling less pressure and of better interpersonal relations. But in situations where competitive pressures are high, and hence the costs of such trades are also high, they will exchange less of the disutility of effort for the utility of freedom from pressure.... The data suggest that in a great many instances the amount to be gained by increasing X-efficiency is frequently significant.

Further attempts[2] have been made to introduce greater

---

[1] Ibid., p. 413.

[2] See for example W. S. Comanor and H. Leibenstein, 'Allocative Efficiency, X-Efficiency and the Measurement of Welfare Loss', *Economica* (Aug 1969); M. A. Crew and C. K. Rowley, 'On Allocative Efficiency, X-efficiency, and the Measurement of Welfare Loss', *Economica* (May 1971). M. A. Crew, C. K. Rowley and M. W. Jones-Lee, 'X-Theory versus Management Discretion Theory', *Southern Economic Journal*, vol. 38 (Oct 1971); Y.-K. Ng and R. Parish, 'Monopoly, X-Efficiency and the Measurement of Welfare Loss', *Economica* (Aug 1972) pp. 301–8.

sophistication into the analysis. These are too technical for our purposes here. It can, however, be said that most economists are now in basic agreement as to the existence of X-inefficiencies in large firms, although they may differ about their extent. Remember that under conditions of perfect competition no X-inefficiencies can exist, otherwise the inefficient firm will be driven out of business. But if a competitive industry is monopolised, and X-inefficiencies subsequently appear, this presents a prima facie case for anti-monopoly legislation. Notice that this argument is completely independent of the neo-classical attack upon monopoly, although it comes to the same conclusions. Thus it would appear overall that a judgement upon the desirability or otherwise of monopoly rests upon a trade-off between, on the one hand, the neo-classical case against monopoly together with the X-inefficiency case against monopoly, and on the other hand the scale-economies argument in favour of monopoly. Informed opinion at the present time appears to agree that the former in general outweighs the latter in economic terms, and hence monopolies should be suppressed. A useful summary of available evidence appears in Rowley.[1] The welfare losses to consumers from price and output changes resultant from monopolisation are insignificant according to every available study. The evidence on scale effects is, as we have seen, by no means unanimous, but benefits from large-scale operations normally outweigh any welfare losses to consumers due to monopolisation. The evidence also suggests, however, that losses due to X-inefficiency after monopolisation occurs will often negate such benefits, so that overall, as Rowley suggests,[2] 'X-inefficiency considerations may yet reverse the trend in public policy towards encouraging large-scale production which has been such a prominent feature at least of the U.K. economy during the past decade.'

Thus we find that a policy of monopoly control within the United Kingdom, although based upon the weakest argument of the above three, namely the neo-classical case against monopoly, is in practice economically justifiable for other reasons, although each case will have to be judged upon its merits.

[1] Rowley, *Anti-trust and Economic Efficiency*, chap. 8.
[2] Ibid., p. 55.

H

SUGGESTED APPROACHES TO MONOPOLY CONTROLS

There are several possible approaches to the question of monopoly controls. The first of these is to eschew controls altogether and let the free market decide.[1] Beacham and Jones appear to favour this policy[2] when they comment: 'Finally it has been too easily assumed that a sufficiently strong case exists to control mergers.'

Few other economists appear, however, to want to do away with controls altogether. As Newbould has pointed out[3] 'If the evidence of this study with respect to the self-generating nature of merger activity and the desires of management to dominate and gain increased size is correct, the result of the abandonment of a merger policy will be to increase, substantially and quickly, the number of firms holding monopoly positions in U.K. markets.'

But a statement to the effect that both existing and prospective monopolies should be controlled begs the question as to how best to go about it. We shall be looking briefly at the legislation in existence a little further on. Since this legislation is based upon traditional rather than modern ideas as to why monopoly power is undesirable it is possible that it needs to be re-thought.

Much of the existing legislation can be said to be based upon a cost–benefit approach to market power, where it is explicitly recognised that both gains and losses will accompany any attempt to control markets. Thus it is necessary for the authorities to investigate the actual or expected performance of the company or companies concerned in such actions, and to assess the net benefits or otherwise associated with them.

Such an approach is favoured by several commentators, but is explicitly rejected by Crew and Rowley[4] on the grounds of its expense and lack of precision.

[1] A full discussion of this approach appears in ibid., pp. 72–5.

[2] A. Beacham and J. Jones, 'Merger Criteria and Policy in Great Britain and Canada', *Journal of Industrial Relations* (Apr 1971) p. 117.

[3] G. D. Newbould, *Management and Merger Activity* (Guthrie Press, 1970) p. 222.

[4] Crew and Rowley, *Moorgate and Wall St Review* (Autumn 1970) p. 28 onwards.

It is evident, for example, that the revenue and cost curves used for calculating the costs and benefits from a merger (as illustrated in Fig. 7.4) must be drawn with absolute accuracy. Yet in practice this simply cannot be done. Furthermore, where the exercise is being done by an investigatory body, co-operation and impartiality are unlikely to be the rule and more likely the exception. Hence the authors conclude that: 'There can be little doubt that the costs of a thorough efficiency audit of the kind required would far outweigh the expected benefits.' Crew and Rowley then go on to suggest two possible alternatives. 'The first alternative is that of allowing unfettered market forces to determine the degree of market power to be accepted within the economy, but of applying regulatory devices in the form of price controls to prevent excessive profits arising from monopolistic practices.'

This suggestion they discard on several grounds, noting in particular that if, under a system of price controls, cost increases are a justification for allowable price rises, X-inefficiencies producing higher average costs would simply lead to higher prices unless the controlling body could identify the cause of the increased costs. This is, however, unlikely to prove possible in practice.

The authors therefore opt for a 'vigorous anti-trust policy in which rules for the most part replace discretionary intervention'. A typical rule might be to the effect that no merger proposal is allowable which raises the potential market share of the merged companies above a certain limit. Such rules the authors suggest could be judicially applied.

In much the same way Sutherland[1] proposes that mergers involving the largest twenty-five companies within the United Kingdom should be automatically disallowed. Less rigorous structural rules have been suggested by various commentators. Sutherland would also like to have investigated a merger involving any company already one of the largest 100 in the United Kingdom which wishes to merge with another company, or any proposed merger which will make a company one of the United Kingdom's largest 100 companies. Utton[2] suggests

[1] A. Sutherland, 'The Management of Mergers Policy' in *The Managed Economy*, ed. A. Cairncross (Blackwell, 1970).

[2] M. Utton, 'Future Prospects for Merger Policy', *Bankers' Magazine* (Sep 1970) pp. 123–7.

that the Monopolies Commission should investigate mergers likely to lead to acquired assets of £25 million or more or which produce a market share of 67 per cent. Hindley agrees but does not pin down the precise scope of his criteria.[1]

A dissenting opinion has been put on record by Howe[2] who agrees with the Board of Trade[3] that such rules as are suggested by Crew and Rowley are inappropriate for Great Britain. His first argument is that it is not possible to correctly define what is meant by 'market share'. Hence it is inappropriate to recommend that a proposed merger should not produce more than a specified share of the relevant market.[4]

Secondly he doubts that a 'line can be drawn at some critical level of market share of a single or group of large firms, such that it can be reasonably accepted that the performance of firms whose shares are above the line will be undesirable, whereas the reverse holds for the performance of firms with smaller than the critical share'.

Howe does not himself accept the X-efficiency argument *per se,* arguing that X-inefficiency will exist in all firms except those in a (never to be found in practice) perfectly competitive industry. Hence merging several small companies to produce a situation of monopoly power will not necessarily imply a degree of X-inefficiency greater than that already existing in the small firms. Indeed he would argue that 'the larger firms with market power may be more able to provide internal stimuli...through such devices as incentives and bonus schemes for workers, stock options or share incentive plans for managers...which raise internal efficiency close to the maximum'.

Howe further notes that care must be taken not to rely on data collected in the U.S.A. where what would be called a

[1] B. Hindley, *Industrial Merger and Public Policy*, Hobart Paper No. 50 (1970).

[2] M. Howe, 'Anti-trust Policy, Rules or Discretionary Intervention?', *Moorgate and Wall St Review* (Feb 1971) pp. 39–68.

[3] Board of Trade, *Mergers, A Guide to Board of Trade Practice*, para. 4.

[4] See also M. Howe, 'British Merger Policy Proposals and American Experience', *Scottish Journal of Political Economy* (Feb 1972) pp. 50–4 and 58–9.

'large' firm would be 'very large' in Britain and so forth. Hence he believes that scale economies may be very important in Britain and also that monopolisation might be highly advantageous from the viewpoint of technical progress.

As we have seen, the evidence either way is somewhat scanty. This fact perhaps militates in favour of a pragmatic judge-each-case-on-its-merits approach, accompanied by some sort of attempt to overcome Crew and Rowley's objections stated above. Howe suggests that 'positive benefit to the public be shown by any challenged increase in market power rather than simply the absence of public detriment'. According to Pass[1] a desirable approach would be that 'only those mergers that could be shown to be *actively* in the public interest in terms of yielding substantial benefits...be approved'. Also with reference to mergers Beacham and Jones[2] suggest that

> If the models of micro theory *per se* are of little help in forecasting the impact of mergers it becomes difficult to define criteria by which they may be categorized and judged. The implication is twofold: first, in most instances, case by case examination is necessary. Second, since mergers cannot be judged *in vacuo*, some fairly arbitrary criteria must be written into the Acts.

The issues are clearly open to several interpretations[3] so that it is perhaps appropriate to consider how in practice monopoly policy has been administered in the United Kingdom.

It should be borne in mind when reading further that there is a significant difference between measures designed to prohibit actions likely to lead to a reduction in competition, and measures designed to remove already existing market power. We shall have more to say on this point later.

[1] C. L. Pass, 'The Control of Mergers in the UK', *Journal of Business Policy* (Winter 1971) pp. 45–58.

[2] A. Beacham and J. Jones, 'Merger Criteria and Policy in Great Britain and Canada', *Journal of Industrial Relations* (Apr 1971) p. 103.

[3] See for example K. D. George, *Industrial Organisation* (Allen & Unwin, 1971) pp. 150–4.

MONOPOLY POLICY IN PRACTICE

During the nineteenth century the business sector was almost totally left to its own devices. It was felt that attempts by entrepreneurs to maximise their profits would be in the long-run interests of the economy (though not presumably of the working classes at the time). Unfettered competition would ensure that only the most efficient would survive. Such an approach to market behaviour became increasingly unsuited to twentieth-century needs. Not only did the need to take cognisance of social welfare become widely accepted, embodied in various pieces of social legislation which impinged directly upon the entrepreneur, but the onset of the great depression in the early 1920s provided a stimulus to various arrangements for controlling markets. At a time when very few firms were able to prosper without tempting competitors into price wars and the like, competition was generally felt to be ruinous. In the early post-war period, however, public opinion swung the other way, and a greater degree of competitive spirit was felt to be an advantage in the difficult years ahead. The first monopoly legislation was accordingly introduced in 1948 as the Monopolies and Restrictive Practices (Inquiry and Control) Act. This Act did not define a monopoly as such, but applied to markets where:

(1) at least one-third of all the goods supplied or processed in the United Kingdom were supplied by a firm and its subsidiaries;

(2) two or more firms, which together supplied at least one-third of the market, were parties to a restrictive agreement (whether oral, written, tacit or overt) or so conducted their affairs as in any way to prevent or restrict competition.

The existence of monopoly power was not condemned out of hand. Instead the Board of Trade was empowered to refer to a Monopolies Commission any firm or firms falling within the above categories. The Board of Trade could either request the Commission to report back to it without judging the issues involved, or to also attach a judgement as to whether or not the public interest was being contravened (in which case the Commission was to suggest remedies). It was then up to the Board of Trade to take action upon the report. The Commission was set up to be an independent administrative tribunal. It was up to the Board of Trade to draw up a Statutory Order if it so wished, subject to Parliamentary approval, asking the parties concerned to desist from their undesirable practices. Alternatively the Board could settle the matter without recourse to law where the firm under investigation was willing to co-operate voluntarily.

It can perhaps be said that the 1948 Act was testing the market for monopoly legislation. The emphasis was on inquiry, and investigations were conducted at a snail's pace. In theory the procedures were intended to be flexible, each case being judged on its merits, and no penalties were laid down. The Commission was also empowered to conduct follow-up enquiries to determine whether or not the condemned practices had in fact been terminated.

In practice, it proved impossible to define what was meant by the 'public interest'. Hence the clause in the Act giving guidance to the Commission on this topic turned out to be far too general to have any practical validity. In effect the Commission was left to its own devices in determining what was or was not economically or socially desirable.

The Commission proceeded to do this in twenty instances between 1948 and 1956. Nevertheless their investigations were slow, only taking place one at a time, and many of the references were to small industries or to small parts of larger industries. No investigations of nationalised industries were permitted and it is difficult to see any particular rhyme or reason about the choice of references.

Of the above twenty industries investigated, three industries were not condemned in any major way, whereas in sixteen cases a majority of the Commission found evidence of malpractices. Exclusive dealing and tying arrangements were condemned in almost every case, as were other measures to exclude competitors, such as brand proliferation and measures to control supply or productive capacity. As a consequence of these condemnations public opinion was undoubtedly influenced, but if the same applied to the Government it was not in any hurry to act upon its beliefs. Only one Order was submitted to Parliament restraining an industry from certain practices. In most other cases voluntary agreements were made with the industry concerned, but it is not possible to determine the extent to which the industries in question honoured these agreements.

THE RESTRICTIVE TRADE PRACTICES ACT, 1956

This Act in part arose out of the discovery of widespread restrictive practices in use in industries investigated under the 1948 Act.[1] Hence the Monopolies Commission was left to deal with specific monopoly situations while provision was made for the registration of trade-association agreements with the Registrar of a Restrictive Practices Court. Such agreements included those between two or more parties concerned with the production or supply of goods who agree upon prices to be charged, the terms or conditions of sale, quantities or types to be produced, the process of manufacture, the persons to whom they sell or the persons from whom they buy. Such agreements did not have to be explicitly laid down in writing but could be of a more informal nature.

A rather different approach to that of the 1948 Act was embodied in the decision to treat a firm under investigation as guilty unless it could prove otherwise by claiming exemption from controls upon its behaviour under one of the so-called 'gateways'. Even where such an exemption was claimed, however, the Court had to satisfy itself that no further disadvantages arising out of the restrictive agreement outweighed the benefits claimed for it.

The onus placed upon firms conducting restrictive practices to prove themselves innocent of malpractices stems from the fact that scale benefits can very rarely be significant in such circumstances, because the individual firms are not joined together into larger operating units.

[1] These practices were set out in the publication entitled *Collective Discrimination. A Report on Exclusive Dealing, Collective Boycotts, Aggregated Rebates, and other Discriminatory Trade Practices*, Cmd 9504 (1955).

The gateways through which a firm may pass are as follows:

(1) That the restriction is reasonably necessary to protect the public against injury in connection with the consumption, installation or use of goods.

(2) That the removal of the restriction would deny to the public as purchasers, consumers or users of any goods, specific and substantial benefits.

(3) That the restriction is reasonably necessary to counteract measures taken by someone not party to the agreement with a view to preventing or restricting competition in the relevant trade.

(4) That the restriction is reasonably necessary to enable parties to the agreement to negotiate fair terms with major suppliers or customers.

(5) That the removal of the restriction would be likely to have a serious and persistent adverse effect upon unemployment in the locality of the firms concerned.

(6) That the removal of the restriction would be bad for exports.

(7) That the restriction is reasonably required for the purposes of supporting other restrictions deemed to be in the public interest.

Unfortunately the nature and extent of the gateways, and in particular of gateway (2) above, left the Court with no option but to make widespread decisions about how to measure in some meaningful way the benefits and detriment associated with any given agreement. This was a somewhat unreasonable requirement for obvious reasons, and it is hardly surprising that the decisions were rather unpredictable. In effect the Court was obliged 'not only to make economic predictions and forecasts, but also to evaluate the economic effects of agreements in the light of the interests of different groups and of competing policy objectives'.[1] Unfortunately although there was much to be said for an attempt to codify what was or was not to be deemed a restrictive trade practice, the Court's decisions did not allow of this eventuality. Hence the piecemeal approach had to be retained, leading in the end to some rather dubious

[1] R. B. Stevens, and B. S. Yamey, *The Restrictive Practices Court* (Weidenfeld & Nicolson, 1965) p. 142.

decisions often associated with gateway (2) above.[1] However, the Court was initially unwilling to let anything much through the gateways at all, so that many firms, not wishing to be bothered with presenting a seemingly hopeless case before the Court, let the restrictive agreements go by the board. Although this might appear at first sight to be highly beneficial, it did not, regrettably, imply of necessity that there were any subsequent changes in operating practices so as to bring about a more competitive atmosphere in the trades involved. The fact that an agreement was no longer officially in existence did not imply that the parties to it no longer behaved in accordance with its provisions.[2] Besides which the high level of demand during the period was hardly a stimulus to competitive behaviour. This has led Beacham and Cunningham[3] to conclude that 'it may be too soon to congratulate ourselves on the demise of cartel agreements'. They also consider[4] that

> It is difficult therefore to offer any very definite verdict on the success of the 1956 Act. It has considerably enlarged our knowledge of the occurrence and functioning of cartels. It has forced a widespread abandonment of agreements covered by the Act. There is some evidence of more competitive attitudes and some evidence that restrictions on competition are merely taking different forms. The Court itself has proved to be a somewhat blunt instrument in the arsenal of anti-monopoly.

George[5] is not altogether dissatisfied with this conclusion, feeling that 'there may be circumstances where the encouragement of short-run competition will not lead to a satisfactory outcome in terms of the longer-term development of an

---

[1] See for example, A. Sutherland, 'Economics in the Restrictive Practices Court', *Oxford Economic Papers,* vol. 17 (Nov 1965).

[2] A breakdown of registrable cases under the terms of the 1956 Act appears in C. Rowley, 'Monopoly in Britain. Private Vice but Public Virtue?', *Moorgate and Wall St Review* (Autumn 1968) p. 45.

[3] A. Beacham and N. J. Cunningham, *Economics of Industrial Organisation,* 5th edn (Pitman, 1970) p. 172.

[4] Ibid., p. 174.

[5] K. D. George, 'Concentration and Specialisation in Industry', *Journal of Industrial Economics* (Apr 1972) p. 165.

industry, so that there may be something to be said in favour of restrictive agreements'. He acknowledges, however, that 'to allow firms to operate a restrictive agreement which could be used to improve market performance always carries the danger that it will actually result in monopolistic exploitation'.

Rowley[1] also considers that 'In practice the impact of the 1956 Act, in so far as registrable agreements are concerned, has been impressive'.

The 1956 Act was amended by the Restrictive Trade Practices Act of 1968 which empowers the Board of Trade to require registration of 'information agreements' by which firms inform one another of their prices and occasionally of their costs. On the other hand the 1956 Act has been weakened by the addition of a further gateway to the effect that an agreement is exempted where it 'does not directly or indirectly restrict or discourage competition to any material degree in any relevant trade or industry, and is not likely to do so'. Certain other agreements have also had to be exempted in the national interest largely because they resulted from the attempts by the Economic Development Committees to speed up the United Kingdom's growth rate by getting firms to work more closely together and to share certain information with one another.

The Economic Development Committees were set up under the central control of the National Economic Development Council, with the avowed aim of examining the operations, both present and future, of various industries, with a view to improving their performance. The work of the Committees inevitably caused them to transgress the terms of the 1956 Act.

This difficulty recurs in the context of the 1965 Monopolies and Mergers Act. On the one hand the Board of Trade is, as we shall see, attempting to control mergers, while on the other hand the Industrial Reorganisation Corporation was set up under a statute of December 1966 with the prime purpose of assisting or promoting mergers in order to avoid duplication, and to achieve scale economies in production, marketing and research. Such sponsored mergers fall theoretically under the terms of the 1965 Act which produces something

[1] Rowley, *Moorgate and Wall St Review* (Autumn 1968) p. 44.

of a conflict of ideas. In fact this is precisely the conflict which we were at pains to discuss in detail in the earlier part of the chapter, which we referred to as the trade-off between scale economies and X-inefficiency. The Economic Development Committees and the I.R.C. were set up presumably in the belief that the scale economies argument was vitally important for certain sectors of industry (especially those with export ramifications such as the automotive industry). Under these circumstances we have seen that it is probably idle to suppose that X-inefficiencies will not later appear. But if they do appear, is one then to refer the firms in question to the Monopolies Commission for abuse of market power? Would it be in the public interest to ignore X-inefficiencies even if the firm was originally the result of a merger in the public interest? As we can see monopoly policy in practice poses some rather awkward questions, to which we shall return a little later.

THE MONOPOLIES AND MERGERS ACT, 1965

This Act was introduced because the previous legislation had done nothing to prevent the acquisition of market power by means of mergers. It is worth noting that a firm which has grown through internal expansion must have done so despite some degree of competition, and must therefore be efficient in some or all spheres of its operations. Growth by merger, however, has prima facie no such implications for efficiency, and may simply result from a desire to reduce competitive pressures. Furthermore, many commentators had been expressing disquiet at the scale of merger activity and its implications for industrial concentration.[1] The Monopolies Commission was once again to be the body to which cases would be passed by the Board of Trade, although its membership was expanded somewhat. The Commission was empowered to investigate monopolies and restrictive practices in the service sector, and the powers of the Board of Trade to act upon the Commission's reports was extended to enable it to require the publication of price lists, to regulate prices, and to prohibit or impose

[1] See Appendix 3, 'General Observations on Mergers'. Annex to Monopolies Commission report on the proposed merger between Rank/De la Rue (H.M.S.O., 1969) pp. 60–1.

conditions on acquisitions. Specifically the Board of Trade
can either dissolve a business, sell a part of its assets, or forbid a
prospective merger to take place. A proposed merger qualified
for investigation either where it produced a firm having a share
of more than one-third of the available market for any given
commodity or where the value of the assets to be taken over
exceeded five million pounds. This was much the same
approach as is embodied in the 1948 Act although the Commission was free to refer to other yardsticks of market power
when conducting specific merger inquiries. The market share
criterion was designed broadly to cover the eventuality of
horizontal mergers, whereas the asset value criterion covered
vertical and conglomerate mergers. It is interesting, however,
that the value of assets criterion should have been introduced,
since it obviously reflected a belief in certain quarters that
company size and monopoly power went hand in hand.

Broadly each investigation had to be completed within six
months (whereas many of the investigations under the 1948
Act had taken several times as long to complete). Companies
considering a takeover bid would hardly have been willing to
wait five years for a decision, and it would have been unreasonable to let all proposed mergers go by default irrespective
of the eventual decision by the Commission. Furthermore,
Rowley points out[1] that if the merger had taken place and
rationalisation followed subsequent upon it, then 'however
undesirable the merger, the cost of divestment might then
outweigh the benefits which would ensue'.

As with the Act of 1948 the public interest was not defined
clearly, despite the attempts to do so through the system of
gateways under the 1956 Act. Pragmatism once again held
sway (perhaps because it was felt that the 'gateways' had not
done their job all that well).

By the end of 1970 the Board of Trade had investigated
roughly 500 proposed or actual mergers.[2] Of these 500 or so,
some 60 per cent appeared to satisfy the size criteria.[3] Approxi-

[1] C. K. Rowley, 'Mergers and Public Policy in Great Britain',
Journal of Law and Economics (Apr 1968) p. 80.

[2] See table II in Howe, *Scottish Journal of Political Economy* (Feb
1972) p. 43.

[3] Pass, *Journal of Business Policy* (Winter 1971) p. 49.

mately 85 per cent of these mergers were predominantly horizontal in nature.[1] Only thirteen cases were, however, actually passed on to the Monopolies Commission for investigation, of which two were special cases under the provisions of the 1965 Act because they were newspaper mergers. Of the remaining eleven mergers four were found to be sufficiently against the public interest for the Board of Trade to step in.[2]

A fifth merger, that between Barclays Bank, Lloyds Bank and Martins Bank,[3] was found to be against the public interest, but the Board of Trade did not activate its powers.[4] On this evidence the chances of a proposed or actual merger being found to be against the public interest are slim.

As a result of its various efforts the Board of Trade was enabled to produce a guide to mergers in July 1969 in which various imponderables are balanced one against the other. So far the Monopolies Commission has been concerned with prospective mergers only and has been forced to guess what might happen were the merger to take place. Rowley[5] has doubts about the validity of such an exercise.

> The Commission is required to predict the impact of the merger upon affected markets not merely at the time of the merger but for the foreseeable future. Predictive ability of a very high order is required for this task. [Furthermore with mergers] the past performance of the separate entities is largely irrelevant as a guide to their likely future conduct as a single enterprise. There is a very real danger of the Monopolies Commission being pressed into reliance upon intuition and presentiment as a substitute for scientific

[1] Ibid.

[2] Ibid., p. 50 for the full list.

[3] See M. A. Crew and C. K. Rowley, *Moorgate and Wall St Review* (Autumn 1970) pp. 30–2 for an analysis of the Commission's Report in terms of the Scale-Economies vs X-Efficiency controversy. This also appears more briefly in A. Beacham and N. J. Cunningham, *Economics of Industrial Organisation*, pp. 169–70.

[4] Nevertheless the merger did not take place.

[5] Rowley, *Journal of Law and Economics* (April 1968) p. 86. See also a more general view of complaints about the working of the 1965 Act in Howe, *Scottish Journal of Political Economy* (Feb 1972) pp. 37–61.

analysis in its assessment of the future consequences of mergers.

With this opinion Beacham and Jones[1] cannot help but agree, commenting that 'the reports suggest a very rapid and impressionistic survey of the situation likely to arise if the merger went through'.

THE FAIR TRADING ACT, 1973

This Act set up a new body known as the office of the Director-General of Fair Trading. This body has firstly taken over the functions of the Registrar of Restrictive Trading Agreements in registering restrictive agreements and referring them to the Restrictive Practices Court. Secondly the Director-General of Fair Trading has taken over from the Department of Trade and Industry (previously called the Board of Trade) the bulk of the responsibility for referring cases to the Monopolies and Mergers Commission (previously called the Monopolies Commission). The office of Fair Trading will normally initiate monopoly enquiries, and will also provide the necessary background information for the responsible Minister in the case of merger enquiries, although this latter Minister retains the specific power of reference to the Commission.

The new Act sets out to remedy some of the most obvious anomalies which arose under the terms of reference of previous Acts. Firstly, the responsible Ministers, acting upon the advice of the office of Fair Trading, can instigate enquiries into both the activities of Nationalised Industries, and also other publically sponsored bodies such as Marketing Boards, such enquiries to be conducted by the Monopolies and Mergers Commission. The Commission is also empowered to investigate restrictive labour practices, although no legally enforceable remedies are available where such practices are found to exist.

A monopoly situation is now taken to exist where a firm controls one-quarter rather than one-third of the market for a particular product. A proposed merger is open to investigation where the new company either controls one-quarter of the

[1] Beacham and Jones, *Journal of Industrial Relations* (Apr 1971) p. 114.

relevant market or where the value of assets taken over exceeds five million pounds. The six-months' rule for the completion of merger enquiries remains in force, but the responsible Ministers are also empowered to impose time limits on monopoly enquiries.

Potentially more significant are firstly the avowed intention to narrow down the scope of investigations to consider only whether or not specific aspects of monopoly conduct or of a proposed merger are against the public interest, and secondly the re-definition of the 'public interest' which now includes a reference to the desirability of maintaining and promoting effective competition.

CONFLICTS IN MONOPOLY POLICY

It is probably fair to suggest that monopoly policy in the United Kingdom is characterised more by its conflicts than by its achievements. There is to begin with a certain lack of harmony between the theoretical case for monopoly controls, which suggests that monopolies should be treated as being in principle against the public interest, and the approach of the legislation, which, with the exception of the Act of 1956, places the onus upon the investigatory body of proving that the public interest is suffering significant detriment. More logically such detriment should be assumed to exist and the firm under investigation should be required to defend its behaviour. Perhaps the authorities are still undecided as to the relative importance of the Scale Economies and X-Inefficiency arguments, and seek to resolve their doubts by giving companies under investigation the benefit of the doubt. Typically the Board of Trade has skirted around the problem by, for example, suggesting that[1] 'The behaviour of the merged company can be examined at a later date to see that it does not conflict with the public interest.'

Not surprisingly the ambivalence of the authorities is reflected in the results of the legislation. As we have seen above the figures largely speak for themselves, and only the Act of 1956 can reasonably be said to have made any real inroads into the dissipation of monopoly power, and even this is not

[1] Board of Trade, *Mergers* (H.M.S.O., 1969).

certain since many agreements have possibly gone underground.

This obvious conflict between principle and practice shows up also in the way that the authorities have been busily setting up organisations which have aims diametrically opposed to the intentions of the monopoly legislation. The I.R.C. and E.D.C.s were presumably brought into being with the pious hope that it would be possible to produce larger operating units without any subsequent abuse of market power. The authorities can hardly have been unaware, however, of the odd appearance of policies which on the one hand attacked the abuse of market power which had appeared as a direct result of the formation of enlarged operating units, and which on the other hand utilised the E.D.C.s and I.R.C. to increase market power in other, or even similar, industries[1] by encouraging mergers and the like. In fact companies which came under the auspices of the I.R.C. were generally informed quite openly that the chances of their ever being investigated under the monopoly legislation were negligible. The I.R.C., it is true, was abolished in the summer of 1970, but this was almost certainly due more to the political need to show reductions in government expenditure at the time, rather than to a recognition that the role of the I.R.C. could not be readily justified in the light of the pre-existing anti-mergers legislation.

A third major area of conflict appertains to the public sector. Nationalised Industries are responsible to the relevant Minister for their actions, but the public sector comprises such an important part of the whole industrial sector that to exempt it wholesale from investigation under the terms of the monopoly legislation seems at best inappropriate. The public sector is after all generally more secure in its operations than commensurately large firms in the private sector because free competition is not permitted, and losses are subsidised by the Treasury. Furthermore, the day-to-day operations of public companies are not subject to supervision, so that abuse of market power, particularly in the form of growing levels of

---

[1] In one case, for example, the Monopolies Commission found the Ross–Associated Fisheries proposed merger to be against the public interest. Yet subsequently the Board of Trade allowed an I.R.C. sponsored merger of Ross and A.F. trawler interests to take place without further reference to the Commission.

X-inefficiency, is as likely as not to result. Nationalised Industries are now subject to investigation under the terms of the Fair Trading Act, but it is not yet possible to tell whether or not this extension of the scope of monopoly legislation will have a significant impact.

THE NEED FOR A NEW APPROACH

As has already been suggested above, there is all the difference in the world between preventive and corrective anti-trust. Rowley sums up the difference as follows[1]

> Preventive anti-trust emphasises the prohibition of both conspiracies between formally independent companies, and of activities which fall short of conspiracy but which nevertheless lessen competition, and the restriction of developing single-firm monopoly power, be it by merger or by internal expansion. Corrective anti-trust encompasses measures such as divestment of assets, prohibitions in company expansion, penalties for conspiracy, improvements in the information market, and even tariff reductions in circumstances where direct intervention is impossible.

The emphasis in Britain has always fallen squarely on preventive measures. For this reason monopoly policy is widely regarded as somewhat of a charade. Nevertheless the necessary corrective measures are already available within the terms of the existing legislation, so it is not really a question of ignorance as to appropriate responses to monopoly power but rather an unwillingness to undertake appropriately severe counter-measures, possibly of a structural nature.

It has been argued in defence of this approach[2] that in the eyes of the Board of Trade 'cost savings and dominance of the U.K. market are relatively unimportant by comparison to the "financial, organisational, technological and marketing" size requirements for survival and growth in a highly competitive international arena'.

---

[1] Rowley, *Anti-trust and Economic Efficiency*, pp. 11–12.
[2] C. L. Pass, 'Horizontal Mergers and the Control of Market Power in the U.K.', *Anti-trust Bulletin*, p. 833.

Newbould, however,[1] reckoned that only 9 per cent of mergers were proposed for reasons dear to the heart of the Board of Trade, whereas over 60 per cent were proposed with a view to the acquisition of market dominance and the elimination of competition.

This suggests that the onus should be placed upon firms to prove that they are acting in the public interest. George for example[2] would like to see it made the responsibility of firms to meaningfully demonstrate the benefits of a proposed merger, and further that such benefits, even where proven, should only be accepted as a justification for a proposed merger where firstly they are substantial, and where secondly they could not easily be achieved by means of internal growth. Similar views are held by Howe[3] and Beesley.[4] For its part the Monopolies Commission does not have a good record in interpreting the extent of competition faced by different firms. As Rowley has pointed out[5]

> The Commission itself places excessive importance upon the share of the market accounted for by the company under investigation, thereby neglecting or under-rating the impact both of competitive substitutes falling outside the reference field and potential competition provided both by large multi-product companies prepared to diversify into profitable areas, not to mention companies and commodities not yet in existence at the time of the investigation.

This suggests that there is a need for any investigatory body to carefully re-define what it is trying to discover, and how best to interpret such information as is available. If the wrong questions are being asked, the wrong conclusions will inevitably result. Several other aspects of the Monopoly Commission investiga-

---

[1] G. Newbould, *Management and Merger Activity* (Guthstead, 1970).

[2] George, *Industrial Organisation* (Allen & Unwin, 1971) pp. 156–7.

[3] Howe, *Moorgate and Wall St Review* (Feb 1971) pp. 39–68.

[4] M. Beesley, 'Economic Effects of National Policies towards Mergers and Acquisitions' in *Corporate Long-Range Planning*, ed. B. Denning (Longman, 1969).

[5] Rowley, *Moorgate and Wall St Review* (Autumn 1968) p. 41.

tions have been criticised as inappropriate, in addition to the question of the meaning of competition[1] so there is clearly room for improvement in this direction also.

It was always rather hard to defend the now discontinued exemption of public corporations from the terms of the various Acts. The fact of their public ownership does not by definition imply a devotion to the public interest, and their relative security may well go hand in hand with significant X-inefficiencies. The rationale for the exemption policy may well have been associated with the economics of politics, as is persuasively argued by Rowley.[2] He suggests that there are too many vested interests in the continuation of monopoly power which include 'not only the management and shareholders of the firms with great market power, but also the trade unionists and workers they employ, as well as state officials accustomed to statutory shelter from competitive pressures'. Meanwhile the 'median voter' whom all political parties must pander to, remains indifferent to the issue of monopoly policy.

It is interesting to note that in the United States, which has monopoly legislation dating back to 1890, the presumption has always been that if you allow a firm to develop market power, by whatever means, it will abuse it. The authorities there have not been concerned with the niceties of the meaning of 'the public interest', which is regarded as being directly associated with the degree of competition to be found within an industry. Thus if the degree of competition is adversely affected by some specific business arrangement or practice then the public interest is assumed to have suffered detriment. The merits of this approach over that traditionally adopted in the United Kingdom are set out, for example, in Bernhard.[3] The

[1] See for example C. K. Rowley, 'The Monopolies Commission and Rate of Return on Capital', *Economic Journal* (Mar 1969) pp. 42–66; 'The Monopolies Commission and Rate of Return on Capital. Reply', *Economic Journal* (Sep 1971) and A. Sutherland, 'The Monopolies Commission. A Critique of Dr Rowley', *Economic Journal* (June 1971) pp. 264–72.

[2] Rowley, *Moorgate and Wall St Review* (Autumn 1968) pp. 65–8.

[3] R. Bernhard, 'The Law and the Economics of Market Collusion in Europe, Great Britain and the United States. An American Point of View', *Journal of Industrial Economics* (Nov 1965) pp. 121–2.

efficacy of the approach is open to question[1] but it is generally
agreed that the various amendments introduced during the
post-war period have made the legislation a serious threat to the
continued existence of monopoly power within the U.S.A.

The Fair Trading Act has now introduced to Britain the
notion that the 'public interest' is closely associated with the
extent of effective competition within the U.K. economy. It is,
however, too early to say whether or not the experience of
anti-trust in the U.S.A. will be paralleled by future developments in the United Kingdom. In Canada also, where the
law relating to dominant firms had long been based upon a
definition of the public interest similar to that used in the
United Kingdom, the criteria against which to judge a proposed
merger are, as a result of the introduction of the Combines
Investigation Act of 1960, now similar to those adopted in the
U.S.A. It is now an indictable offence under criminal law to
form a merger in non-service trades which leads to public
detriment.[2] Once again this does not necessarily imply that the
legislation is more effective in practice than that of the United
Kingdom,[3] but the experience of the U.K. Restrictive Trade
Practices Act itself tends to suggest that the efficacy of monopoly legislation is likely to be significantly increased where the
firms under investigation are required to defend themselves
against the presumption that they have been acting against the
public interest, however defined.

Thus it may be said that there is no reason to expect satisfactory results from monopoly legislation unless firstly, market
power and public detriment are assumed to be directly associated with one another, and unless secondly there exists a
clear willingness to impose structural remedies where market
power is subject to abuse. Interpreted in the light of these

[1] See for example C. Eis, 'The 1919–1930 Merger Movement in
American Industry', *Journal of Law and Economics* (Oct 1969)
pp. 267–96 or K. G. Elzinga, 'Mergers: Their Causes and Cures',
Anti-trust Law and Economics Review (Fall 1968) pp. 53–104.

[2] See for example Beacham and Jones, *Journal of Industrial Relations* (April 1971) pp. 97–117 or L. A. Skeoch, 'Merger Issues in
Canada', *Anti-trust Bulletin* (Summer 1971) pp. 131–51.

[3] Beacham and Jones, *Journal of Industrial Relations* (Apr 1971)
p. 110.

criteria monopoly controls in Great Britain have inspired but little confidence.

There is, however, rather more hope for the future in the light of the passing of the 1973 Fair Trading Act. The office of the Director-General of Fair Trading is the first body to have widespread responsibility for examining defects in market structure or conduct over a wide range of economic activities. It therefore has the opportunity to build up a continuing dossier on all major markets within the United Kingdom. Such a dossier would be invaluable, because the degree of effective competition within any market can change over quite short time periods. In the past lengthy monopoly investigations have been carried out at the completion of which the state of competition within the industry under investigation bore no great resemblance to that appertaining at the commencement of the investigation. This resulted in a major wastage of the limited resources of the Monopolies Commission. The 1973 Act provides the opportunity to clarify the criteria for selecting industries for investigation, but whether or not this opportunity will be grasped is as yet unclear. Further clarification will also hopefully be forthcoming as to the reasons for the selection of certain industries for investigation.

One cannot, however, even now be unduly hopeful that a clear-cut approach to the vexed question of what to do about market power will be forthcoming. Although the 1973 Act has introduced the criterion of effective competition, this is intended to be only one among other, sometimes unspecified things, which the investigatory bodies are to take into account in each individual case. When one considers the significant about-faces on the question of the free market which have been the hallmark of the present government, a degree of ambivalence towards monopoly controls is to be expected. All in all the heritage of the 1948 Act, which favoured competition in principle but not necessarily in practice, appears to be with us still.

BIBLIOGRAPHY

W. ADAMS and J. DIRLAM, 'Big Steel, Invention and Innovation', *Quarterly Journal of Economics* (May 1966) pp. 167–89.

J. S. BAIN, 'Survival-ability as a Test of Efficiency', *American Economic Review*, no. 59 (May 1969).

A. BEACHAM and N. J. CUNNINGHAM, *Economics of Industrial Organisation*, 5th edn (Pitman, 1970).

A. BEACHAM and J. C. JONES, 'Merger Criteria and Policy in Great Britain and Canada', *Journal of Industrial Relations* (Apr 1971) pp. 97–117.

R. BERNHARD, 'The Law and the Economics of Market Collusion in Europe, Great Britain and the United States. An American Point of View', *Journal of Industrial Economics* (Nov 1965) pp. 101–23.

W. S. COMANOR and H. LEIBENSTEIN, 'Allocative Efficiency. X-Efficiency and the Measurement of Welfare Loss', *Economica* (Aug 1969).

M. A. CREW and C. K. ROWLEY, 'On Allocative Efficiency. X-efficiency, and the Measurement of Welfare Loss', *Economica* (May 1971).

——, 'Anti-trust Policy – Economics versus Management Science', *Moorgate and Wall St Review* (Autumn 1970).

M. A. CREW, C. K. ROWLEY and M. W. JONES-LEE 'X-Theory versus Management Discretion Theory', *Southern Economic Journal*, vol. 38 (Oct 1971).

H. DEMSETZ, 'Information and Efficiency. Another Viewpoint', *Journal of Law and Economics* (Apr 1969) pp. 1–23.

C. EIS, 'The 1919–1930 Merger Movement in American Industry', *Journal of Law and Economics* (Oct 1969) pp. 267–96.

W. J. EITEMAN and G. E. GUTHRIE, 'The Shape of the Average Cost Curve', *American Economic Review* (Dec 1952) pp. 832–9.

K. G. ELZINGA, 'Mergers: Their Causes and Cures', *Anti-trust Law and Economics Review* (Fall 1968) pp. 53–104.

——, 'The Anti-Merger Law. Pyrrhic Victories', *Journal of Law and Economics* (Apr 1969) pp. 43–79.

C. FREEMAN, 'Research and Development. A Comparison

238   MANAGERIAL ECONOMICS

between British and American Industry', *National Institute Economic Review* (May 1962) pp. 21–39.

K. D. GEORGE, 'Concentration and Specialisation in Industry', *Journal of Industrial Economics* (Apr 1972).

——, *Industrial Organisation* (Allen & Unwin, 1971).

D. HAMBERG, 'Invention in the Industrial Research Laboratory', *Journal of Political Economy* (Apr 1963) pp. 95–115.

B. HINDLEY, *Industrial Merger and Public Policy*, Hobart Paper No. 50 (1970).

M. HOWE, 'Anti-trust Policy. Rules or Discretionary Intervention?', *Moorgate and Wall St Review* (Feb 1971) pp. 39–68.

——, 'British Merger Policy Proposals and American Experience', *Scottish Journal of Political Economy* (Feb 1972) pp. 37–61.

R. JACKSON, 'Market Structure and the Rewards for Patented Inventions', *Anti-trust Bulletin* (Fall 1972) pp. 911–26.

P. S. JOHNSON, 'Firm Size and Technological Change', *Moorgate and Wall St Review* (Spring 1970).

R. E. JOHNSTON, 'Technical Progress and Innovation', *Oxford Economic Papers* (July 1966) pp. 158–77.

H. LEIBENSTEIN, 'Allocative Efficiency versus X-Efficiency', *American Economic Review* (June 1966).

B. LLOYD, 'Invention, Innovation and Size', *Moorgate and Wall St Review* (Autumn 1970).

E. MANSFIELD, 'Industrial Research and Development: Characteristics, Costs, and Diffusion of Results', *American Economic Review*, Papers and Proceedings (May 1969) pp. 65–71.

——, *Industrial Research and Technological Innovation* (Longman, 1969).

——, 'Size of Firms, Market Structure, and Innovation', *Journal of Political Economy* (Dec 1963) pp. 556–77.

——, 'Industrial Research and Development Expenditures Determinants, Prospects and Relation to Size of Firm and Inventive Output', *Journal of Political Economy* (Aug 1964) pp. 319–41.

R. R. NELSON, 'The Economics of Invention. A Survey of the Literature', *The Journal of Business* (Apr 1959) pp. 101–27.

Y.-K. NG and R. PARISH, 'Monopoly, X-Efficiency and the Measurement of Welfare Loss', *Economica* (Aug 1972) pp. 301–8.

N. Owen, 'Competition and Structural Change in Unconcentrated Industries', *Journal of Industrial Economics* (Apr 1971).

C. L. Pass, 'The Control of Mergers in the UK', *Journal of Business Policy* (Winter 1971) pp. 45–58.

——, 'Horizontal Mergers and the Control of Market Power in the UK', *Anti-trust Bulletin,* pp. 811–34.

R. Posner, 'A Statistical Study of Anti-trust Enforcement', *Journal of Law and Economics,* pp. 365–419.

C. K. Rowley, 'The Monopolies Commission and Rate of Return on Capital', *Economic Journal* (Mar 1969) pp. 42–66.

——, 'Monopoly in Britain. Private Vice but Public Virtue?', *Moorgate and Wall St Review* (Autumn 1968) pp. 37–68.

——, 'The Monopolies Commission and Rate of Return on Capital. Reply', *Economic Journal* (Sep 1971).

——, *Anti-trust and Economic Efficiency* (Macmillan, 1973).

——, 'Mergers and Public Policy in Great Britain', *Journal of Law and Economics* (Apr 1968) pp. 75-132.

J. M. Samuels, D. J. Smyth and J. Tzoannos, 'Patents, Profitability, Liquidity and Firm Size', *Applied Economics,* vol. 4 (1972) pp. 77–87.

T. R. Saving, 'Estimation of Optimum Plant Size by the Survivor Technique', *Quarterly Journal of Economics* (Nov 1961) pp. 569–607.

F. M. Scherer, 'Firm Size, Market Structure, Opportunity, and the Output of Patented Inventions', *American Economic Review* (Dec 1965) pp. 1097–126.

J. P. Shelton, 'Allocative Efficiency versus X-Efficiency. Comment', *American Economic Review* (1967) pp. 1252–5.

W. G. Shepherd, 'What does the Survivor Technique show about Economies of Scale?', *Southern Economic Journal* (July 1967) pp. 113–22.

A. Silberston, 'Economies of Scale in Theory and Practice', *Economic Journal* (Special issue; Mar 1972) pp. 369–91.

L. A. Skeoch, 'Merger Issues in Canada', *Anti-trust Bulletin* (Summer 1971) pp. 131–51.

G. J. Stigler, 'The Economies of Scale', *Journal of Law and Economics* (Oct 1958).

A. Sutherland, 'The Monopolies Commission. A Critique of Dr Rowley', *Economic Journal* (June 1971) pp. 264–72.

240   MANAGERIAL ECONOMICS

A. P. THIRLWALL and C. KENNEDY, 'Surveys in Applied
Economics: Technical Progress', *Economic Journal* (Mar
1972).

M. A. UTTON, 'Future Prospects for Merger Policy', *Banker's
Magazine* (Sep 1970) pp. 123–7.

O. E. WILLIAMSON, 'Allocative Efficiency and the Limits of
Anti-trust', *American Economic Review* (May 1969).

——, 'Economies as an Anti-trust Defense', *American Economic
Review* (Mar 1968) pp. 18–36.

B. YAMEY, 'Monopoly, Competition, and the Incentive to
Invest. Comment', *Journal of Law and Economics,* pp. 253–6.

Index

5774